The Politics
of Black Joy

The Politics
of Black Joy

Zora Neale Hurston and Neo-Abolitionism

✦

Lindsey Stewart

NORTHWESTERN UNIVERSITY PRESS
EVANSTON, ILLINOIS

Northwestern University Press
www.nupress.northwestern.edu

Printed in the United States of America

10 9 8 7 6 5 4 3 2 1

Library of Congress Cataloging-in-Publication Data

Names: Stewart, Lindsey (LIndsey L.), author.
Title: The politics of Black joy : Zora Neale Hurston and neo-
    abolitionism / Lindsey Stewart.
Description: Evanston, Illinois : Northwestern University Press, 2021. |
    Includes bibliographical references and index.
Identifiers: LCCN 2021009869 | ISBN 9780810144132 (paperback) |
    ISBN 9780810144118 (cloth) | ISBN 9780810144125 (ebook)
Subjects: LCSH: Hurston, Zora Neale—Criticism and interpretation. |
    African American philosophy. | Joy—Political aspects—Southern States. |
    Joy—Philosophy.
Classification: LCC B947.A37 S74 2021 | DDC 191.08996073—dc23
LC record available at https://lccn.loc.gov/2021009869

To Cheryl A. Wall, whose mentorship and
scholarship showed me the way

CONTENTS

ACKNOWLEDGMENTS

There are so many people to thank. Thanks to the time and energy and love that many of the faculty at Calvin College showed this highly inquisitive student during their years as an undergraduate student. Thanks to the faculty at Pennsylvania State University who managed to make a philosopher out of me, despite the odds. And thanks to the faculty at Wellesley College for their generosity of time and spirit in helping me to get the mentoring and intellectual stimulation I needed—and a special thanks to Mary Kate McGowan for arranging our monthly feminist studies meetings with yummy treats! Many thanks to the students and faculty of the University of Memphis, who have provided a wonderful environment for me to continue my work on Black southern life. Thanks especially to my student, Jasper St. Bernard, for his help in editing the first draft of this manuscript.

Thanks to the many Black women in the professional discipline of philosophy who went before me and mentored me, both near and far: Kathryn Sophia Belle, Kristie Dotson, Denise James, Anita Allen, Kris Sealey, Devonya Havis, Jacqueline Scott, and Denise Melton. Also, many thanks to my Black feminist colleagues who have encouraged, pushed, and sustained me on this journey: Axelle Karera, Jameliah Shorter-Bourhanou, Tempest Henning, Imani Perry, Cynthia Greenlee, Kameelah Martin, Kinitra D. Brooks, Birgitta Johnson, Alexandria Smith, and Regina Bradley. And thanks very much to the group that participated in the feminist research seminar on Beyoncé at the University of Michigan's Institute for Research on Women and Gender for lively and fruitful conversations about *Lemonade*.

None of this would have been possible without the steadfast support of my family, friends, and wonderful husband, Danny J. Smith. Thanks to you all for your patience, energy, time, and love.

Introduction

The Trouble of Black Southern Joy

> Finally, in this long trek through three hundred years of Black life, there was joy, which is what I mostly remember. The part of our lives that was spent neither on our knees nor hanging from trees.
>
> —Toni Morrison, "Rediscovering Black History"

The red beans were in a salad. As I stared at the cold, dry beans in a diffident salad bar at a typical college cafeteria up North, I could not fathom why they had not been slowly simmered in their own sauce, as I was accustomed. Back in Louisiana. Truth be told, it was not until that moment that I truly understood that the South was not the whole world. And as I moved through various halls and classrooms, coffee shops and dinner parties, I learned, soon enough, that "the South" was instead a world of paradoxical meanings for those I encountered. Although many northerners, Black and white, heartily agreed that there was surely good food and good times to be had "down South," it was also simultaneously assumed that Black life down here is ultimately untenable.[1] These paradoxes were present when a white professor politely accused me of cheating on an essay, saying "I just had to meet you because you wrote this excellent essay *and* you come all the way from Louisiana." The paradoxes were present in the exotic excitement of colleagues when they learned I was from Louisiana and in the disappointment that crowded their faces as soon as I gracefully declined to tell them horror stories of Hurricane Katrina. They were present when Black northern friends would tell me all about their grandmama's pound cakes that filled their dreams and the Mississippi police cars that fueled their nightmares. In many of these interactions, I found myself relying upon ways of evasion that I had learned growing up: feigning bewilderment, downplaying pain, or pretending not to know much about the things they asked after. I didn't know why I didn't want to give them these stories. It's not as if I didn't have these stories to tell. What I did know was that I ought to reject the pity they slid toward me, even when it was hidden behind apparent praise. This pity attached to Black southern life made it difficult to assert the joy that Toni

Morrison mentions in the epigraph, the joy that had sustained my life, my mother's, and her mother's in the face of many toils and troubles we endured "down South."

These paradoxical views of "the South" are deeply rooted in our national imaginary. In our schools, media, and national stories, Black life in the South is sometimes pitched as so devastating that no one would ever seriously entertain the thought of living here. At the same time, Black life in the South is also rendered in nostalgic terms, as the "good old days" or a place to have a "real good time." On the one hand, the South is presented as the site of Black tragedy, bearing the brunt of the nation's sin of racism. On the other hand, the South is often portrayed as a land of Black enchantment, as the hub and home of much-celebrated Black cultural products, such as our food, music, and dance traditions. However, the type of joy that Morrison speaks about cannot be captured by such schemas of devastation or nostalgia, tragedy or enchantment. Although the South burgeons through and through with racism, our oppression is not so totalizing that it chokes out every tender shoot of Black joy. And that Black joy cannot be reduced to the truncated versions served up to tourists in Popeye's commercials, Bourbon Street parades, and voodoo dolls. I know this because of my own upbringing.

To be sure, my upbringing included some experiences that my northern friends assumed. I remember the jolt of being called a "nigger" by a small white boy in my youth. He'd launched the word at me without either of us knowing what it truly meant, but we knew sure enough that it was not a thing to be said. And once he had said it, he got the results he wanted. I ceased to play with the little white girl he had boldly deemed to be his "girl-friend." I also remember the fear that gripped me when my mother took me to a barbecue shop that was, unofficially, whites only. Upon our entrance, I immediately sensed our unwelcome in the frowns that graced those in the restaurant. When we reached the front counter to order, we were asked if we were "sure [we] didn't want to go around back to wait." My mother was a study in stubbornness and refused to budge, even as I begged her to let us leave without staying for the food we had ordered. I was too young to understand why she stayed put, but I was old enough to be afraid for our welfare. I shook with fear in the backseat of our car the whole way home.

But the place where I grew up was also shaped in ways that extended beyond the tragic stereotypes my northern friends imagined. My childhood was largely spent crisscrossing the Mississippi River to spend time with my maternal grandfather in Darrow, Louisiana, and my maternal grandmother (or *maman* as we call them) in Donaldsonville, Louisiana. Both are largely Black communities situated between Baton Rouge and New Orleans. Both have rich, complicated histories that are not simply ones of Black death and devastation. Sporting the largest free Black population outside of New Orleans during slavery as well as the first Black mayor (in the nation) during Reconstruction, Donaldsonville especially has a legacy of Black political agency, cultivated in the heart of the "sugar parish," that often gets eclipsed by our assumptions of Black devastation in the South.[2]

Moreover, my upbringing is sown with scenes of Black joy. The simply sinful spread of crawfish, corn, and potatoes under the oaks in my grandfather's yard as my extended family ate and ate until the cicadas chimed in with our music late in the evening. Birthday horse rides at the stable of my great-uncle, the (self-proclaimed) first Black cowboy in Ascension Parish. The glee my *maman* exhibited when she searched newspapers for dear, dead friends, eager to participate in the veneration of the dead through celebratory "homegoing" rituals. The seriousness with which my *maman* delivered a bit of wisdom when I was frightened by her beloved horror films: "it's not the dead you have to fear, but the living." The hushed tones with which my mother informed me that my *maman* had only seen a "hoodoo woman" once and how that woman "sure did fix" a loved one. Above all, I had a fierce sense that what I witnessed and participated in could not be reduced to merely a reaction against the racism that brands this region in our national imagination. In fact, I was acutely aware of how much of our everyday lives seemed to not revolve around white folks.

While some might not deny that such experiences of Black joy in the South exist, many remain wary of the political uses of Black southern joy in our national, public sphere. Black southern joy, for instance, was once used to justify our enslavement. Slave masters pointed to singing slaves as if a sliver of joy meant that we were content with our oppression. Used in this way, Black joy was reduced to enchantment, stripped of its critical power, and fashioned as the romance of Black life in the South. Though it is less often used to bolster an argument for slavery these days, Black joy in the South is still sometimes used against us. This can be seen in how a narrative of Black southern enchantment is frequently spun to evade the civil rights movement's demands for political inclusion and recognition in our institutions across the nation.

Consider the tourism narratives (or curated national stories) of post-civil rights New Orleans. As Lynnell Thomas notes, the inclusion of Black culture in current New Orleans tourist narratives is largely due to pressure from the civil rights movement. During the civil rights movement in south Louisiana, local African Americans lobbied for more inclusion in public stories about the region. The irony, however, is that Black southern "culture" came to be widely celebrated in the post-civil rights public sphere, even as Black communities continued to struggle with forms of institutional racism.[3] As such, these tourist narratives began to overrepresent Black southern culture in the national public sphere while also "displac[ing] and distort[ing] the political and moral project of the civil rights movement."[4] That is, the tourist industry (and, I would say, the national public sphere more broadly) answered the political demand for inclusion merely symbolically, not institutionally. The tourist industry included rosy stories of Black southerners in the brochures and tours as if Black faces in pamphlets would absolve the insidious legacy of slavery. To tell the story in this way makes it look as if the disparities in wealth and health that Black New Orleanians are still facing is due to their own accord, not the racist institutions that persist in the nation. For Thomas, this is how the tourist industry in New Orleans could market the "desire" for a nostalgic southern past of Black culture, while also denouncing the current Black population of New Orleans as a zone of "disaster."[5] In other words, Black southern culture came to be heralded, even as Black southerners continue to be looked down upon nationally.

It's a curious tension: the vast celebration of Black southern culture right alongside wide pronouncements of the political devastation of the Black people who continue to live here. This dialectic of Black enchantment and Black tragedy can be seen in both popular culture and the academy. In both arenas, Black southern culture is often teased apart from Black emancipatory politics, so that Black southerners are rendered artistically enchanting but (ultimately) politically tragic. For instance, a celebration of Black southern culture can be seen in the public fervor over Beyoncé Knowles's visual album, *Lemonade*. Many have devoted much analysis to the rich, jubilant allusions to Black southern culture in this visual album. Many have also praised Beyoncé's stances on Black politics in snippets of the album—such as her references to Malcolm X, the Black Panther Party, and Black Lives Matter. However, in popular culture, the connection between Beyoncé's Black southern joy and her progressive politics is more ambiguous, even tenuous. Considering a political climate in which overrepresentations of southern Black culture are used to temper complaints of racial injustice, some question the motives behind Beyoncé's engagement with southern Black culture. Some suggest that Beyoncé's engagement with southern Black culture simply reflects her shrewdness as a capitalist; as such, her album is not the pro-Black or Black feminist anthem it is frequently taken to be.[6] Seen in this way, Beyoncé's engagement with southern Black culture is mere commodification, rather than the wellspring from which her Black emancipatory politics issues.

While there is some value to this critique, it also reminds us that there is a deep reluctance to link southern Black culture with Black emancipatory politics in the public sphere. Perhaps this reticence can be seen more starkly in the shock that northern white liberals displayed at the recent election of Alabamian Democratic Senator Doug Jones, which was brought about largely by southern Black women's votes.[7] As Cynthia Greenlee observes, "the surprise and awe of Americans over the Alabama outcome reinforces the ludicrous notion that Black Southerners have been out here twiddling our thumbs and waiting for the liberation bus to stop in Dixie."[8] The shock reveals the assumption that we lack political agency. As such, Greenlee rightly criticizes those who assume "that Black Alabamians have been ground into passive dust by the potent and public racism for which their home state has long been known—and were going to be MIA at the polls."[9]

We can also see this tension in the academic recovery of Zora Neale Hurston's work in the 1980s and 1990s. Although initially erased from her place in the Harlem Renaissance, Hurston has largely been recovered by Black feminists since Alice Walker's 1975 essay "In Search of Zora Neale Hurston" in *Ms.* magazine. And in the 1980s and 1990s, Hurston's work came to be widely celebrated. For example, her work on Black southern culture became integral to academic curriculums in high schools and colleges.[10] As Hazel Carby notes in "The Politics of Fiction, Anthropology, and the Folk: Zora Neale Hurston," this ecstatic celebration of Hurston and Black southern culture in the 1980s and 1990s occurred alongside the further entrenchment of institutional racism in our communities. In this fashion, Hurston was used in school curriculums to increase Black representation, even as racism stubbornly persisted in those very same institutions. Especially in the South, where some were working to present a "new" image of the region as one that had learned from and been strengthened by its history of violent racial strife.

Like Beyoncé's reception in popular culture, the connection between Hurston's southern Black joy and her progressive politics in academic scholarship is ambiguous, and much more tenuous. Although Hurston is widely celebrated for her contributions to southern Black culture, her racial politics have a more complicated legacy. So complicated that we often shirk going near it. There have been few book-length treatments of Hurston's expository work devoted to tracing her development as a philosophical and political theorist of race.[11] Her essays have especially been undertheorized. Perhaps this is because, in her essays, her commitment to southern Black joy caused her to take political positions that put her out of step with her contemporaries, such as her public denunciation of the *Brown v. Board* Supreme Court decision to desegregate schools.[12]

Due to these (often vexing) polemical stances, Hurston's theoretical contributions to racial politics have often been rendered murky, at best, or dismal, at worst.[13] For instance, in her 1978 essay "Sexual Politics and the Fiction of Zora Neale Hurston," Barbara Smith introduced an important distinction to facilitate the recovery of Hurston's politics. Smith showed that Hurston's fictional works exhibited a "sexual politics" that informed intra-racial rather than interracial politics.[14] This was an important point to make in the larger context of debates about Black liberation. For during this time, Hurston became a powerful symbol of the intra-racial gender politics that often got erased in appeals to a Black nationalist agenda or models of Black power.[15] This method of recovery was also highly successful; we would not have so much of Hurston's work available to us without it. And since Hurston's recovery in the 1980s and 1990s, there has been a proliferation of works devoted to further developing the intra-racial, and especially feminist, politics in her literature and folklore material. However, this tactic of recovery included conceding to Hurston's critics that some of her interracial political views were tragically mistaken, even if we were sympathetic to the logic behind those views.[16]

There is some benefit in placing Hurston and Beyoncé side by side in this discussion. The two have striking similarities. With strong connections to the blueswoman tradition, both are invested in creating a southern Black aesthetic, especially one with ties to the Gulf Coast region.[17] And although Hurston and Beyoncé are separated by long decades of Black political movements, racial gains in the public sphere, and radical shifts in society due to legal desegregation, there remain strong similarities regarding both the conditions of Black life and their use of Black affect in the public sphere. For instance, both in Hurston's time and Beyoncé's own, violence against Black and brown peoples often still proceeds without legal repercussions. And while Jim Crow legally expired with the Civil Rights Act of 1964, it has been resurrected through the mass incarceration of Black and brown peoples since the 1970s. The most salient similarity for us is how Hurston and Beyoncé both insist upon performing southern Black joy in the public sphere. Their magnum opuses, *Their Eyes Were Watching God* and *Lemonade*, have both faced criticism on this score, due to concerns over the dangers of publicly performing Black joy amid our oppression.[18] While their critics may appreciate the role of Black joy in Black liberation, some remain reluctant to elevate southern Black joy to an emancipatory political tradition. Much like the erotic and deeply gendered, southern Black joy has come to be devalued in Black political discourses.

The Dialectic of Black Enchantment and Black Tragedy

The political devaluation of southern Black joy has its roots in an emancipatory Black political tradition that mandates an emphasis on our racial oppression in the public sphere. This political tradition is one that stretches back to the abolitionist movement, where the suffering of the enslaved was used to prove the moral reprehensibility of slavery. During the antebellum-abolitionist period, we were right to be wary of how some fashioned southern Black joy into an argument for our enslavement. And we are right to remain wary of how this argument continues to be used: when the celebration of Black southern culture in the public sphere becomes a way to evade addressing structural oppression. However, there is an important insight that gets lost in all our wariness of southern Black joy. In our haste to rid the public sphere of southern Black joy, we miss the danger in confining our stories to racial sorrow. Put another way, we miss how the aesthetic exaltation of Black southern culture and the political depreciation of Black southern agency, the displays of Black enchantment and Black tragedy, are linked. Certainly, the overrepresentation of Black southern culture can be used to bolster racism. But so too can the reduction of Black life to the oppression we face, which constitutes a severe underrepresentation of our agency. While we have become savvy at noting how Black joy is used to uphold racial oppression by our opponents, we are less apt to diagnose how the racism of our liberal allies is fed by stories of our abjection as well.

Grappling with the political effects of southern Black joy, assessing when and how it might be useful in the public sphere, means revisiting the context in which the dialectic of Black southern enchantment and tragedy first emerged: the abolitionist's staging of Black sorrow and the minstrel's show of Black joy. As a dialectic, there is an underlying logic that holds the two positions together in tension. Namely, there is shared anxiety about how whites perceive the inner lives of Blacks. Moreover, both sides share a presumption that Black life is tragic without white intervention. On the part of the slave owners, Black life is seen to be tragic without the "civilizing" benefits or forced "guidance" of enslavement. On the part of the abolitionists, Black life is seen to be tragic without northern, white political intervention to secure our emancipation. It seems that in the end, both sides are deeply afraid that when you cut open the hearts of Black folk, you will not, as they assume, find white folks there. The abolitionist's forecast of tragedy and the minstrel's chicanery of joy continue to echo in our representations of southern Black life as well.[19] On the one hand, due to the persistence of abolitionist discourse, Black joy in representations of southern Black life is rendered politically and morally suspect as "nostalgia" or as an evasion of Black suffering. On the other hand, due to lingering vestiges of pro-slavery southern sentiments, Black southern culture is celebrated as an achievement of racial progress, masking the way that racism persists in the nation. However, to fully delve into Hurston's contributions to racial politics and philosophy, we must be willing to wade into the uncomfortable waters of southern Black joy.

In *The Politics of Black Joy*, I develop Hurston's contributions to political theory and philosophy of race by introducing the *politics of joy* as a response to this dialectic of Black enchantment and Black tragedy. That is, I read Hurston's performances of southern Black joy in the public sphere as her way navigating the dialectic representations of southern Black life in our national imaginary, as just noted. In Hurston's treatment of southern Black joy, she lays bare the terms upon which the southern dialectic of Black tragedy and Black enchantment proceeds—centering how white folks define our lives. Her performance of joy in the public sphere refuses, rather than entertains, those terms. As a concept, the politics of joy also aims to capture the corrective that Hurston provides by bringing southern Black joy into the public sphere in this way. While both sides of the dialectic persist in our national imaginary, it is the North that won the Civil War. It was thus the northern abolitionist that got to dictate how "progressive" stories of southern Black life were told nationally. As such, Hurston's performances of southern Black joy also reveal the lingering hold of abolitionist discourse in the public sphere. In other words, her performances of southern Black joy reveal the implicit requirement of demonstrations of Black abjection for political recognition in our national public sphere.

During our own time, the political significance of Hurston's emphasis on southern Black joy is a refusal of the neo-abolitionist mandate that we emphasize sorrow in our representations of Black life. When it comes to representations of Black life, neo-abolitionism captures the impulses (or, more strongly, mandates) to emphasize sorrow and mute joy, to dial down our pleasure and turn up our pain, in pursuit of white, northern liberal allies. I use the term "neo-abolitionism" to hearken back to the abolitionist discourse that informed Black writing during the antebellum period and to shed light on the lingering abolitionist norms and rhetorical strategies in contemporary Black political discourse. The prefix "neo-" here registers that the originating condition for these strategies (slavery) has been significantly altered (upon the "emancipation" of the enslaved), while also marking the afterlife of these strategies in US public discourse.

I develop the term "neo-abolitionism" from Hurston's criticisms of abolitionist discourse in her essays. We can see Hurston taking up some of these themes in her 1938 essay "Art and Such," part of her contribution to the Florida Federal Writers' Project.[20] The Writers Project's vision for the essay was a history of the artistic contributions of African Americans in Florida. Perhaps out of immense frustration, Hurston instead chose to write an essay that criticized a contemporary racial politics that restricted Black art to portrayals of Black suffering. "Art and Such," along with Hurston's other writings for the Florida Federal Writers' Project, was ultimately dropped from the manuscript and left unpublished for decades. The recovery of this essay has lent much-longed-for insight into Hurston's views on art for scholars.[21] As Cheryl Wall remarks, the essay provides "rare and useful insights into Hurston's understanding of African American literary and artistic traditions and of herself as an artist."[22] Seen in this light, "Art and Such" also presents something of a puzzle to Hurston scholars. Who exactly is her target in this essay? Some scholars argue that Hurston is critiquing her fellow Harlem Renaissance writers, such as Alain Locke and Richard Wright, in the essay.[23] However, as Wall notes, "she does not mention the Harlem Renaissance here or anywhere in her writings. Given its subject, the omission in this essay seems especially curious."[24] While I agree that Locke and Wright are in the background of "Art and Such," Hurston explicitly names the abolitionist Frederick Douglass, which suggests that abolitionists are the main target of her criticism. Indeed, in this essay, Hurston attributes the mandate to center oppression in our stories of Black life to the tradition of abolitionism. As such, I aim to move scholarly discussions of Hurston's racial politics away from the Harlem Renaissance and toward the influence of abolitionism (through her refusal of it) within her writing.[25]

Although my development of the politics of joy and my critique of neo-abolitionism take place within the context of Hurston's racial politics, these concepts touch upon broader topics and trends in race and gender studies. For instance, many feminist and race scholars have argued that a narrow focus on resistance has caused us to miss other modes of agency that the oppressed exhibit.[26] When we reduce agency to resistance, we act as if our reaction to oppression is the only thing that defines us. By reconceiving Hurston's views on race through the politics of joy, I also aim to critique the dominant trend of reducing agency under oppression to resistance. I do this not only by emphasizing the dangers of limiting our emancipatory imaginary to resistance, but also by offering other modes of agency for analysis and study, such as joy. While resistance foregrounds an oppositional relation between oppressed and oppressors, joy foregrounds a flourishing relation of the self to the self (or, in the case of Black joy, how Black folks relate to each other). In this way, my understanding of joy is like what Audre Lorde describes as the "erotic," which functions as a critical source of self-definition. The erotic, which provides "the open and fearless underlining of [our] capacity for joy," encourages us to "live from within outward" and "illuminate[s] our actions upon the world around us" so that "we are responsible to ourselves in the deepest sense."[27] Seen in this way, the truly erotic for Lorde, along with the Black joy which I am advocating, can become much more than naive nostalgia or exotic enchantment. Rather, Black joy can become an internal barometer by which we assess the ways our social environment inhibits or enhances our flourishing.[28] Moreover, this view suggests that Black joy is often reduced to minstrelsy in popular culture, similar to how the erotic is shrunk to the pornographic, precisely *because* of its potential power.[29]

The theorization of joy in *The Politics of Black Joy* also has strong resonances with scholars working to shift the discussion of agency under oppression from acts of resistances to practices of refusal.[30] In cultural anthropology, Carole McGranahan has stressed that refusal is not simply "another word for resistance."[31] Rather, these are distinct modes of agency. In indigenous studies (Audra Simpson) and Black feminist scholarship (Saidiya Hartman), the politics of recognition is one way that refusal is distinguished from resistance.[32] While resistance can, as Angela Davis argues, enable us to switch positions in the game of recognition, refusal is a rejection of the game altogether.[33] And that rejection is both world-breaking and world-making, both negation and generation.[34] Similarly, the mode of agency signaled by the politics of joy cannot be captured by the category of resistance. Instead of directly protesting oppression, Hurston's emphasis on Black joy was more like a refusal to entertain the white gaze. That is, she strove to maintain an emotional indifference toward whites, relegating them to the periphery of a Black world.[35] Rather than actively fight against whites, she refused to pay them attention. And her refusal, I argue, exposes the terms and limits of political recognition from whites when pursued as a remedy for social injustice. In other words, Hurston's insistence upon Black joy places pressure on the public demand of Black abjection for political recognition. This allows her to raise the question that Hartman also raises in her critiques of abolitionist discourse: "for whom does one expose the [pained Black] body?"[36] As such, to embrace the politics of joy is also to participate in a "refusal to offer Black suffering as the raw material of white pedagogy and enjoyment."[37]

Although negative, refusal is also deeply generative because it prompts us to, as Hartman says, "produce a thought of the outside while in the inside."[38] I argue that this is an important issue with which to grapple, given the resurgent popularity of the formulation of Blackness as "social death."[39] Such formulations force us to ask, as Christina Sharpe does in *In the Wake*, "what exceeds the hold?"[40] My primary example of what may indeed exceed the hold is *root work*, those practices of conjure that Hurston analyzed as an anthropologist.[41] Root work is a touchstone of West African religious practices that persisted even as slavery sought to erase our cultural ties to the continent.[42] Root work has also been a source of innovation in the New World through its blending with Native American and European folk traditions.[43] For Hurston, root work is an important site for working out the politics of joy. These practices are often, in her essays, one space where Hurston can decenter whiteness or refuse the white gaze in her analyses of Black southern life. In this way, she draws upon the rich reserve of refusals that root work stores in African American culture: refusals of respectability politics, of religious patriarchy, of the state, of cultural assimilation, and even of the Black tragedy that neo-abolitionism assumes.[44]

The Politics of Black Joy develops Hurston's theoretical contributions to racial politics primarily through her essays. Three prominent texts that have also worked through Hurston's gender and racial politics using her essays are Deborah G. Plant's *Every Tub Must Sit on Its Own Bottom*, Susan Meisenhelder's *Hitting a Straight Lick with a Crooked Stick*, and Lynda Marian Hill's *Social Rituals and the Verbal Art of Zora Neale Hurston*. Covering a wide range of Hurston's fiction and essays, Plant incorporates Spinoza and Nietzsche into her analysis in order to situate Hurston's "individualist philosophy."[45] Contextualizing Hurston's views on race and gender through the lens of individualism, Plant argues that Hurston's individualism was an approach that helped her "survive systematic sexism, racism, and classism, strengthened her will to resist negative controlling images, and empowered her to overcome Anglo-American cultural hegemony."[46] Criticizing previous scholarship for analyzing race and gender "in isolation from one another" in Hurston's work, Meisenhelder interprets Hurston's writing on race and gender as "hitting a straight lick with a crooked stick."[47] Drawing upon Hurston's 1943 essay "High John de Conquer," Meisenhelder's interpretation highlights how Hurston "developed her themes from a position of racial and sexual subordination that required indirection, masking, and ambiguity too often seen simply as conventionality and conservatism."[48] As such, Hurston's written views on race and gender are more trickster than truth, relying upon "a much more subversive approach to the problem of audience, one based on a shrewd assessment of complex power relations."[49] In her *Social Rituals and the Verbal Art of Zora Neale Hurston*, Hill brings together several disciplines (anthropology, theater, literature, women's studies) to theorize Hurston's controversial views on race, culture, and class as part of verbal artistry and performance, rooted in Black cultural expressions.[50] After several of the above texts were published, many of Hurston's lost essays, letters, and nonfiction were published in Cheryl Wall's anthology *Zora Neale Hurston: Folklore, Memoirs, and Other Writings*, Carla Kaplan's *Zora Neale Hurston: A Life in Letters*, Pamela Bordelon's *Go Gator and Muddy the Water: Writings by Zora Neale Hurston from the Federal Writers' Project*, and, most recently, Hurston's *Barracoon: The Story of the Last "Black Cargo,"* edited by Plant.

My own method in *The Politics of Black Joy* has been informed by Cheryl Wall's recent *On Freedom and the Will to Adorn*, to whom this book is dedicated. Drawing upon Hurston's 1934 essay "Characteristics of Negro Expression," Wall further develops Hurston's concept of the "will to adorn," a register of Black aesthetics. Wall argues that African American essays as a genre also exhibit the "will to adorn," which is an "attitude towards language . . . an impulse towards embellishment, an understanding that language did more than convey information, and a commitment to beauty as a cardinal value."[51] I am interested in this register, "the will to adorn," because it does not fit squarely into the mode of protest writing. Adornment enables us to shift away from reactive responses and toward a kind of relation to the self that joy exhibits. During the Harlem Renaissance, this turn to adornment was related to an acute awareness of the intransigence of racism. As such, the will to adorn also reflects a pessimism toward racial politics that Black essayists felt at that time. "It was a lack of progress," Wall writes, "rather than an absence of interest that led Black leaders to concentrate on arts rather than politics."[52] This is important to stress, for without such racial pessimism, the southern Black joy for which Hurston advocates whittles down to the minstrel's nostalgia or Black enchantment. Hurston's essays are an especially rich site where this pessimism over political recognition and performances of ecstatic Black joy interact in ways that produce a strong dissonance with our common conceptions of racism and racial politics.[53] As such, in *The Politics of Black Joy*, I privilege Hurston's essays rather than her fiction in my analysis of the political dissonance that her displays of Black southern joy wreaked in the public sphere.

The Politics of Joy

The politics of joy is rooted in the ways that Black southerners have often negotiated the dialectic outlined above: the tension arising from the simultaneous romanticizing and catastrophizing of our lives down here. In *This Ain't Chicago*, sociologist Zandria Robinson has described this negotiation as "country cosmopolitanism" which "draws on the tropes of the rural

South . . . but decenters, reconfigures, and relocates them for consumption and production in the urban South and beyond."[54] When it comes to the national narrative of the "racist South," Robinson found that many respondents performed a peculiar indifference regarding their experiences of racism, claiming not to "study" white folks.[55] Moreover, respondents claimed not to need to "study" white folks due to the intimate, intergenerational knowledge of racism that they have gained by living in the South.[56] This response of indifference enabled respondents to turn the negative associations of rural, "country" America (i.e., racism) into a positive type of "cosmopolitanism." That is, respondents were able to turn their collective experiences of rural, southern racism into a kind of cultural, cosmopolitan capital, whereby they "claim[ed] an epistemological superiority over non-southern Blacks."[57]

This performance of indifference also drew an emotional boundary, carving out a space in their inner life that whites could not determine. Put another way, respondents drew a line where white folks supposedly could not go or get to them emotionally. Robinson writes that through their indifference, or "in denying or rejecting the feeling" of the pain of racism, respondents "contended [that] they are overcoming the feeling, not letting the debilitating effects of racism take hold."[58] In this way, their response of indifference plays down the pain of racism in order to "emphasize their agency."[59] As a result, their performances of indifference demonstrate "a way in which [they] ha[ve] the upperhand."[60] Their responses were also framed by a spiritual backdrop. Instead of "studying" white folks, they often "studied" a "higher Master." "Regardless of their relationship to spirituality or religion, respondents draw on decidedly religious and/or spiritual language to navigate race, class, and regional tensions," Robinson reports, and "[respondents] contend that a divine power orders their interracial steps."[61] Put more strongly, the spiritual turn made possible their performance of indifference—their "studying" of spiritual matters made it possible to *not* "study" white folks.[62]

The respondents in Robinson's study neither deny that racism occurs in the South (romanticize) nor affirm that racism has devastated them (catastrophe). They acknowledge that racism occurs, but they choose not to "study" it. In this way, their response of indifference maneuvers through the dialectic of Black catastrophe or Black romanticism, Black tragedy or Black enchantment, without the entanglement of either side.

This is a response that we see modeled, decades earlier, in Hurston's essays on racial politics. For instance, Hurston feigns indifference to the pain of racism in her 1928 essay "How It Feels to Be Colored Me." Rather than allow the racism of whites to determine her sense of self, Hurston writes that she "does not mind at all":

> But I am not tragically colored. There is no great sorrow dammed up in my soul, nor lurking behind my eyes. I do not mind at all. I do not belong to the sobbing school of Negrohood who hold that nature

somehow has given them a low-down dirty deal and whose feelings are all hurt about it. Even in the helter-skelter skirmish that is my life, I have seen that the world is to the strong regardless of a little pigmentation more or less. No, I do not weep at the world—I am too busy sharpening my oyster knife.[63]

We can also see Hurston performing this kind of indifference in her 1943 essay "The 'Pet Negro' System." In this essay, she describes how racism in the South operates very differently than racism in the North.[64] And yet, in a curious encounter with a northern white liberal friend, Hurston feigns ignorance of these very dynamics:

It has been so generally accepted that all Negroes in the South are living under horrible conditions that many friends of the Negro up North actually take offense if you don't tell them a tale of horror and suffering. They stroll up to you, cocktail glass in hand, and say, "I am a friend of the Negro, you know, and feel awful about the terrible conditions down there." That's your cue to launch into atrocities amidst murmurs of sympathy. If, on the other hand, just to find out if they have really done their research down there, you ask, "What conditions do you refer to?" you get an injured, and sometimes a malicious, look. Why ask foolish questions?[65]

Rather than confirm or deny her northern white liberal counterpart's assumption of Black racial tragedy due to southern racism, Hurston feigns indifference, throwing them off guard. When her interlocutor insists upon stories of Black calamity, Hurston simply asks, "What conditions do you refer to?" And instead of observing the social cue to provide a tale of Black southern suffering, Hurston "drag[s] in the many Negroes of opulence and education" in the South.[66] In this way, she redirects her interlocutor to the local conditions in the South where some African Americans have turned the "Pet Negro" system to their advantage.

As an anthropologist, Hurston also witnessed this response of indifference in her own interactions with respondents. The game she seems to be playing above is embedded in the daily negotiation of power dynamics in the South, where certain things simply cannot be said to white folks without retaliation. Hurston reports in the introduction to her 1935 *Mules and Men*:

[Respondents] are most reluctant at times to reveal that which the soul lives by. And the Negro, in spite of his open-faced laughter, his seeming acquiescence, is particularly evasive. You see we are a polite people and we do not say to our questioner, "Get out of here!" We smile and tell him or her something that satisfies the white person because, knowing so little about us, he doesn't know what he is missing.[67]

The interaction Hurston describes is informed by a deep understanding that the playing field between whites and Blacks is not equal. Her respondents cannot simply say "no" to nosy whites here. Instead, there is a performance of indifference that limits the emotional harm that whites can invoke in this scenario. "We let the probe enter," Hurston writes, "but it never comes out. It gets smothered under a lot of laughter and pleasantries."[68] Put another way, we pretend we are not bothered by or are indifferent to their probing, but we never truly answer the questions they posed in the first place. It is here that we can also see how the politics of joy diverges from a politics of recognition. The tactic described in this passage is aimed at evasion of white folks and thus relies upon a deft calculation of white *misrecognition* (or not knowing "what he is missing"). Black respondents are not attempting to facilitate true understanding and respect within the other. Instead, Black respondents ascertain that the racism of their white interlocutors undermines even the possibility of recognition. So these respondents do what it takes to make white folks "go away" instead.[69] In this way, this response is more about creating and preserving the inward space to "say [our] say and sing [our] song" rather than "stud'n white folks."[70]

The introduction of the concept of the politics of joy, developed out of Hurston's essays, offers us many things politically, analytically, and aesthetically. Politically, the politics of joy includes a shift toward self-determination and a shift away from the pursuit of white political recognition; a refusal of assumptions of Black southern tragedy and inferiority; and a keen awareness of racial dynamics that remain intransigent, even while Black representation in the public sphere increases. Analytically, the politics of joy offers a change in focus and perspective, from the relations between oppressed and oppressor to the intragroup relations among the oppressed. Doing so positions us to analyze how we relate to each other, not just how we relate to our oppressors. Moreover, the politics of joy encourages us to engage with the cultural practices that make self-definition possible in our analyses of agency under oppression. The guiding example for this book is practices of root work, where the difference in interpretation (joy vs. resistance) is perhaps most stark. Aesthetically, the politics of joy positions us to approach Black southern cultural expression in a way that acknowledges yet decenters the racism of white folks. It broadens our engagement with Black southern cultural practices, so that we appreciate, as Hurston put it, that "Negroes love and hate and fight and play and strive and travel and have a thousand and one interests in life like other humans."[71] Rather than mine Black southern cultural expression for moments of protest, the politics of joy casts Black southern cultural expression in a different register, such as the "will to adorn," which foregrounds the relation to the self.[72] This aesthetic decentering of whiteness (i.e., Black-white relations in the South) can also render more visible the knowledge production of Black southerners.[73] That is, rather than portray us as victims of white southern horrors, this aesthetic decentering privileges the kinds of lives we have made in spite of it.

Neo-Abolitionism

Hurston's emphasis on southern Black joy is jarring precisely because it violates a norm of Black political representation: a show of Black sorrow. In her work, Hurston ascribes this norm to neo-abolitionism. Breaking this norm, insisting upon southern Black joy, is not only a criticism of neo-abolitionism for Hurston, but a way to lay bare its problematic foundations. As such, Hurston's emphasis on southern Black joy in the public sphere paves the way for certain questions that are often neglected in scholarship on Black liberation. That is, much of feminist and race scholarship currently focuses on analyzing the various ways that slavery lives on in our public discourse, government policies, and day-to-day practices in the United States.[74] Less an object of study are the negative ways that abolitionist discourse continues to inform progressive, liberal politics. Ironically, neo-abolitionism can work to further entrench racism in liberal politics rather than abolish it.

We can see this in the relationship of neo-abolitionism to Black abjection. In her 1943 essay "Negroes without Self-Pity," Hurston suggests that abolitionist discourse implicitly made Black abjection the terms of our political recognition and advancement in the national public sphere. She writes:

> Look back over your shoulder for a minute. Count the years. If you take in the twenty-odd years of intense Abolitionist speaking and writing that preceded the Civil War, the four war years, the Reconstruction period and recent Negro rights agitations, you have at least a hundred years of indoctrination of the Negro that he is an object of pity.[75]

One way to understand Hurston's claim (i.e., that abolitionist discourse renders "the Negro" into "an object of pity") is to consider what Audra Simpson notes about the stakes of gaining political recognition from a state that continues to oppress you. In *Mohawk Interruptus*, Simpson asserts that, for Indigenous peoples in North America, there are stories that are "always being told" about them. These are stories that settler-colonial states fashion about the Indigenous and reaffirm in public discourse to normalize their oppression.[76] Assent to these stories that are "always being told" about them is also the terms by which such a state will recognize the Indigenous politically.[77] For Hurston, abolitionist discourse, too, fashioned a story that is "always being told" about African Americans, a story to which we must assent in order to gain political recognition. That story is that we are "object[s] of pity."

Consider the ways that African Americans were historically constrained in their testimonies about their enslavement. Several scholars note that the marriage of slave narratives to the abolitionist cause overdetermined these testimonies of enslavement.[78] As Dwight McBride notes in his *Impossible Witness*, the overdetermination of their stories put these Black writers in a double bind. On the one hand, the potency of slave narratives relied upon their being the genuine "truth" about experiences of enslavement. On the other hand, the authenticity or "truthfulness" of such narratives was measured by how closely they aligned with the abolitionist message. In other words, these narratives were considered "authentic" narratives, or secured uptake in their northern white audience, only if they bore witness to the abolitionist cause. As such, abolitionist discourse produced constraints upon exactly what Black writers could report of their own experiences of enslavement. Under these circumstances McBride asks, "how does one negotiate the terms of slavery in order to be able to tell one's own story?"[79] In a slightly different way, when a story is "always being told" about "the slave" (whereby we "know them before they even speak"), how are Black writers to tell their *own* story?[80] For the intelligibility of their story is conditioned upon how well they adhere to the readerly expectations of sympathetic northern whites—or, as McBride puts it, the "prophecy of abolitionist discourse."[81] For these reasons, McBride argues that the position of the "slave" is that of an "impossible witness." The "slave" must tell the "truth" about slavery, but that "truth" has already been determined by the cause of abolitionism.

And the "truth" or "prophecy" of abolitionist discourse is Black suffering. For example, in her *Scenes of Subjection*, Saidiya Hartman draws attention to the spectacle of Black suffering in fugitive slave narratives.[82] Hartman observes that the "pained" Black body often stood as a testimony to the evils of slavery in abolitionist discourse.[83] Drafted within the genre of sentimentalism, slave narratives rhetorically staged the suffering Black body as a way to marshal the moral sentiments of white readers.[84] And so, several tropes of Black tragedy were mobilized in abolitionist discourse to evoke sympathy, such as the auction block, demoralizing whippings, and the idealization of motherhood.[85] These tropes established certain norms of representation in abolitionist literature, so that our stories were considered "truthful" only if we adhered to an abolitionist script of Black suffering and pain. Hartman rightfully questions why pain became the terms of identification with the enslaved in abolitionist discourse, such that abolitionists demanded a show of suffering as a requisite for their recognition of our humanity.[86] Moreover, Hartman worries that abolitionist discourse also ran the risk of naturalizing Black suffering by linking such pain to the (ontological) condition of Blackness.[87] Put another way, does not the very abjection that made us recognizable as humans to white abolitionists also endanger our access to the very category of human subjectivity? For if part of what it means to be a human subject is agency and a sense of autonomy, stories of Black abjection may, in effect, undermine Black claims to such agency and autonomy. The question is not whether slavery was wrong (it was) or whether we suffered under it (we did), but what happens when a show of suffering becomes a requirement for political recognition.

For instance, in his *My Bondage and My Freedom*, Frederick Douglass is explicit about the racism he faced within the abolitionist movement.[88]

Douglass tells us that white abolitionists insisted that he continue to play "the slave," even after his successful escape. Instead of being encouraged to tell his own story, Douglass's scarred Black body was used by white abolitionists as a "text" to confirm the "truth" of their cause. This can be seen when Douglass attempted to deviate from the abolitionist script. When Douglass tried to move away from divulging painful tales of his enslavement and toward a more philosophical indictment of whites, white abolitionists balked.[89] Douglass was to "give [them] the facts," white abolitionists said, and they "will take care of the philosophy."[90] In other words, he is simply evidence, a "fact," for their cause; he is not a legitimate political actor or theorist in their eyes. As long as Douglass sticks to the message they have authorized, as long as he rehearses the suffering he experienced as a slave or shows the scars on his back, his story is considered authentic, their cause legitimate.[91] Douglass rightly struggled against his reduction to the figure of the "slave" when he addressed abolitionist audiences.[92] But he found that when he resisted this image, his credibility to speak for the antislavery cause was questioned. As Douglass reports, the more his story did not match up to "all the facts" his white abolitionist audiences already held concerning the nature of "slaves," the less credible he appeared.[93] In search of room to grow, Douglass eventually broke with radical white abolitionists such as William Lloyd Garrison.[94]

Douglass, however, did not leave behind abolitionist rhetoric and tropes. Rather, he refashioned them for his own purposes. Consider, for example, his interpretation of Negro spirituals in *Narrative of the Life of Frederick Douglass* and *My Bondage and My Freedom*. Jon Cruz argues that Douglass was responsible for a cultural shift in the interpretation of Black song-making. Once considered "alien noise" by whites, Douglass introduces Negro spirituals as "sorrow songs" that pack a powerful political message.[95] For example, in *Narrative of the Life of Frederick Douglass*, Douglass admits that it would seem to some (i.e., white folks) that these songs are "unmeaning jargon" and "apparently incoherent."[96] As such, Douglass inserts *abolitionist* meanings into these songs to render them intelligible to his audience. In this passage, Douglass claims that "the mere hearing of those songs would do more to impress some minds with the horrible character of slavery" than volume upon volume of antislavery philosophy.[97] This is because, Douglass writes, "every tone was a testimony against slavery . . . the hearing of these wild notes always depressed my spirit, and filled me with ineffable sadness."[98] By linking the meaning of the spirituals to this enslaved "tale of woe," Douglass makes the spirituals comprehensible to his abolitionist audience.[99] That is, the interpretation that Douglass proposes "makes sense" of these songs within the existing abolitionist discourse of the time: the abolitionist "prophecy" of Black suffering due to the moral evils of slavery.[100] "To those songs," Douglass asserts, "I trace my first glimmering conception of the dehumanizing character of slavery."[101]

Part of what made Douglass's interpretation of Negro spirituals so successful is that he tapped into the ways that Black affect was already being weaponized in the national debate over slavery. Instances of Black song-making were often used as evidence of Black joy. And Black joy, in turn, was weaponized by pro-slavery advocates to ensure our oppression. If slaves were happy, so the pro-slavery argument goes, then slavery must not be some moral evil. Because pro-slavery agitators often enlisted the "happy darky" image of minstrelsy to bolster this argument, Douglass sought to reverse the minstrel's message in his interpretation of Negro spirituals.[102] By emphasizing the sorrow in Negro spirituals, Douglass turned the joyous Black song-making that was once ammunition for pro-slavery arguments into a weapon that abolitionists could wield.

Although the minstrel's grasp of Black song-making was a gross caricature of Black culture, minstrel shows were politically potent enough to provoke anxiety in abolitionists over any suggestion of joy in the enslaved.[103] This anxiety over Black joy can be seen, for example, in how Douglass takes great pains to banish joy in his interpretation of Negro spirituals. "It is impossible to conceive of a greater mistake" than attributing joy to Black song-making, Douglass argues, for "slaves sing most when they are most unhappy."[104] Against the tradition of minstrelsy, Douglass asserts that Black joy was uncommon during slavery. Regarding his own life, Douglass reports that he "ha[s] often sung to drown [his] sorrow, but seldom to express [his] happiness. Crying for joy, and singing for joy, were alike uncommon to [him] while in the jaws of slavery."[105] In *My Bondage and My Freedom* Douglass follows up on this point, arguing that the "it is a great mistake to suppose [the enslaved] happy because they sing," for "the songs of the slave represent the sorrows, rather than the joys, of his heart."[106] Under this interpretation, any appearance of joy in the life of the enslaved is a farce. If we only look deeper, we will see that *even the appearance of joy* is really a witness to the evils of slavery.

Hurston took great exception to this banishment of Black joy within progressive, liberal circles. As several scholars have noted, Hurston's refusal to center sorrow in representations of southern Black life played a crucial role in her critique of other Black writers. In her 1938 essay "Art and Such," Hurston thematizes that refusal. She complains that the Black artist is placed under a political mandate to center sorrow in Black life:

> Can the black poet sing a song to the morning? Upsprings the song to his lips but it is fought back. He says to himself, "Ah this is a beautiful song inside me. I feel the morning star in my throat. I will sing of the star and the morning." Then his background thrusts itself between his lips and the star and he mutters, "Ought I not to be singing of our sorrows? That is what is expected of me and I shall be considered forgetful of our past and present. If I do not some will even call me

a coward. The one subject for a Negro is the Race and its sufferings and so the song of the morning must be choked back. I will write of a lynching instead."[107]

As Wall points out, in this essay Hurston is criticizing a tradition that "silences artists . . . who do not adhere to its dictates" forged during slavery.[108] Hurston also suggests that this mandate of Black sorrow was especially reinforced in the period just after the abolition of slavery. For instance, early on in "Art and Such," Hurston identifies the period after Emancipation as a central moment when the privileging of tragedy in representations of Black life became crystallized into a "folk pattern."[109] This period, writes Hurston, was the "age of cries." "[The Black writer] rejoiced with the realization of old dreams and he cried new cries for wounds that had become scars," Hurston writes. "If it seems monotonous, one remembers the ex-slave had the pitying ear of the world. He had the encouragement of Northern sympathizers."[110]

This "age of cries," the first twenty-five years after Emancipation, is extremely important for Hurston, since it encompasses the rise of neo-abolitionism. "This post-war generation time," she writes, "was a matrix from which certain ideas came that have seriously affected art creation as well as every other form of Negro expression, including the economic."[111] And Hurston is very specific about which "ideas" she is criticizing:

> Out of this period of sound and emotion came the Race Man and Race Woman: that great horde of individuals known as "Race Champions." The great Frederick Douglass was the original pattern, no doubt, for these people who went up and down the land making speeches so fixed in type as to become a folk pattern.[112]

This "folk pattern" resulted in a "Race attitude" that mandates that we emphasize sorrow in our representations of Black life.[113] And if we are in doubt as to just who she is talking about, Douglass started it, and those who "call spirituals 'Our Sorrow Songs'" (i.e., W. E. B. Du Bois) have continued it.[114]

There are many reasons why Hurston might have alluded to both Douglass and Du Bois as targets of criticism in this essay. As many scholars have noted, the essay also harbors critiques of Black male leadership—especially Du Bois's model of the "Talented Tenth."[115] For instance, Hurston mocks the phenomenon of "double-consciousness" that informs their leadership. Instead of accepting that double-consciousness is representative of all Black life, Hurston attributes this phenomenon to the internalized racism of the elite class of Black men who got into Ivy League schools. "It was assumed that no Negro brain could ever grasp the curriculum of a white college, so the Black man who did had come by some white folk's brain by accident," Hurston surmises, "and there was bound to be conflict between his dark body and his white mind."[116] Moreover, Hurston criticizes the assumption that this elite class could know enough about the experiences of all Black folk to speak for them. "Any Negro who had all that brains to be taking a degree at a white college was bound to know every thought and feeling of every other Negro in America, however remote from him," Hurston writes sarcastically, "and he was bound to feel sad."[117] This latter criticism also characterizes how Hurston thought her approach to Black life differed from Black thinkers such as Du Bois. As she writes in a letter, "I tried to deal with life as we actually live it—not as the Sociologists imagine it."[118] While Hurston attempts to "work from the middle of the Negro out," she complains that Du Bois's method is "propaganda," a method that "never follow[s] actual conditions very accurately."[119]

These criticisms (ironically) place Hurston on the "realist" side of a realist-romantic debate that Yogita Goyal notes structures much of Black political discourse. Although romanticism is exceedingly difficult to define given its multiple references—"as a genre, a mode, a set of representational strategy, a host of narrative concerns"—Goyal uses "romanticism" to refer to "a shift outside of realism into the sphere of the marvelous rather than the mundane, often organized around the motif of a quest into unknown territories (both physical and the uncanny zone of the self)."[120] Contemporary Du Bois scholars have noted how romanticism shaped not only *The Souls of Black Folk*, but the model of racial politics that Du Bois embraced in his early years.[121] As Goyal writes, "tracking Du Bois's use of romance" can help "refin[e] our understandings of his famous conception of double-consciousness and the role of the Talented Tenth."[122] One of the major benefits that romanticism lent to Du Bois was the ability to conceptualize Blackness, to unify our racial identity, in a way that would get uptake in liberal public discourse. As Goyal observes, Du Bois "finds romance at the core of the Black experience, represented most movingly by the sorrow songs." Moreover, for Du Bois, his grasp of this romance "qualifi[ed] him" to be a "representative" of the masses of Black folk.[123] That is to say, the romance of Black sorrow, found in the "sorrow songs," is what enables Du Bois to imagine Black folk as a unified community for which he can speak.

I want to emphasize that the romanticism that contemporary scholars track in Du Bois's work was ultimately mobilized in the service of abolitionism.[124] Similar to slave narratives, Du Bois aimed to usher northern white readers into the "hidden world" of southern Black life, which was "opaque" to them and "prone to vicious misinterpretations" in popular, minstrel entertainment.[125] As such, Hurston's critique of Du Bois's style of leadership does not just refer to the use of romance or "propaganda" in depictions of southern Black life, but also captures how this romanticism was wielded within abolitionism.[126] Hurston seems to grasp the connection of abolitionism between Du Bois and Douglass by her claim that Douglass was the creator of this "folk pattern" of leadership styles that privilege Black sorrow. Although Hurston references Du Bois's moniker for Negro spirituals (i.e., "sorrow songs") in her critique of this style of leadership, Du Bois first inherited this interpretation of Negro spirituals from Douglass. Against the backdrop of political mandates harbored within the moniker "sorrow songs," Hurston asks: "Can the Black poet sing a song to the morning?" My primary foil for the development of Hurston's criticisms of neo-abolitionism will be Du Bois because Hurston saw him as a central Black leader who found ways to refashion abolitionist discourse into a radical political tradition, even after the abolition of slavery. Within the political tradition that Du Bois raised, Hurston's political and philosophical contributions to race theory tend to get buried.

Root Work

Taking seriously Hurston's criticism of neo-abolitionism, refusing the mandate that we reduce Black life to sorrow in the public sphere, means altering our analyses of southern Black life. It means, in Hurston's work, shifting from a focus on our oppression to other areas of Black life. One example of how Hurston does this is her discussions of root work in her essays. Even now in scholarship, when root work is discussed in the context of emancipatory politics, it is most often interpreted as a means of resistance, which centers our relationship to our oppressors.[127] In contrast, Hurston uses root work to signal the politics of joy, a different model of political action that centers our relationship to ourselves. This model of political action emphasizes refusal over resistance, and strategic ruse over political recognition.

As Imani Perry observes in her *Vexy Thing*, root work has long been a staple of a feminist imaginary that challenges our conceptions of political order, progressive politics, and state recognition. Noting that the language of "witchcraft" was "applied to global spiritual forms that lay outside Judeo-Christian traditions," Perry argues that the persecution of "witches" was "driven by a fear of what witches knew about different possibilities of social ordering, specifically those in which the feminine would not necessarily be subject to patriarchal authority."[128] Blending the woodsy hags of Europe with the southern conjure woman, Perry draws upon a rich tradition in Black feminist thought where root work or conjure has often captured our emancipatory imagination.[129] Within the lexicon of witchcraft, Perry finds ways to "push us beyond integrationist feminism that simply calls for inclusion in the political and intellectual grammars of Western personhood" by refusing to equate "seeking patriarchy, ladyhood, or personhood for more people" with political liberation.[130] Indeed, there seem to be resources of refusal in the very stance of the "witch" toward the world. "The witches are engaged in doings that are challenging," writes Perry, "they are presenting ideas and orders that threaten to open up the dominant logic, shift the terrain of what is regarded as mattering."[131]

Hurston, too, draws upon the lexicon of witchcraft, via root work, to signal a shift in "what is regarded as mattering." In her 1943 essay "High John de Conquer," Hurston models a shift away from a politics of resistance to a politics of joy. Both a trickster folk figure and a root used in hoodoo practices, John de Conquer stands as a kind of "patron saint" in the tradition of hoodoo.[132] In this essay, Hurston uses John de Conquer to remind us that resistance against oppression is not all there is to our liberation. She writes:

> And all the time, there was High John de Conquer playing his tricks of making a way out of no- way. Hitting a straight lick with a crooked stick. Winning the jack pot with no other stake but a laugh. Fighting a mighty battle without outside-showing force, and winning his war from within. Really winning in a permanent way, for he was winning with the soul of the Black man whole and free. So he could use it afterwards. For what shall it profit a man if he gains the whole world, and lose his own soul?[133]

In other words, what is the point of winning the battle against oppression if you are not well in the end too? The question itself implies a distinction between resistance and joy, for it suggests that it is possible to resist our oppression and still "lose [our] own soul" in the process. In this passage on emancipation, resistance to or abolition of our oppression recedes into the background, while our relation to ourselves, our inward struggle for well-being, is cast into the center.

Rather than banish Black joy or recast it in terms of resistance, Hurston points to how the laughter that John de Conquer brings can help us to "win within." "Winning within" has little to do with our oppressors. "Winning within" is not accomplished by outward shows of force against the system (or "carr[ying] [our] heart in [our] sword"), but by being "armed with love and laughter."[134] "Winning within" is not about the battle, but our inward state beyond the battle. It is a mode or an orientation that prioritizes our self-development, so that, as poet Alexis Pauline Gumbs put it, we will not be "saving up for a freedom we will be unfit for when we get there."[135] For Hurston, if we neglect this realm of self-development we risk becoming "nothing but a cruel, vengeful, grasping monster come to power."[136] We risk becoming the very thing we are opposing.

Hurston's emphasis on laughter, love, and beauty in her analysis of root work in this essay suggests the register of adornment—where the relation to the self is primary—for interpreting these practices. By using this register, she can foreground how we relate to each other. And by focusing on what John de Conquer means to us, rather than how John de Conquer can be used against our oppressors, Hurston can refuse the tragedy that is at the heart of neo-abolitionism. For instance, she refuses the abjection of Black life by showing us the joy that John de Conquer brought to the enslaved. Hurston writes that in the slave quarters, "Old John, High John could beat the unbeat-able. He was top-superior to the whole mess of sorrow. He could beat it all, and what made it so cool, finish it off with a laugh."[137] The ways that John de Conquer was used in enslaved Black life, as a source of strength, comfort, and humor, show that our lives were not wholly subsumed under sorrow as the abolitionist proclaimed.

Moreover, Hurston's analysis of root work not only asks us to broaden our emancipatory imaginary beyond resistance, but it also encourages a wariness toward the political goal of state recognition. We can see this in how Hurston fashions John de Conquer into a Black southern aesthetic that contests versions of racial progress that would leave Black southerners behind. She writes:

> So after a while, freedom came. Therefore High John de Conquer has not walked the winds of America for seventy-five years now. His people had their freedom, their laugh and their song. They have traded it to the other Americans for things they could use like education and property, and acceptance. High John de Conquer knew that that was the way it would be, so he could retire with his secret smile into the soil of the South and wait.[138]

During Hurston's time, John de Conquer had indeed been "traded to the other Americans" for gains of political recognition in the public sphere, such as "education and property, and acceptance." For many of Hurston's contemporaries, root work was a dangerous superstition that held Black people back by confirming white assumptions of our inferiority and pathology.[139] The path to state recognition, the full gains of American citizenship, meant some amount of cultural assimilation, such as relinquishing these practices of root work. But High John's "secret smile" suggests that perhaps the joke was on us in following this path. What would representation in the public sphere—education, property, and acceptance—cost us? And would it, in the end, only be a raw deal? Hurston did not live long enough to see how the coming civil rights movement indeed got the state to avow greater education, property, and acceptance, but she may have ascertained that these promises would cost us dearly. Hurston also seemed to know, as the "secret smile" suggests, that High John may have been buried, but he has certainly not been forgotten in the South. This is why Hurston references the "thousands upon thousands" in the South who still "do John reverence" by continuing root work practices.[140] And amid the racial violence and strife of our current moment, it appears that John de Conquer may have risen again through the recent turn of Black millennial faith practices to conjure.[141]

Book Overview

The Politics of Black Joy makes the arguments outlined above in a series of chapters organized by close readings of Hurston's essays. I have chosen these essays as entryways into debates within Hurston scholarship and African American philosophy more broadly, such as issues of Black representation and political recognition, the use of Negro spirituals as a model of politics, white epistemic access to Black interior life, and modes of agency beyond resistance. Before each chapter, I provide interludes from Beyoncé's visual album, *Lemonade*. These interludes offer an example of the inner workings of the politics of joy in popular culture and are a contemporary illustration of the contortions that must be made to avoid both abjection and enchantment when expressing southern Black joy in the public sphere. Each contortion in the interlude is a microcosm of the larger analysis of Hurston's racial politics enclosed in the following chapter.

The book's first chapter, "Sing[ing] a Song to the Morning," begins with the famous debate between Richard Wright and Hurston over Black art. Within this debate, I develop a relationship between Hurston's performances of indifference toward racism and the politics of joy. While Wright took Hurston's emphasis on Black joy and her downplaying of interracial violence in *Their Eyes Were Watching God* as evidence of her nostalgia, naivete, and/or political conservatism, Black feminists have been arguing for decades that Hurston's work was inherently political. I build upon these Black feminist insights by highlighting the neo-abolitionist background that motivated Hurston's desire to present Black southern life as a site of joy through a close reading of Hurston's 1944 "My Most Humiliating Jim Crow Experience" and 1945 "Crazy for This Democracy" at the end of the chapter. I argue that this strategy (the politics of joy via principled indifference toward white folks) is not an evasion of racism. Rather, it is motivated by a radical insight concerning the intransigence of racism when it comes to certain models of Black liberation.

In the next two chapters, I offer an extended development of the politics of joy in response to neo-abolitionism. In "An Object of Pity," I analyze how Du Bois uses Negro spirituals to refashion abolitionism in *The Souls of Black Folk*. I argue that it is this neo-abolitionist context to which Hurston objects in her criticisms of Du Bois's moniker, "sorrow songs." At the end of the chapter, I provide a close reading of Hurston's 1934 "Spirituals and Neo-Spirituals" to demonstrate how the politics of joy informs the debate between Hurston and Du Bois over Negro spirituals. This move broadens the terms of their disagreement to the nature of racial progress, the refusals present in root work, and the political feasibility of cultural assimilation. In "Tak[ing] the Indian Position," I more fully develop an account of refusal in Hurston's work. As an extended interview with an ex-slave, Hurston's *Barracoon* is a direct point of contact with abolitionist discourse. Placing Hurston in conversation with the contemporary anthropologist Audra Simpson, I read *Barracoon* as an "ethnographic refusal" of the neo-abolitionist presumption of white epistemic access to Black interior life.[142] Drawing upon the insight that *Barracoon* was written alongside Hurston's famous and controversial 1928 essay "How It Feels to Be Colored Me," I end with a close reading of this essay through the ethnographic refusals found in *Barracoon*.

In the final chapter, "Winning [Our] War from Within," I take up insights in Hurston's essay "High John de Conquer" to consider what mode of agency root work exhibits. When neo-abolitionism constrains us to read Black life through the lens of oppression, we end up privileging the mode of resistance in our discussions of Black political agency. Drawing upon the work of Toni Morrison as well as cultural anthropologists, I contest interpretations of root work that center resistance. By revisiting the context and cosmology of these spiritual practices, I aim to dislodge the preoccupation with resistance in our analyses of agency under oppression. I end the chapter by providing an interpretation of Hurston's "High John de Conquer" as a meta-hoodoo tale that warns us of the dangers of neo-abolitionism, which reduces Black southern life to tragedy. In addition, aligning "winning within" with the politics of joy draws upon Black feminist insights concerning the emancipatory resources found within root work. To spin a conception of agency from the folds of root work is to, as Perry urges us, "rest our thoughts, at least for a moment, on [the witch's] symbolic value for feminist thought."[143] It shows us how root work can be a way to edify ourselves rather than "study" the oppressor. Moreover, as an exemplar of the politics of joy, root work highlights the central crossroads that Hurston traversed while writing about southern Black life: the contravening frameworks of minstrelsy and abolitionism that continue to eclipse Black southern joy in our political imaginary.

Scene 1

✦

"I Ain't Thinkin' 'Bout You"

Rather similar to "I ain't studyin' you," "I ain't thinkin' 'bout you" is a central refrain throughout the song "Sorry" in Beyoncé's visual album *Lemonade*.[1] At this point in the album, the protagonist's husband has been offering half-hearted attempts at reconciliation. I say "half-hearted" because, as Beyoncé sings, the husband is still cheating on her ("I see them boppers in the corner / They sneaking out the back door") and is not truly sorry for his wrongs ("He only want me when I'm not there"). Her response to his half-hearted apology is a refusal to entertain his attempts at reconciliation.[2] It is tempting to read the album as simply a tiff between lovers. However, if we read the "you" that Beyoncé is addressing here as America, the ironic eulogy that opens the album's "Apathy" chapter (under which "Sorry" falls) takes on a much darker valence.[3]

"So what are you gonna say at my funeral now that you've killed me?" Beyoncé asks. "Here lies the body of the love of my life, whose heart I broke without a gun to my head." What if Beyoncé is suggesting not only a personal betrayal, but a national betrayal? America has long relied upon our love and labor and killed us in return. Beyoncé not only draws these stronger resonances with references to Black Lives Matter throughout the album, but she also takes us to the primary scene of national betrayal in the song "Sorry"— the plantation. To start "Sorry" at the site of the plantation may suggest why the protagonist is not "thinkin' 'bout" America's current half-hearted attempts at social remedies, promises of addressing racial injustices, or gestures at granting us political recognition.[4] Put another way, seeking the methods of political redress available in our public discourse may not be appropriate if our national counterpart has yet to truly change its bad behavior.

However, the response to America's betrayal that is modeled in "Sorry" is not only pessimism, but southern Black joy.[5] The song is partitioned by an apathetic "enthronement" at Destrehan plantation, a joyous spiritual bus ride, and a ceremonious swamp meeting.[6] What might we make of racism, the South, and abolitionism given this imagery in "Sorry"? There are two things to note here. First, Beyoncé's "enthronement" at the plantation suggests the authority or control gained from observing an emotional boundary over the trauma that whites invoked through slavery. Her body language on the throne—slouching, smirks, and flips of the wrists—suggests that she is not bothered. That is, she is not rehearsing the pain of enslavement; she is performing dominion over it by not "studyin' it." Perhaps this is the best you can do to take care of yourself when you are dealing with a nation that won't deal with the wrongs of its past. Acknowledge it, but don't "study it" on your own time. This may be why the protagonist insists upon not "thinkin' 'bout" her wayward lover (or the nation)—she is aware of how all that can "interrupt her grindin.' "[7]

What is more, this imaginative remaking of plantation life (i.e., Beyoncé's "enthronement") pushes against the neo-abolitionist mandate that Black southern life should be represented in terms of tragedy. Her enthronement at the plantation contests the very site where tragic images of Black life were first produced in abolitionist discourse. And her emotional state on the throne rebuffs the pity that abolitionists sought to stir in their white audience. In contrast to the abolitionist appeals to white consciences, this stance of apathy implies a lack of interest in the pursuit of racial recognition. This lack of interest, again, is due to a racial pessimism with regard to our national counterpart. Perhaps unusually, I read Beyoncé's apathetic enthronement and her joyous bus ride as intimately connected with her participation in root work. That is, root work on the bus ride is what enables her performance of apathy or indifference at the plantation. This is because the root work on the bus ride provides another register of knowledge by which to assess her worth in this world (i.e., her "ori" or destiny). In other words, the protagonist can be indifferent toward (not "thinkin' 'bout") her lover (or the nation) precisely because root work provides another thing for her to "study."

In the chapter that follows, I provide an interpretation of Hurston's racial politics that is predicated on racial pessimism and riddled with Black joy. Hurston's response, like Beyoncé in *Lemonade*, also connects a performance of indifference with the development of southern Black joy. In response to white racism, Hurston often took the stance of "I ain't thinkin' 'bout you." Instead of rehearsing narratives of Black southern tragedy, her stories more often than not focused on Black people "headed to the club." While this tendency often got Hurston accused of nostalgia or naivete, I argue that this tendency is informed by a deep pessimism of recognition politics when it came to her white counterparts. Rather than seek white recognition by appealing to stories of Black southern tragedy, Hurston often chose to "study" how African Americans managed to create a life for themselves in spite of their oppression, such as through root work. Through her insistence upon not "studyin' " white racism, Hurston seemed to grasp the intimate connection between southern Black joy and the principled indifference that Beyoncé artistically renders in *Lemonade*.

Chapter 1

✦

"Sing[ing] a Song to the Morning"
The Politics of Joy

> Can the black poet sing a song to the morning? Upsprings the
> song to his lips but it is fought back. He says to himself, "Ah
> this is a beautiful song inside me. I feel the morning star in
> my throat. I will sing of the star and the morning." Then his
> background thrusts itself between his lips and the star and he
> mutters, "Ought I not to be singing of our sorrows? That is
> what is expected of me and I shall be considered forgetful of
> our past and present. If I do not some will even call me a cow-
> ard. The one subject for a Negro is the Race and its sufferings
> and so the song of the morning must be choked back. I will
> write of a lynching instead."
>
> —Zora Neale Hurston, "Art and Such"

In the epigraph, Hurston complains about the pressure African American
artists feel to only relay stories of Black tragedy and oppression. Throughout
her career, she often criticized African American writers who succumbed to
that pressure. Consider, for instance, Hurston's 1938 "Stories of Conflict,"
a harsh review of Richard Wright's *Uncle Tom's Children*.[1] Although Hurston's critique of Wright reads as deeply personal, a "discursive throw down,"
the themes present in this short review exemplify how Hurston's refusal of
tragic depictions of southern Black life dovetailed with issues of gender and
class.[2] Moreover, the review is a site where the tragic depictions of southern Black life are implicitly linked to neo-abolitionism, such as the legacy of
Harriet Beecher Stowe's *Uncle Tom's Cabin*.[3] In her review, Hurston criticizes Wright's novel for fitting into a pattern of tragic representation of Black
southern life as "[a] dismal, hopeless section ruled by brutish hatred and
nothing else."[4] I stress that this pattern of tragic representation not only had
regional dynamics but gendered ones as well. For example, Hurston argues
that Wright's "sentences" which "have the shocking-power of a forty-four"
are designed to satisfy the tastes of a male audience.[5] "There is lavish killing

29

here," Hurston writes, "perhaps enough to satisfy all male Black readers."[6] Hurston also notes that this writing style is raced and gendered by considering Wright's storyline: the Black male hero is one who "gets his man" (i.e., the white man) and avenges "his woman."[7]

While Wright accused Hurston of participating in the minstrel tradition for emphasizing Black joy, she claims here that Wright makes Black southern life a tragic spectacle to satisfy both a white, northern (or rather, neo-abolitionist) audience and his Black male readers.[8] That is, white publishers preferred stories that portrayed Blacks as tragic heroes or violent victims in their confrontation with, and protest of, racism.[9] This preference can be traced back to abolitionist discourse, from which arose the mandate that "the one subject for a Negro is the Race and its sufferings."[10] Moreover, Black male audiences expected this confrontation with white men to be showcased. In her review Hurston admits that Wright has tremendous talents, but she wonders "what he would have done had he dealt with plots that touched the broader and more fundamental phases of Negro life."[11] Hurston's emphasis on the "broader and more fundamental phases of Negro life" echoes her complaints in her 1938 essay "Art and Such," written the same year as this review. In "Art and Such," Hurston bemoans that Black writing is often restricted to the sorrow and tragedy of southern Black life, "despite the obvious fact that Negroes love and hate and fight and play and strive and travel and have thousand and one interests in life like other humans."[12] Her struggle to present more nuanced depictions of southern Black life was intimately tied to her more controversial positions on racial politics—positions that often put her at odds with her contemporaries.

Black Feminist Interventions

One of Hurston's most controversial positions can be found in her later essay, "Court Order Can't Make Races Mix." In this 1955 essay, she denounces the Supreme Court's *Brown vs. Board* decision to desegregate the nation's public schools. She was well aware that this position was controversial, that "a great clamor will arise in certain quarters [that] I seek to deny the Negro children of the South their rights."[13] However, what was at stake for Hurston was a depiction of Black southern life that robbed us of self-respect. Hurston writes:

> If there are not adequate Negro schools in Florida, and there is some residual, some inherent and unchangeable quality in white schools, impossible to duplicate anywhere else, then I am the first to insist that Negro children of Florida be allowed to share this boon. But if there are adequate Negro schools and prepared instructors and instructions, then there is nothing different except the presence of

white people. For this reason, I regard the ruling of the U.S. Supreme
Court as insulting rather than honoring my race. Since the days of
the never-to-be-sufficiently-deplored Reconstruction, there has been
current the belief that there is no greater delight to Negroes than
physical association with whites.[14]

For Hurston, the Supreme Court decision harbored insulting assumptions
about Black life, such as the desire for white association or the belief in Black
inferiority. For Hurston, these assumptions also seem to be implicitly linked
with abolitionist propaganda.

For example, Hurston links the reasoning behind the Supreme Court
decision with the "Race Men" whom she criticizes in "Art and Such" for
making a political platform out of Black tragedy. These "Race Men" "stand
around and mouth the same trite phrases, and try their practiced-best to
look sad," Hurston writes, even though they face "a situation as different
from the 1880s as chalk is from cheese."[15] Hurston assures her readers that
the "Race Man is still with us—he and his Reconstruction pullings. His job
today is to rush around and seek for something he can 'resent.' "[16] It is this
same platform of sorrow and resentment that Hurston criticizes later in her
"Court Order Can't Make Races Mix": "It is well known that I have no
sympathy or respect for the 'tragedy of color' school of thought among us,
whose fountain-head is the pressure group concerned in this court ruling."[17]
To emphasize her point, Hurston asserts that she "can see no tragedy in being
too dark to be invited to a white school social affair."[18]

It is important to note that Hurston does not contest desegregation itself,
but the terms upon which it proceeds in "Court Order Can't Make Races
Mix." She advocates for "ethical and cultural" desegregation instead of
the legal desegregation advanced by the Supreme Court.[19] This pivot is an
example of the kind of deflection on southern racism that often infuriated
and drew sharp criticism from Hurston's intellectual contemporaries. That is,
rather than take up criticism of southern segregation, Hurston deflects, pointing to how segregation is a national, ethical, and cultural problem rather
than a "sectional" or regional one that can be solved by tinkering with legal
codes. However, as Hurston writes in a letter to Claude Barnett, her frequent
attempts to nuance life in the South were often "twist[ed]" into support for
Jim Crow.[20] These controversial positions of Hurston concerning southern
Black life often caused ambivalence regarding her racial politics even as we
continue to celebrate her work today.[21]

Over the decades, feminists (especially Black feminists) have used a variety of approaches to contextualize and make sense of Hurston's politics.
For instance, Black feminists first recovered Hurston in the 1970s by highlighting the intra-racial politics that Hurston's work exhibits. This strategy
was especially important at this time because this was a period of bringing
Black feminist criticism into the academy. The erasures that Black women

were experiencing in both the political arena and academic disciplines at this time were exemplified in the earlier erasure of Hurston from the Harlem Renaissance.[22] As such, Hurston's recovery by these Black feminists was also a catalyst for the political and intellectual recovery of Black women's lives.[23] For example, Black feminists used Hurston's interventions to expose how the current Black liberation movements (such as Black nationalism and the Black Arts Movement) exhibited a masculinist project that privileged inter-racial politics (i.e., Black men warring against white men) over intra-racial concerns of gender and class.[24]

An example of this strategy can be found in Barbara Smith's essay "Sexual Politics and the Politics of Zora Neale Hurston." With regard to Hurston's racial politics, Smith concedes that "Hurston can fairly be described as indi-vidualistic and conservative."[25] However, "[Hurston's] insights into sexual politics indicate that she was inherently feminist, a radical stance for a Black woman in any era."[26] With this approach, the apparent contradictions within Hurston's stances on race are nuanced by privileging Hurston's intra-racial political insights over her interracial politics. Her criticisms of "Race Men" noted earlier are understood to expose the violent suppression of Black wom-en's voices and issues in the political arena.[27] And in Smith's account of *Their Eyes Were Watching God*, space for Black joy is carved out by Hurston's pursuit of self-fulfillment, love, and happiness in the character Janie's journey to come to terms with and transcend the various oppressions that are spe-cific to Black women. This journey is not representative of the entire Black race, but a foray into the intra-racial dynamics that inform our lives. This is part of what it meant, Smith writes, for Hurston to "tak[e] Black women seriously."[28] It means "that Janie's life is seen as inherently valuable," Smith notes, and "there is the assumption that she has the right to search for happi-ness and freedom, however she may define them."[29]

Closely tied to the privileging of intra-racial politics is the importance of individual expression within the collective. This emphasis on individuality has informed another approach to contextualizing Hurston's racial and gen-der politics. An example of this approach can be found in Deborah Plant's *Every Tub Must Sit on Its Own Bottom*. Hurston's "political philosophy of uncompromising individualism," Plant writes, "helped her survive systematic sexism, racism, and classism, strengthened her will to resist negative control-ling images, and empowered her to overcome."[30] Moreover, Plant sees the collective and the individual in connection rather than opposition. "Hurston's philosophy of individualism was firmly rooted in an African American folk ethos, which is a fundamental 'site of resistance,' " she writes.[31] As a result, Plant insists that Hurston "understood profoundly the significance of African American culture as a vital component in the full emancipation of African American people, individually and collectively."[32] This is because African American culture was a repository for "alternative images, self-definitions, and strategies necessary to resist Anglo-American cultural domination and to reclaim Black life."[33] For Plant, this reclamation of Black life takes place on the level of the self in Hurston's work, even as African American culture provides the alternative self-definitions that Hurston sought. In this way, Hurston's drive for individual expression, where the Black poet can exist as "an individual" and not just as "another tragic unit of the Race," is a crucial lens for interpreting her racial politics.[34]

In both approaches, Hurston's portrayals of Black joy in the South (such as in *Their Eyes Were Watching God*), which were a major departure from the political mandate of representations of southern interracial strife, are linked to various refusals: a refusal to politically prioritize fights between Black men and white men; a refusal to define Black life in terms of the racism we face; and a refusal to let the racism and sexism of the world define how Hurston relates to herself.[35] This same emphasis can be seen, for example, in the work of the earlier recovery period of the 1970s, such as in June Jordan's "Notes toward a Black Balancing of Love and Hatred." In this essay, Jordan links political protests with affirmations of Black culture (or joy).[36] We can also see these themes of refusal in contemporary Hurston scholarship, such as Carla Kaplan's *The Erotics of Talk*, Erica Edwards's *Charisma and the Fictions of Black Leadership*, and Cheryl Wall's *On Freedom and the Will to Adorn*.[37] I want to follow suit, using the language of refusal to explore the political effects of Hurston's emphasis on southern Black joy in the public sphere. Using the language of refusal in my analysis enables me to do two things. First, I will put Hurston's insights on race into conversation with contemporary discussions of recognition politics, liberalism, and the importance of refusal in race scholarship. Second, the language of refusal enables me to foreground the implicit neo-abolitionist context of her politics of joy.

Resistance, Refusal, and Root Work

I want to stress that I do not see "refusal" as a synonym for "resistance." One of the main differences between refusal and resistance is how each concept treats the search for political recognition.[38] Resistance locks us into a life-and-death struggle with our oppressor for recognition. In contrast, refusal *withholds* recognition of the oppressor's power or authority to define our lives. Instead of seeking recognition from a state that continues to oppress us, to refuse, as the cultural anthropologist Audra Simpson observes, is to decide *not* to "let go, roll over, or play this game."[39] Moreover, by refusing the terms of recognition issued by an oppressive state, we can render those terms more explicit.[40] As noted in the introduction, Hurston understood that political recognition from northern white liberals required that we contort ourselves into an "object of pity."[41] Hurston rejected those terms of recognition (Black abjection) by maintaining a state of indifference toward whites. In contrast to the images of abjection that arise from neo-abolitionism, Hurston found alternative sources of self-definition and recognition in African American folklore and cultural traditions, such as root work. By providing a possible alternative source of recognition, root work operates as the ground or conditions of possibility for refusals to be defined (or recognized) by our oppressors.

To illustrate the differences between resistance and refusal, as well as the role of root work in distinguishing the two, consider the character Sixo in Toni Morrison's novel *Beloved*. Sixo is a slave of Indigenous and African origin. When Sixo is caught stealing, he argues with the slave master (Schoolteacher) about who is actually stealing from whom, the slave or the master. This is an example of resistance, direct engagement with the oppressor. And the result is an important one for Sixo: "clever, but schoolteacher beat [Sixo] anyway to show him that definitions belonged to the definers—not the defined."[42] Sixo's argument with Schoolteacher can be contrasted with refusal, such as when Sixo "stopped speaking English because there was no future in it."[43] This shift in Sixo's behavior is preceded by his participation in practices of root work, his going out "among the trees at night. For dancing, he said, to keep his bloodlines open."[44] And Sixo's refusal to communicate with the master (i.e., "speak English") is the beginning of his "unsuitableness" for slavery.[45] Put another way, Sixo's refusal gives way to an "enjoyment" that often accompanies such acts, an enjoyment that wreaks havoc upon the order imposed by domination.[46] For example, while he is being burned to death by Schoolteacher, Sixo's laughter and song-making mark his participation in the practice of "juba," a dance and praise-song to the gods.[47] It is this juba that makes Schoolteacher, who "knew the worth of everything," regard Sixo as now "unsuitable."[48] For "who could be fooled into buying a singing nigger with a gun? . . . What a laugh. So rippling and full of glee it put out the fire."[49] Rather than struggle for recognition from Schoolteacher, e.g., by arguing with him over the definition of stealing, Sixo's refusal withholds recognition of Schoolteacher's valuation and estimation of his life. This can be seen in Sixo's shout as he dies in the fire with Schoolteacher watching. Sixo dies "shouting Seven-O! Seven O!" Morrison writes, "because his Thirty-Mile Woman got away with his blossoming seed."[50] His triumphant shout, steeped in juba, refuses recognition of Schoolteacher's reduction of his life to calloused breeding and increasing white male property. I maintain that this discussion of refusal, resistance, and root work can even provide a different entryway into the Hurston-Wright debate than the usual framework of apolitical individualism (Hurston) versus political protest (Wright).[51]

While Hurston and Wright were both southerners who were deeply interested in the emancipatory potential of Black folklore, their chosen folk heroes fell along the fault lines of resistance and refusal.[52] In his 1937 "Blueprint for Negro Writing," Wright notes how Black folklore "embodies the memories and hopes" of our "struggle for freedom."[53] It is interesting to consider the example of Black folklore that he uses to demonstrate this point:

> In the absence of fixed and nourishing forms of culture, the Negro has a folklore which embodies the memories and hopes of his struggle for freedom. Not yet caught in paint or stone, and as yet but feebly depicted in the poem and novel, the Negroes' most powerful images of hope and despair still remains in the fluid state of daily speech. How many John Henrys have lived and died on the lips of these Black people?[54]

The legend of John Henry has its roots in the construction of the Chesapeake and Ohio Railroad in West Virginia in the 1870s. It branched outward through song and oral storytelling well into the 1930s.[55] One of many Black male chain-gang workers, John Henry was known for a mythic victory where he, by natural strength alone, won a contest with his hammer against new machines introduced for construction. The songs and tales surrounding John Henry depict the dismal conditions of the workers, as well as the encroachment of industrialization that further alienated them from their labor.[56] In many versions of the story, John Henry defeats a white man who uses the new machines. In nearly all versions, John Henry dies of exhaustion after the battle. Some versions recast John Henry as a Jesus-like figure, where he is resurrected days later.[57] Additionally, some versions of the tale make John Henry's hammer a symbol for his penis, drawing a parallel between his ability to drive a hammer and his sexual prowess.[58]

I argue that John Henry is preferred by Wright because he is emblematic of the mode of agency that Wright prefers, resistance. In *Black Culture and Black Consciousness*, Lawrence Levine claims that John Henry is especially loved by Blacks because he "defeated white society on *its* own territory and by *its* own rules."[59] That is, he played the white man's game and won, exemplifying a resistant mode of agency. John Henry is also no trickster figure. Rather, he "defeat[s] rivals . . . directly and publicly," being "contemptuous of guile and indirection."[60] As we have noted earlier, some Black men are very interested in this type of confrontation, direct and open, public and individualized. Moreover, this confrontation is often sexualized as well. Part of John Henry's allure and strength are derived from his powerful penis in folktales. To tie John Henry's sexuality to the defeat of the white man is to perform a symbolic reverse castration. Wright may have also been motivated to symbolically participate in this reverse castration by promoting John Henry since, as James Baldwin observes of Wright, the "root" of the violence that proliferates in Wright's texts is "the rage, almost literally the howl, of a man who is being castrated."[61] Given the direct and central confrontation with the white man in John Henry's tale, Wright's focus on John Henry reflects his *gendered* preference for protest as exemplified in his *Uncle Tom's Children*. In other words, it intimates his depiction of Black life as fundamentally a violent struggle against racism.

Contrary to Levine's claim that John Henry is *the* central figure of Black folklore, Hurston claims that a very different John "runs through all our folk-lore."[62] In many ways, John de Conquer, who is both a hoodoo root and a folk figure, is the opposite of John Henry. Consider Hurston's comments on John de Conquer in her 1943 essay "High John de Conquer." While Wright emphasizes our being separated from Africa through John Henry, Hurston notes that even while the ships "hauled [slaves] across the water to helplessness" during the Middle Passage, John de Conquer "was walking the very winds that filled the sails of the ships."[63] While John Henry was a stranger in the North (West Virginia), John de Conquer is the ancestor who "retire[d] with his secret smile into the soil of the South."[64] While John Henry is isolated, reliant upon only his natural strength to combat racism, Hurston emphasizes John de Conquer's spiritual role within the community. More specifically, John de Conquer was invoked through spiritual practices that offered the enslaved an "inside thing to live by."[65] This "inside thing to live by," in turn, connected the enslaved to each other and fostered a sense of community.[66] And while John Henry signals open, public, and direct confrontation with whites, John de Conquer "has evaded the ears of white people" and is loved for his many ruses and tricks.[67]

John de Conquer is also a symbol of the laughing juba that intoxicated Sixo in the fire.[68] As such, John de Conquer provided the grounds for the enslaved to refuse the terms of reality that the master supplied, and instead furnish their own. Hurston writes:

> The sign of [High John de Conquer] was a laugh, and his singing-symbol was a drum-beat. No parading drum-shout like soldiers out for a show. It did not call to the feet of those who were fixed to hear it. It was an inside thing to live by. It was sure to be heard when and where the work was the hardest, and the lot the most cruel. It helped the slaves endure. They knew that something better was coming. So they laughed in the face of things and sang, "I'm so glad! Trouble don't last always." And the white people who heard them were struck dumb that they could laugh. In an outside way, this was Old Massa's fun, so what was Old Cuffy laughing for? Old Massa couldn't know, of course, but High John de Conquer was there walking his plantation like a natural man. He was treading the sweat-flavored clods of the plantation, crushing out his drum tunes, and giving out secret laughter.[69]

There are several things to note from this passage. First, the laughter that John de Conquer brings signals a contrast in perceptions of reality between the enslaved and whites, who were "struck dumb" by such laughter. Second, not only are whites "struck dumb" at our laughter, but they are implicitly threatened. That is, the laughter of the enslaved invokes a power shift, whereby the enslaved partake of something that the slave masters presumed was firmly in their domain, or "Old Massa's fun." In this way, John de Conquer was "walking [the slave master's] plantation," undermining the slave master's authority by "giving out [his] secret laughter." Similar to Sixo's laughter in the fire, this secret laughter challenges the authority of the slave master or the staying power of his definitions. Indeed, John de Conquer tells the enslaved, when it comes to the slave master, "[d]on't pay what [the slave master] say no mind. You know where you got something finer than this plantation and anything it's got on it."[70] And third, the work that John de Conquer is doing is taking place on a different register than resistance or direct confrontation. Root work is neither the "parading drum-shout like soldiers for show" nor does it "call to the feet of those who were fixed to hear it." To put it another way, root work, or John de Conquer, operates in terms of secrecy, thus *avoiding* recognition from whites. Rather than wage a direct war with whites, John de Conquer shifts the battle to one within the very souls of Black folk. As Hurston writes, John de Conquer helped the slaves "fight a mighty battle without outside-showing force" and "win [their] war from within."[71]

Capturing the political effects of this pivot, from seeking the recognition of the oppressor to the struggle for self-definition, is one of the resources that the language of refusal offers. And one political effect is that refusing the recognition of the oppressor puts the authority of the oppressor in question, shifting (and perhaps undermining) the power dynamic. As Morrison observes,

> there are lots of ways to destabilize racism, and protest novels are only one way. Maybe they're the best way, and maybe they aren't. I'm not interested in that. I'm interested in Black readers and me. I think that when you constantly focus on the Nazi, you give him more power than he should have. That's what confrontation in art sometimes does. It's like asking a jazz musician to play his music so white people will like it, and I don't think that's what's going on with Black women.[72]

In other words, one of the political effects of this pivot can be "destabilizing racism" (rather than eradicating it). This turn toward "Black readers and me" that Morrison invokes parallels Hurston's focus on Black joy, to the point of appearing indifferent to interracial conflict. Within interpersonal contexts, this performance of indifference is often marked by strong, negative affectual responses by oppressors, for they experience it as an affront. Indeed, Hurston's performances of indifference often registered antagonist affects within her northern white liberal counterparts.[73] Moreover, her contemporaries and critics saw her indifference as an ignorant evasion or a perverse misunderstanding of racism. However, as I will demonstrate with the politics of joy, she only ascertained that the game was rigged, and so she chose to play a different one altogether.[74]

"Picking Up" Her Points

In the case of Sixo, refusal becomes a political option when all good faith departs from our endeavors with the other.[75] This often happened when Hurston encountered the racism disguised as regionalism among her northern white liberal counterparts.[76] Hurston's response, in these scenarios, was similar to Sixo's decision to "no longer speak English." That is, Hurston saw the futility in trying to "reason" with whites who have not reckoned with their own racism. Instead of trying to "reason" with whites who veiled their racism by invoking a racist, white southerner, Hurston often refused the terms of the conversation. She did so by appearing indifferent to southern racism and playing up instances of Black joy. Put another way, the politics of joy often occurs in Hurston's work as a practice of principled indifference or active disinterest in narratives of tragic southern Black life due to racism.

This strategy is closely related to what Hurston describes in her introduction to her 1935 *Mules and Men*. What do you do when you don't have the option of removing yourself from racist whites, but you also don't want to play their game? Hurston wrote that her southern Black respondents are often

> most reluctant at times to reveal that which the soul lives by. And the Negro, in spite of his open-faced laughter, his seeming acquiescence, is particularly evasive. You see we are a polite people and we do not say to our questioner, "Get out of here!" We smile and tell him or her something that satisfies the white person because, knowing so little about us, he doesn't know what he is missing . . . That is, we let the probe enter, but it never comes out. It gets smothered under a lot of laughter and pleasantries.[77]

Wielding the power of laughter like Sixo or John de Conquer did, Hurston's Black southern respondents subtly refuse their interviewers. They "let the probe enter" through a performance of indifference, such as when they "smile and tell him or her something that satisfies the white person" rather than telling interviewers to "Get out of here!" And through that performance of indifference, they subtly refuse to answer these questions that probe into Black interiority or how they/we *really* feel.

The type of refusals that I am tracking through the politics of joy has a different context than that of Hurston's respondents in *Mules and Men*. I am specifically interested in those moments when Hurston is engaged with northern white liberals who are trying to probe her southern Black interiority. Hurston was aware that northern white liberals were primed for stories of southern Black tragedy due to the "phraseology of the Abolition struggle" exhibited in novels like *Uncle Tom's Cabin*.[78] In abolitionist discourse, Black suffering was the terms upon which whites recognized our humanity. Rather than confirm these narratives, Hurston often syncopated, accenting what was

normally left out of these conversations, such as scenes of southern Black
joy. This joyous syncopation shifted the accent of these conversations by
downplaying or appearing indifferent to what was normally stressed in these
exchanges, southern white racism and Black southern tragedy.

We can see this in action, for instance, in Hurston's essay "The 'Pet Negro'
System":

> It has been so generally accepted that all Negroes in the South are
> living under horrible conditions that many friends of the Negro up
> North actually take offense if you don't tell them a tale of horror
> and suffering. They stroll up to you, cocktail glass in hand, and say,
> "I am a friend of the Negro, you know, and feel awful about the ter-
> rible conditions down there." That's your cue to launch into atrocities
> amidst murmurs of sympathy. If, on the other hand, just to find out if
> they've really done some research down there, you ask, "What condi-
> tions do you refer to?" you get an injured, and sometimes a malicious,
> look. Why ask foolish questions? Why drag in the many Negroes of
> opulence and education? Yet these comfortable, contented Negroes
> are as real as the sharecroppers.[79]

In this conversation, Hurston appears indifferent or pretends not to know
"what conditions they refer to," evading the probe of her northern white
interlocutor, who is in search of a personal story of southern suffering. Rather
than play along the beat dictated by this northern white liberal or "friend of
the Negro up North," Hurston shifts the accent, from southern "sharecrop-
pers" to "comfortable, contended Negroes." There are two crucial aspects
of racial politics that inform this joyous shift for Hurston. The first aspect
describes the *conditions* that prompt a refusal: the intransigence of racism
to certain liberation strategies. The second aspect is the *enactment* of refusal
through a performance of indifference, or decentering racism in representations of Black life by shoring up Black joy. Both aspects appear in Hurston's
essays "My Most Humiliating Jim Crow Experience" (1944) and "Crazy for
This Democracy" (1945).

The Intransigence of Racism

For Hurston, white supremacy is a national, institutional, and psychological structure.[80] In "My Most Humiliating Jim Crow Experience," Hurston
recounts an experience of racism in order to challenge common beliefs about
race and racism. Due to Hurston's frequent digestion problems, her patron,
Mrs. R. Osgood Mason, arranged a visit to a white specialist. However, upon
her arrival at the doctor's office, Hurston was hastily swept into a broom
closet and handled quickly by the doctor. Sensing that the staff was embar-
rassed to have a Black customer, Hurston deliberately stayed longer to see

"what would happen, and further to torture [the doctor] more."[81] There are two comments in this essay that are central to how Hurston thought about white supremacy and region.

In the opening lines of the essay, Hurston remarks that this humiliating experience "came in New York instead of the South as one would have expected."[82] Throughout her body of work, Hurston consistently reminds us that racism is present in both the South *and* the North. As she remarked to Alain Locke in a letter on July 23, 1943, to pretend that racism is a regional problem is to ignore that racism is a national issue.[83] Therefore, she insists that racism is not the result of the taste of "uncivilized" southerners, but a characteristic of Western civilization itself: "The truth of the matter is that the Anglo-Saxon is the most intolerant of human beings in the matter of any other group darker than themselves."[84] In answer to those who blame racism on the South, Hurston asks, "Did the southerners colonize Africa and India, and put over the outrages based on race there? Were these slave holders southerners in the beginning?"[85] To view racism as a regional problem is to fail to address the real scale of the problem.

In "Crazy for This Democracy," Hurston develops these points further in the context of segregation in the South.[86] Rather provocatively for the time, Hurston argues that ending segregation in the South will not be enough to dismantle racism. Likening racism to a disease, Hurston claims that to mistake segregation for the sickness is a "sentimental oversimplification in diagnosis," for "segregation and things like that are the bumps and blisters on the skin, and not the disease, but evidence and symptoms of the sickness."[87] For those who think that moving North would end their troubles with racism, Hurston writes that "some strangely assert that a change of climate is all that is needed to kill the virus in the blood!"[88] For those whose think that appeals to the conscience of northern white liberals will be our salvation, Hurston admonishes that "the business of some whites to help pick a bump or so is even part of the pattern. Not a human right, but a concession from the throne has been made."[89] Hurston names "Jim Crow" as the disease itself, a legal and social institution that is both a national and global system of oppression.[90] It is worth quoting Hurston in full here:

> Jim Crow is the rule in South Africa, and is even more extensive than in America. More rigid and grinding. No East Indian may ride first-class in the trains of British-held India. Jim Crow is common in all colonial Africa, Asia, and the Netherland East Indies. There, too, a Javenese male is punished for flirting back at a white female. So why this stupid assumption that "moving North" will do away with social smallpox?[91]

This "disease" especially renders the experiment of democracy ineffective in the United States. And it makes the United States the "arse-and-all" in all our international relations. "The Ass-and-All of Democracy has shouldered the load of subjugating the dark world completely," Hurston observes.[92] Having never truly experienced the democracy of which the United States boasts, Hurston writes, "I am crazy about the idea of Democracy. I want to see how it feels."[93]

If racism is truly the global, social pathology that Hurston claims in this essay, then the strategies for liberation (i.e., integration) employed by her contemporaries will never match the scale or quality of the problem at hand.[94] And so, Hurston remarks:

> So why the waste of good time and energy, and further delay the recovery of the patient by picking him over bump by bump and blister to blister? Why not the shot of serum that will kill the thing in the blood? The bumps are symptoms. The symptoms cannot disappear until the cause is cured.[95]

Hurston rejects southern integration as the cure because the social and legal conventions of "Jim Crow" (i.e., white supremacy) work on a "physical and emotional" level to normalize racism.[96] The separate seats, houses, the exclusion from certain activities and places are all part of a national web of ways to bolster whites' sense of superiority.[97] As such, white children who grow up under "Jim Crow" are taught that they are superior to Blacks simply by their birth.[98] If this is the case, even if we were to dwell in the same spaces, how could we possibly be considered equal actors in the experiment of democracy?

Hurston ends "My Most Humiliating Jim Crow Experience" on a similar note, which is the second central comment about white supremacy for our discussion. Rather than internalize the pain of her experience and succumb to a sense of inferiority, she "set[s] [her] hat at a reckless angle and walk[s] out . . . feeling the pathos of Anglo-Saxon civilization."[99] By *pathos*, she means *pathological*. "And I still mean pathos," she writes, "for I know that anything with such a false foundation cannot last. Whom the gods would destroy, they first make mad."[100] I argue that Hurston stresses this point because a common liberation strategy during her time assumed that whites could be reasoned with, their consciences called upon, if only they could be convinced of our humanity.[101] However, if whites truly are "mad" due to the effects of racism, this strategy is never enough. Tinkering with a few laws and offering heartfelt humanistic appeals will not help us in the end if "all of it"—the *entire* social fabric of our society—"is wrong."[102]

With these comments in mind, we can outline the contour of conditions that prompt the refusal which lies at the heart of the politics of joy. That is, the politics of joy arise out of an awareness that certain strategies are limited, depending on our vision of liberation. Hurston was deeply suspicious of the regionalism that allows us to map the nation's racism solely onto the South. In her 1943 letter to Alain Locke noted earlier, Hurston contends that this regionalism is part of the legacy of abolitionist discourse, or an instance of neo-abolitionism. Because northern white liberals had "carried over the phraseology of the Abolition struggle," Hurston found that they were

> caught between the folk-lore [they] ha[ve] been raised on about Negroes, and [their] actual feelings. But so much has happened, including the Civil War, that [they] hate to admit it. So [they] take refuge in saying that southerners moving north did it. This is ridiculous on the face of it. The Negroes who have gloried in the nort[h] are also caught, so they join in the chorus, "Them southerners snuk up here and done it."[103]

Such a tactic blinds us to the fact that racism is a national and global institution. Hurston was also wary of a white, northern liberalism that only "picks the bumps" of racism, leaving the pathology of racism to rage throughout the body politic. And Hurston understood that racism is much too deep-seated to be fixed by appeals to the conscience or compassion of racist whites. In fact, such appeals might even reinforce the psychological dynamics of superiority and saviorism that often plagues whites. These insights make the confrontation of racism necessary but ultimately insufficient in successfully navigating interacting oppressions. That is to say, these factors make racism intransigent to certain liberation tactics. Due to racism's complex and multifaceted underpinnings, it might be better to "allow the probe to enter" but never find its way back out when encountering such whites.

Decentering Racism in Representations of Southern Black Life

The second crucial aspect of the politics of joy is that of decentering racism in representations of southern Black life. By "decentering racism," I mean that Hurston deliberately emphasized other aspects of southern Black life over racism, thus violating the neo-abolitionist norms of representations of southern interracial strife. In her attempts to decenter racism, Hurston seemed to be in contradiction with her views on race as provided above. These apparent contradictions have led some critical scholars to either dismiss Hurston's views on race or to engage in diatribes that attack her personality, sanity, and gender. For instance, Andrew Delbanco claims that "Crazy for This Democracy" contradicts Hurston's earlier public views on race. To support his claim, he provides a quote from an interview two years earlier where Hurston says, "the lot of the Negro is much better in the South than in the North."[104] He concludes that "Hurston's politics had never been coherent, and it is a mistake, really to take her opinions too seriously. She tended to shoot off letters to the editor and to blurt things out in interviews."[105] This paints Hurston as a quick-tempered, irrational blabbermouth whose racial convictions are spun for personal advantage. However, if we turn to Hurston's letters written during the same period as "My Most Humiliating Jim Crow Experience" and "Crazy for This Democracy," we can gain more insight into the logic that undergirds her racial polemic in these essays.

For instance, Hurston commented on the 1943 interview to which Delbanco is referring in a letter to Claude Barnett.[106] In this letter, Hurston expresses outrage at how the editors distorted her words. "You can see him cutting out, and substituting," Hurston asserts, while "he hints at some of the things I really did say, but twists them into something else."[107] Moreover, she explicitly states in the letter that she did not "approve of segregation in the South or anywhere else."[108] She also wrote a letter to the interviewer, Douglas Gilbert, on February 4, 1943, to complain about the misrepresentation of her views.[109] "Now, I have the three copies of the interview with you at the Algonquin Hotel," Hurston begins in complaint to Gilbert.[110] She then proceeds to remind him of what she *actually* said. Namely, that racism is a national rather than a "sectional" problem, and that Black southern communities often have more resources to cope with racism than northern ones.[111] Her attempts to tell a more complex story about Black life in the South that did not center whiteness, or to point out Black southern joy as well as intra-group class dynamics, were turned into support for Jim Crow.[112] As an explanation of Gilbert's misunderstanding, Hurston offers: "Perhaps my saying that the North was prejudiced too, was too far off from the norm, and too distressing after all the fine phrases have been poured over us up there."[113] Hurston notes that there is a national pattern of disregard for Black life, as the nation is "too sentimental about us to know us. It has a cut-and-dried formula for us which must not be violated."[114] Again, I stress that for Hurston, these "norms" and "formulas" come out of abolitionist discourse just as much as they do out of the minstrel tradition. Hurston's choice to decenter racism in representations of Black life is aimed at disrupting these national narratives, to introduce complexity into discussions of Black life under oppression.

Hurston also links the public demand for the spectacle of Black suffering to the need to prop up a sense of superiority in whites. For example, in a letter to Burton Rascoe on September 4, 1944, Hurston bemoans the implicit racism present in some of her "liberal" (northern, white) associates who make it their mission to become "friends of the Negro."[115] "I told them that their condescension in fixing us in a type and place is a sort of intellectual Jim Crow," Hurston writes, "and is just as insulting as the physical aspects."[116] In this same letter, we see that what many pose as Hurston's individualism can also be read as a refusal to seek recognition from her white counterparts. Hurston argues that "put[ting] us all in a lump" as a group—a needy, helpless group at that—actually does northern white liberals a service. "It feels *so* good to them," Hurston writes, to be able to "pity [us]."[117]

However, Hurston refuses to allow these "friends of the Negro" to build their sense of self upon her acceptance of inferiority:

> They condescend, and then are infuriated if I don't like it, which is just another way of telling me that I am incompetent, and ought to be proud to let them stand watch-and-ward over me, and pity me. It feels *so* good to them. I say, to hell with it![118]

To surrender the ability to define herself for herself, or to allow herself to be defined as a victim, is to succumb to white supremacy. As such, while Hurston could freely admit "the handicaps of race in America," she fought against the portrayal of her life, or Black life in general, as one of complete, debilitating sorrow.[119] "I am no poor, dumb something blundering around with an odor tagged onto me by the all-conquering whites," Hurston asserts.[120] This is why, rather than entertain the latent racism of northern, liberal whites with a response of protest or despair, she pretended to be "astonished."[121] Her indifference rebuffed their pity, exposing their hidden racism.

A major strength of reading Hurston's emphasis on southern Black joy in the public sphere as a posture of refusal is that this interpretation enables us to analyze two important aspects of her views on race. When we consider *what* she was refusing, we can foreground the conditions that often prompted such refusals in her work (i.e., the intransigence of racism). Moreover, the posture of refusal offers an alternative reading of Hurston's apparent indifference to southern racism, about which many of her contemporaries complained. Instead of exemplifying racial naivete, her performances of indifference can be read as a refusal to center racism (or white folks) in her representations of Black life. My analysis also shows how Hurston's concern over artistic representations of southern Black life in her debate with Wright was intimately tied to her broader views of racial politics. That is, for Hurston, both the norms of Black art exemplified by Wright, as well as the solutions to racism posed during her time (such as *Brown v. Board*), are steeped in the legacy of abolitionist discourse—a discourse whose norms she consistently rejected. In the next chapter, I will delve deeper into how these norms of abolitionism were reasserted immediately after the abolition of slavery.

Scene 2

"The Past and the Future Merge to Meet Us Here"

In Beyoncé's attempts to create a southern Black aesthetic, she consistently reaches back to the abolitionist-antebellum period. For example, much of the album takes place on various plantations along the Gulf Coast region.[1] In a stunning reversal of neo-abolitionist norms, her scenes on plantations are not only devoid of white people but are also sites of Black joy such as ancestral communion, feasts, and dancing. Moreover, the address of the album seems to refuse the terms of abolitionist discourse. That is, the album is not interested in shoring up Black suffering to gain sympathy from whites, because the album is not interested in addressing whites at all. We can see this in the gazes of many Black women staged on plantations throughout the visual album. Primarily dressed from slavery and the Reconstruction era, these women signal how the past (i.e., the dead) and the future "merge to meet us" in this southern landscape. But rather than invite the audience into the inner world of Blacks (as neo-abolitionism would mandate), the women stare off—as if they are indifferent to the camera.[2] Their gaze is similar to what Toni Morrison finds in the literature of many Black women writers, a gaze that is "not interested in confrontations with white men" because "there are more important [confrontations] for them."[3] Morrison's description of this gaze in Black feminist literature aptly applies to the stares of these ancestral figures in the album, for their gaze, too, "is unblinking and wide and very steady. It's not narrow, it's very probing and it does not flinch."[4] By decentering our relation to whites, this "unblinking" gaze offers a different entryway into the experiences of slavery, our relation to the South, and the fashioning of a Black southern aesthetic.

While Beyoncé does indeed allude to various types of racial and sexual oppression that stem from plantation life, she is careful to nuance representations of southern Black life on plantations as well.[5] For example, instead of focusing on the relation between slave master and the enslaved on the plantation, Beyoncé's use of ancestral Black women centers our relationship to our dead through root work. In their privileging of the dead, root work practices are one way that Beyoncé can shift scenes of Black plantation life from neo-abolitionist Black sorrow to Black joy.[6] For instance, in the "Apathy" chapter we find Beyoncé enthroned with Serena Williams twerking beside her in a plantation. This reverses the usual practice on plantations, where white slave owners would often make the enslaved dance for their pleasure. Instead, we have Black women dancing for their own entertainment and edification, oblivious to the white gaze.[7] This scene of dancing is tied to and preceded by a spiritual bus ride that is filled with allusions to Yoruba and Voodoo practices.[8] In the "Resurrection" chapter we also find women, dressed from the Reconstruction era, gathered under oak trees to take photos. This scene is striking not only because of the dress, colors, and landscape, but also because it reverses a common trope of photography at the time: tree-lynched Black folks surrounded by decked-out white mobs. This photo-op in the film is interlaced with a recording of a Black woman offering advice on "how to lead our children forward." Her advice is bound up with root work in the sense that she "shouts" as she delivers her message, a practice in the Sanctified Church.[9] Also, in the "Hope" chapter, we find ancestral Black women holding a feast on the plantation grounds, cooking for their own pleasure, and lounging on oaks instead of hanging from them. These scenes are preceded by a root work ritual on the plantation—a Mardi Gras Indian traces the sacred cosmogram in multiple rooms, shaking a tambourine to summon the ancestors.[10] The ritual ends with a voice-over of one word, "magic," and a flashback of the spiritual bus ride mentioned earlier. In these examples, root work provides the scaffolding to begin to imagine spaces of joy in the lives of the enslaved.

In the chapter that follows, I analyze how Hurston also wrestled with the mandates of neo-abolitionism in her writings on Black life. Like Beyoncé, Hurston often strove to change the narrative of Black southern life so that intra-racial relations (like those of ancestry) were privileged over resistance to our oppressors. Moreover, Hurston often turned to root work to bring about this shift in focus, creating room for Black joy. We can see this, for instance, in her criticism of W. E. B. Du Bois's moniker for Negro spirituals, "sorrow songs." Hurston's disagreement with Du Bois highlights the political significance of Beyoncé's remaking of Black southern plantation life. That is, Hurston's disagreement with Du Bois is not merely a question of what to call Negro spirituals, but the nature of enslaved life. Was sorrow the predominant affect? Was there room for joy? While Du Bois refashioned Negro spirituals to further the abolitionist message of Black sorrow, Hurston shored up the aspects of root work that informed Negro spirituals in order to make room for Black joy.

Chapter 2

"An Object of Pity"

Zora Neale Hurston, W. E. B. Du Bois, and the Rise of Neo-Abolitionism

> Look back over your shoulder for a minute. Count the years. If you take in the twenty-odd years of intense Abolitionist speaking and writing that preceded the Civil War, the four war years, the Reconstruction period and recent Negro rights agitations, you have at least a hundred years of indoctrination of the Negro that he is an object of pity.
>
> —Zora Neale Hurston, "Negroes without Self-Pity"

In this epigraph's quote from her 1943 essay "Negroes without Self-Pity," I take Hurston to be identifying an important aspect of what it takes for Black people to gain recognition in the United States' public sphere. While abolitionists rightly lobbied for the recognition of the humanity of the enslaved, this recognition hinged upon shows of Black abjection, or the "indoctrination of the Negro that he is an object of pity."[1] For Hurston, this tradition of tragic southern Black representation extended well after the abolition of slavery. Although it would seem that the abolition of slavery in 1865 has since rendered this tradition obsolete, it has only further entrenched it. This is because the racism that underpinned slavery had only been transformed, rather than eradicated, upon Emancipation. And so, Hurston writes, "the post-war generation time was a matrix from which certain ideas came that have seriously affected art creation as well as every other form of Negro expression, including the economic."[2]

The post-Civil War adherence to this norm of representation from the abolitionist period, that Black folks be represented in terms of tragedy or "pity," is what I have termed *neo-abolitionism*. Many of Hurston's comments on the resurgence of abolitionist norms during the Reconstruction era can be found in clusters of her essays in the mid- to late 1930s (such as "Spirituals and Neo-Spirituals," "Art and Such," and "The Sanctified Church") as well as in the mid-1940s (such as "High John de Conquer," "Negroes without Self-Pity," and "The Rise of the Begging Joints"). Hurston's consistent example of neo-abolitionism comes from the work of W. E. B. Du Bois, a major figure in African American philosophy. For example, Hurston often signals neo-abolitionism by referring to Du Bois's moniker for Negro spirituals, "sorrow songs."[3] Hurston writes in her 1938 "Art and Such":

> Just let [these Black leaders] hear that white people have curiosity about some activity among Negroes, and these "leaders" will not let their shirt-tails touch them [i.e., sit down] until they have rushed forward and offered themselves as an authority on the subject whether they have ever heard it before or not. In the very face of a situation as different from the 1880s as chalk is from cheese, they stand around and mouth the same trite phrases, and try their practiced-best to look sad. *They call spirituals "Our Sorrow Songs"* and other such tomfoolery in an effort to get into the spotlight if possible without having ever done anything to improve education, industry, invention, art and never having uttered a quotable line.[4]

In this passage, the "sorrow songs" moniker operates as a metonym of a tradition of Black political leadership that adheres to the neo-abolitionist norm of Black tragedy.

Indeed, Negro spirituals become the site of contestation between Hurston and Du Bois concerning larger questions of how we represent southern Black life in the public sphere. There are two primary points of contact between Du Bois and abolitionist discourse that I will analyze in this chapter: his discussion of African American religion (in "Of the Faith of the Fathers" and "Of the Coming of John") and his discussion of Negro spirituals (in "The Sorrow Songs"). These essays in *The Souls of Black Folk* not only adhere to the abolitionist script of southern Black tragedy, but they also serve as an example of how region, affect, class, and gender interact in Du Bois's development of neo-abolitionism. I will focus primarily on *The Souls of Black Folk* for this analysis because it seems to be the primary text of Du Bois with which Hurston was most familiar.[5]

Through my analysis of Du Bois's neo-abolitionism, I aim to broaden the target of Hurston's criticisms in her 1934 "Spirituals and Neo-Spirituals." In this essay Hurston denounces Du Bois's moniker, "sorrow songs," as "ridiculous."[6] Moreover, she criticizes the type of Negro spiritual performance that Du Bois lauds (i.e., the Fisk Jubilee Singers), claiming that it is not a "presentation of genuine Negro spirituals."[7] Some have taken these criticisms by Hurston to be, primarily, concerns over authenticity or accuracy.[8] In this view, Hurston's criticism is essentially about the manner of Negro spiritual performance. By contrast, I argue that Hurston's target of criticism should be expanded to include an indictment of neo-abolitionism itself. That is,

Hurston's objection to the moniker "sorrow songs" is one way that she can refuse the image of Blacks under abolitionist discourse: as "objects of pity."[9]

A "Spiritual Son of the Abolitionists"

In her 1945 essay "The Rise of the Begging Joints," Hurston describes a northern-southern migration of educated Black folk working to rebuild the South during the Reconstruction period:

> First, there were those little piney-woods schools opened by the Abolitionist church groups immediately after the Civil War. Fired by the Cause, hundreds, perhaps thousands, of pious Northerners came South and gave themselves to teach the freedmen how to read and write. But the greatest emphasis was on the Bible. Those who were first taught, were urged to go forth and spread what they had learned to others.[10]

These "pious Northerners" had inherited the program of the abolitionists in their mission to regenerate and reform the South after the Civil War. And this group is critical for positioning Du Bois's relationship to abolitionism. That is, Du Bois was not only a member of this group, but he also foregrounds their relationship to abolitionist discourse. For example, in "Of Booker T. Washington and Others," Du Bois introduces the poignant phrase "the spiritual sons of the Abolitionists."[11] Similar to Hurston's "pious Northerners," this phrase refers to those who came back to the South to set up schools at the dawn of Reconstruction.[12] For Du Bois, these "spiritual sons of the Abolitionists" stand at a critical juncture of two different political strategies for liberation: racial submission and racial revolt in the South.[13] Analyzing several strategies for Black liberation, Du Bois's target in this essay is first and foremost Booker T. Washington, who emblematizes racial submission. Washington's approach advocates the gradual adjustment of our political rights by economic gain, so argues Du Bois, while submitting to the regime of Jim Crow in the meantime. In contrast, Du Bois aligns himself with what he takes to be the position of Frederick Douglass and other abolitionists. Their program encompasses the integration of Blacks into American citizenry by asserting our political rights.[14]

The political juncture that Du Bois describes also has gendered, classed, and regional implications. Du Bois writes:

> In the North the feeling has several times forced itself into words, that Mr. Washington's counsels of submission overlooked certain elements of true manhood, and that his educational programme was unnecessarily narrow. Usually, however, such criticism has not found

open expression, although, too, the spiritual sons of the Abolitionists have not been prepared to acknowledge that the schools founded before Tuskegee, by men of broad ideals and self-sacrificing spirit, were wholly failures or worthy of ridicule.[15]

From this quote, we can catch glimpses of region, gender, and class in Du Bois's careful consideration of these "spiritual sons of the Abolitionists." Washington's strategy is criticized by northern Blacks and reinforces problematic white-Black relations in the South. His strategy "overlooks" aspects of "true manhood" by advocating "submission" over "self-assertion," "compromise" over revolt.[16] Furthermore, Washington's strategy embraced an "unnecessarily narrow" educational program that privileged industrial schools over liberal arts colleges, thereby running counter to the racial uplift program that Du Bois espouses in *The Souls of Black Folk*. Put another way, it ran counter to the uplift of lower-class Blacks by middle-class Blacks through liberal arts education and exposure to the fine arts.

If we turn to Du Bois's story "Of the Coming of John"—comprising another chapter in *The Souls of Black Folk*—we can further trace how region, gender, and class come to interact in the lives of these "spiritual sons of the Abolitionists."[17] There are two Johns in this tale, one Black, one white. Both are southern-born and, upon finishing their primary education, are sent "up North" to college. The white folks in their community say that the education up North will "make a man" of the white John.[18] However, the white folks shake their heads over Black John, proclaiming that northern education will "ruin him."[19] Indeed, in this story, we witness Black John's transition from a happy, country boy to a sorrowful, bitter man. And this transition is provoked through an education which makes him deeply aware of the "Veil" that prevents Blacks from accessing the same life chances and opportunities of their white counterparts in the United States.[20] When the North disappoints him, Black John returns to the South (becoming one of Hurston's "pious Northerners") only to find that he no longer fits into his old life. Without a home or a hope, Black John engages in a suicidal battle with a lynch mob at the close of the tale. Fulfilling the abolitionist script of Black southern tragedy, the confluence of gender, race, class, and regional oppression in the story produces an intersectional susceptibility to sorrow rather than joy in Black John. The similarities between Black John's political position and Du Bois's own suggests that Du Bois identifies with this character.[21]

Most insightful are the various transitions that Black John undergoes in this tragic coming-of-age tale. When Black John first arrives at school up North, he violates all sorts of northern norms due to his regional and class background. "He used perpetually to set the quiet dining-room into waves of merriment, as he stole to his place after the bell had tapped for prayers," writes Du Bois.[22] Far from the model student, Black John is often tardy and careless, "loud and boisterous, always laughing and singing, and never able to work consecutively at anything."[23] Loudness, tardiness, and laziness are behaviors and attitudes often attributed to the lower class by those in the middle class (i.e., he was being "ratchet"). With mentions of the general good humor, laughter, and merriment in Black John's southern upbringing, the image of the "happy slave" is evoked.[24] The "white folk of Altamaha voted John a *good boy*," Du Bois observes, "a fine plough-hand, good in the fields, handy everywhere, and always good-natured and respectful."[25] His rural, southern upbringing is such a mismatch with his new environment, this school up North, that Black John gets expelled. Being expelled, however, gives Black John the push needed to become more "serious" in his studies. When he returns the next semester, Du Bois notes that the "serious look that crept over his boyish face" upon expulsion never left it again.[26]

Now, while other students "skipped about merrily," Black John pored over his books. His manner of dress also changed as "his clothes seemed to grow and arrange themselves," Du Bois notes: his "coat sleeves got longer, cuffs appeared, and collars got less soiled."[27] Not only did cuffs appear, marking his emerging middle-class status, but he was cleaner in appearance, registering a distance from his earlier county/rural (read "field hand") status. A new sense of "dignity crept into [Black John's] walk" as Du Bois watched him "transform" into the "tall, grave man" who graduated years later.[28] And alongside Black John's transformation from boyhood to manhood, from southern charm to northern gentility, came the constellation of affects that Du Bois ascribes to double consciousness. Anger, resentment, sorrow.[29] Consequently, "a tinge of sarcasm crept into [Black John's] speech, and a vague bitterness into his life."[30] Du Bois writes:

> He looked now for the first time sharply about him, and wondered he had seen so little before. He grew slowly to feel almost for the first time the Veil that lay between him and the white world; he first noticed now the oppression that had not seemed oppression before, differences that erstwhile seemed natural, restraints and slights that in his boyhood days had gone unnoticed or been greeted with a laugh.[31]

Now, when he is not called "Mister" by white men, or when he is forced to ride "Jim Crow" on the train, Black John gets angry. Now, Black John sits and stews over the social goods and opportunities he is being denied. Now, our John begins to see his life *through* the "Veil," as a newfound awareness of his oppression colors and taints his experiences. As Farah Jasmine Griffin observes, "the tragedy of John is that his acquisition of knowledge, his brief experience of a different, more intellectual way of life, makes him long for freedom beyond the Veil and creates a distance between himself and his community of origin."[32]

There are two things to note in the story so far. First, entrance to Black manhood is marked by cognizance of the "Veil," which produces a constellation of affects such as sorrow, bitterness, and anger in the story. John becomes "a Black man hurrying on with an ache in his heart," full of "buried anger."[33] His awakening to the "Veil," to the opportunities he is being denied, is marked by resentment. I argue that this awakening is highly class-inflected. That is, his awakening occurs when he gains the cultural capital (i.e., a liberal arts education in the North) which should secure his middle-class status. Yet, he is denied the privileges that belong to the middle class due to racial discrimination. For instance, the central example of the "Veil" in this story is when Black John is denied seating at the opera house, a clear indication of the middle-class status to which he aspires. As a result, Du Bois notes that Blacks like John tend to separate themselves from lower-class Blacks and, "feeling deeply and keenly the tendencies of opportunities of the age in which they live, their souls are bitter at the fate which drops the Veil between them."[34]

Second, I want to draw a preliminary relationship between region and masculinity here. Education "up North" is the site where Black John becomes a man in this story. For in the South, Black John remained in a state of constant amusement, rather like a child. In the South, Black John was, and would continue to be, treated like a boy. However, at school "up North," Black John transforms into a man before Du Bois's very eyes. In the transition from South to North, the base "merriment" attributed to the lower class is replaced by the gravitas of middle-class respectability. One implication of Du Bois's reading is that the Black joy of Black John, his original happiness or "general satisfaction with the world" in the South, is born of a childlike ignorance of his oppression, an ignorance manufactured by southern whites.[35] (Recall that the white southerners relish the fact that Black John is a "good boy" and bemoan his being sent "up North" to school because it will "ruin" him.) In this way, Du Bois's story resonates with abolitionist norms wherein Black southern joy is politically disavowed. In this story, Black southern joy is the source of Black John's undoing. Southern Black joy is taken to be exemplary of the ignorance that further entrenches our oppression. Thus, for Black John's liberation, northern liberal intervention (i.e., being sent to school "up North") is needed.

And yet, Black John also finds that the North has made him "a man" only to deny him his rights as such. Therefore, Black John decides to return to the South and help "settle the Negro problems there."[36] But when we leave home, we can never truly go home again. When Black John returns home, he finds himself making all sorts of offensive blunders.[37] Reflecting the middle-class, northern sensibilities to which he has grown accustomed, Black John is austere when he meets his family at the train station. His family, in turn, takes his behavior to mean that he is "stuck up." He is cool and dispassionate when in church, similar to Du Bois's own encounters with Black southern religion in "Of the Faith of the Fathers."[38] The congregation, in turn, takes his behavior as an indication that he has "no religion."[39] So deep-founded is his sense of equality with white men that Black John forgets to go to the back door while visiting the Judge (white John's father) and instead strides boldly to the front of the house, thus defying Jim Crow. For these reasons, when Black John asks the Judge for money to build a school, the Judge's first concern is whether Black John has gotten into his head the "Northern notion" that he is equal to white men.[40]

The climax of this story draws strong parallels with another John we have discussed in the previous chapter. Black John's defining end moment, which initiates his tragic downfall, is more in line with John Henry than with High John de Conquer.[41] Upon finding white John trying to rape his sister, Black John strikes him dead, "with all the pent-up hatred of his great Black arm."[42] Black John steps back, surveys the blood before him, and goes home to say goodbye to his mother. He tells her that he is "going away . . . going to be free."[43] Confused, his mother asks if he going "up North" again. He says yes, he is "going North."[44] And yet, Black John actually returns to white John's body, awaiting the coming lynch mob well into the night. I argue that he has not lied to his mother. He has "gone North" in the sense that he has displayed a type of behavior that is readily identified with freedom in abolitionist discourse. Consider Frederick Douglass, whose struggle for freedom is etched in similar masculine terms. Speaking of his epic fight with the slave-breaker Mr. Covey, Douglass tells his reader: "You have seen how a man was made a slave; you shall see how a slave was made a man."[45] In the story of Black John, region (the North), freedom, and the restoration of his "manhood" are all tied together in this defiant act: facing the lynch mob without guile or fear. Similar to John Henry, Black John faces the racist oppressor directly and publicly, without an ounce of trickery.

It is important to note that this act of "manliness" is provoked by the sexual violence done to his sister. To mark John's "manliness" within the context of the sexual violence of white men toward Black women is also a hallmark of abolitionist discourse. That is, Black feminist scholars have long noted how the staging of Black suffering in abolitionist discourse is often gendered. The freedom secured by Black men in slave narratives was often rhetorically thrown into relief by the sexualized whippings of Black women. Consider the *Narrative of the Life of Frederick Douglass*. As Deborah McDowell notes, the agency of the enslaved was masculinized in Douglass's pursuit of freedom. That is, Douglass's freedom narrative employs the trope of the collective, tortured slave body in a way that is deeply gendered. After all, it is his Aunt Hester's beating that first introduces Douglass to the horrors of slavery, "the bloody scenes that often occurred on the plantation."[46] And throughout the *Narrative*, "[Douglass's] journey from slavery to freedom leaves women in the logical position of representing the condition of slavery," that is, Black suffering.[47] In this way, the abolitionist rendering of Black women as pure victims underscores the masculine framework within which Du Bois is operating.[48] Not only does Black John's reaction to the attempted rape of his sister exemplify the sexual warfare in which Black and white men are engaged to define their masculinity, but I argue that the conclusion to be drawn from this tale is that the South is a place that kills Black "manhood." It murders their very masculinity. If the North becomes the site of aspirational Black manhood in this tale, the South becomes the site where Black men cannot "be a man."

Du Bois is, of course, very concerned about this double bind that Black men face. On the one hand, they are denied the possibility of expressing their "masculinity" openly in the South. In this way, Du Bois shores up abolitionist readerly expectations by pointing to Black John's southern despair. At the story's close, Black John's lynching fulfills the abolitionist script of southern Black tragedy. On the other hand, the North so radically disappoints that Black men, in Du Bois's view, are in danger of becoming bitter and angry to the point of self-destruction. It is this double bind during the Reconstruction period that sets the stage for Du Bois's own navigation through and uptake of abolitionist discourse in his work.

The Rise of Neo-Abolitionism

As several scholars have noted, Du Bois's *The Souls of Black Folk* is, in some ways, patterned after the slave narratives of abolitionist discourse, albeit in reverse.[49] Although Du Bois employs several tropes used in slave narratives, unlike other texts in that genre, he travels from North to South in *The Souls of Black Folk*. There are two aspects of the abolitionist undertaking that I want to analyze in the remainder of this chapter. First, his development of the stages of African American religion in "Of the Faith of the Fathers." In this essay, Du Bois develops the stages of Black religion as a dialectic of opposing modes of response to racism: hypocritical compromise (as exemplified by Booker T. Washington) and radical revolt (as exemplified by abolitionists like Frederick Douglass). These responses are not only regionalized and gendered in Du Bois's account, but they also produce certain affects (sorrow vs. joy) as well. I argue that Du Bois's account of these responses follows the abolitionist script that denounces the South as a site of racial tragedy and failure. That is, the South becomes both feminine *and* the emblem of hypocritical compromise, while the North is masculinized *and* the symbol of direct protest or radical revolt.[50] Second, I want to consider how Du Bois's treatment of the South and differing responses to racism in "Of the Faith of the Fathers" comes to bear on how he interprets Negro spirituals in "The Sorrow Songs." Analyzing Du Bois's discussion of Negro spirituals in this way provides another primary site where abolitionism is reworked and repurposed to address the racism that lingered after the abolition of slavery.

The Dialectic of African American Religion

In "Of the Faith of the Fathers," Du Bois turns to African American religion to analyze Black liberation strategies, for he considers Black religion to be "one expression of [Blacks'] higher life."[51] The essay aims to provide insight into the "ethical attitudes" of Blacks concerning their oppression through an adroit conceptual development of Black religion.[52] I call this Du Boisian development a primarily conceptual one because Du Bois outlines the development of African American religious traditions as a Hegelian dialectic.[53] Reading Du Bois's development of Black religion conceptually has certain implications in how I interpret this essay.[54] When Du Bois presents the essay as "a study of Negro religion *as a development*," a Hegelian reading means that his development is not purely chronological or contingent.[55] It is a spiritual development, in the Hegelian sense. As such, the stages in the history of Black religion are interpreted as necessary cyclical ruptures and reunions that successively and logically bring us closer to the final stage of Hegelian "Spirit." Put another way, Black religion has a telos, an eschatology of meaning, that is wrapped up in the material conditions of the struggle for racial justice as depicted, for Du Bois, in the abolitionist movement.[56] So when Du Bois claims that the essay aims to analyze "what have been the successive steps of this social history[of Negro religion]," "successive steps" means not only temporal progression, but structurally necessary steps (as in a ladder or staircase).[57]

Within Hegel's dialectics, there are (roughly) three movements in the following order: (1) two positions are posited as opposites (or as thesis and antithesis), (2) these two positions (thesis and antithesis) are transformed through an argument where they are shown to share an inner logic, and (3) the two positions (thesis and antithesis) are posited again as a synthesis. The synthesis at which the dialectic arrives is one where aspects of the previously opposing positions (of stage 1) are preserved. In "Of the Faith of the Fathers," the numerous "ethical attitudes" within African American religion can also be cast into the categories of thesis, antithesis, and synthesis. The first complete cycle of the dialectic follows the transition from "voodooism" (thesis) to Christianity (antithesis) to abolitionism (synthesis). The second cycle of the dialectic in Du Bois's essay discusses the development of hypocritical compromise (in the South) alongside radical revolt (in the North). The reconciliation or synthesis of the second cycle of the dialectic is left unfinished. Instead, Du Bois beseeches us to find the middle path that reconciles the latter opposing ethical attitudes.[58]

During the pre-emancipation stage of Black religion (i.e., "slave religion"), we see two ethical attitudes emerge. The first is a "spirit of revolt and revenge" found within "voodooism," or what I have called *root work*. Du Bois writes of the enslaved's use of root work:

> Slavery, then, was to him the dark triumph of Evil over him. All the hateful powers of the Under-world were striving against him, *and a spirit of revolt and revenge filled his heart*. He called up all the resources of heathenism to aid,—exorcism and witchcraft, the

mysterious Obi worship with its barbarous rites, spells, and blood-sacrifice even, now and then, of human victims. Weird midnight orgies and mystic conjurations were invoked, the witch-woman and the voodoo-priest became the center of Negro group life, and that vein of vague superstition which characterizes the unlettered Negro even to-day was deepened and strengthened.[59]

"Voodooism" provided the tools for rebellion, contributing to a "spirit of revolt and revenge" that caused "maroons, the Danish Blacks, and others" to rebel against slavery.[60] At the center of "voodooism" is the "Voodoo Priest," the rock upon which the "Negro Church" was built.[61] While Du Bois lists several functions of the "Voodoo Priest" (or "Medicine-Man"), he privileges resistance. That is, the "Voodoo Priest" became a symbol of "the longing, disappointment, and resentment of a stolen and oppressed people" precisely because root work was a means of revolt and revenge during enslavement.[62] Du Bois argues that the "spirit of revolt" in "voodooism" was gradually snuffed out, due to the "untiring energy and superior strength of the slave masters."[63] Crushed by the violent punishments for revolt, the enslaved no longer attempted direct, open opposition to their slave masters. "By the middle of the eighteenth century," notes Du Bois, "the Black slave had sunk, with hushed murmurs, to his place at the bottom of a new economic system, and was unconsciously ripe for a new philosophy."[64] In place of "voodooism" was a "newly learned Christianity" that preached submission in the here and now and racial justice in the hereafter.[65]

Put another way, the ineffectiveness of some strategies of resistance, such as the open revolt closely aligned with "voodooism," made the enslaved susceptible to the idea that it is impossible to overturn their oppression. As such, some of the enslaved chose to temporarily get ahead by deception, rather than continue to resist their oppression. This is what gives rise to the ethical attitude Du Bois calls "hypocritical compromise."[66] And a docile version of Christianity provided the intellectual and spiritual justification for this hypocrisy, for "a religion of resignation and submission degenerated easily, in less strenuous minds, into a philosophy of indulgence and crime."[67] The system of racial domination in this country had "tamper[ed] with the moral fiber" of Blacks and whites, Du Bois argues, until Blacks who would have once waged war became "criminals and hypocrites" and whites "be[came] ungovernable tyrants."[68] Under such a system, deception and trickery become appealing strategies of racial advancement.

Abolitionism is presented as the synthesis in Du Bois's account, uniting aspects of the previous opposition of "voodooism" (thesis) and Christianity (antithesis).[69] Under abolitionism, the spirit of revolt and revenge was preserved from "voodooism." We can see this in how the tone of Negro spirituals changed during the abolitionist struggle. Du Bois writes that, for the enslaved during this period, "freedom became to him a real thing and not a dream.

His religion became darker and more intense, *and into his ethics crept a note of revenge, into his songs a day of reckoning close at hand*."[70] And while the slave master's version of Christianity turned the "Coming of the Lord," the promised day of vengeance, into a "comforting dream," abolitionism brought this day of reckoning into the realm of the here and now.[71] Du Bois asserts:

> For fifty years Negro religion thus transformed itself and identified itself with the dream of Abolition, until that which was a radical fad in the white North and an anarchistic plot in the white South *had become a religion to the black world*. Thus, when Emancipation finally came, it seemed to the freedmen a literal Coming of the Lord. His fervid imagination was stirred as never before, by the tramp of armies, the blood and dust of battle, and the wail and whirl of social upheaval.[72]

When Black religion "transformed itself and identified itself with the dream of Abolition," the religious fatalism of the slave master's Christianity was transformed into the radical revolt of the enslaved.

This transformation was possible because of the inner logic that Christianity and Du Bois's "voodooism" share. Namely, they both share a sense of justice as retribution or vengeance. Within "voodooism" this is found in the "Voodoo Priest" who is the "supernatural avenger of wrong."[73] Within Christianity, it is found in the "avenging Spirit of the Lord" who brings supernatural vengeance on that "day of reckoning," the "Coming of the Lord."[74] Thus, I argue that it is a focus on vengeance which transforms the religious fatalism of the slave master's Christianity into the abolitionist's "day of reckoning." I want to stress, however, that the revolt and revenge that were once found in the cosmology of "voodooism" ultimately became recast in a Christian cosmology through this abolitionist synthesis. Through this recasting, abolitionism displaces the original context of root work in the formation of revolt and revenge, a disavowal we often see mirrored in the literature of abolitionist discourse.[75] Moreover, for Du Bois, this recasting or transformation takes place in the development of the Negro spirituals.

When he wrote this essay, Du Bois considered us to be in another cycle of the dialectic of African American religion, for we still "live, move, and have [our] being" in these ethical attitudes that arose during our enslavement.[76] On the one hand, some of us are "conscious of [our] impotence and [are] pessimistic" about race relations in the United States. Our pessimism can lead us to become "bitter and vindictive" as a result.[77] On the other hand, there is a faction of us with the other mindset that "sees in the very strength of the anti-Negro movement its patent weaknesses."[78] Without concern for ethics, we choose to game the system. "One [faction] is wedded to ideals remote, whimsical, perhaps impossible of realization," notes Du Bois, while "the other forgets that life is more than meat and the body more than raiment."[79] These two positions, in turn, are regionalized. "To-day the two groups of Negroes, the one in the North, the other in the South, represent these divergent ethical tendencies," Du Bois writes, "the first tending towards radicalism, the other toward hypocritical compromise."[80] Recalling our earlier discussion of Black masculinity and the South in "Of the Coming of John," we are in a position to see how gender and region interact in Du Bois's analysis of African American religion.

According to Du Bois, Black men in the South are only able to advance by submission and deception, as advocated by leaders such as Booker T. Washington. And this strategy ultimately results in racial tragedy for Black men. "Political defense is becoming less and less available, and economic defense is only partial," observes Du Bois.[81] What is left if direct protest is not an option? "Deception and flattery . . . cajoling and lying."[82] As a result, Black men are forced into a hypocritical compromise that results in the "lack of many elements of *true manhood*."[83] Black male youth in the South "cannot be frank and outspoken, honest and self-assertive."[84] Instead, they must "be silent and wary, politic and sly; . . . flatter and be pleasant, endure petty insults with a smile, shut [their] eyes to a wrong."[85] Consider some of the imagery Du Bois uses here: they must be silent, sly, flatter, smile, even speak in whispers. This is behavior typically assigned to women, right down to the posture. And in some ways, it is behavior typically assigned to the wrong type of woman, that is, the southern belle who would manipulate the men with whom she associates. As a result, Du Bois bemoans the fact that "patience, humility, and adroitness, in these growing Black youth, must replace impulse, manliness, and courage" in the South.[86] As we have seen in the story of the two Johns, the South becomes a place where Black men cannot truly be "men." This is, in part, because the South prevents direct confrontation with their oppressors. And such direct confrontation is often equated with honesty, moral wholeness, and masculinity in abolitionist discourse.

Although Du Bois adheres to the abolitionist script in his description of southern Black life in this essay, he does deviate from the script when he discusses northern Black life. While the North does hold the promise of an unhampered performance of Black masculinity, as we have seen in the story of Black John, the North ultimately disappoints. Du Bois writes:

> Driven from his birthright in the South by a situation at which every fibre of his more outspoken and assertive nature revolts, he finds himself in a land where he can scarcely earn a decent living amid the harsh competition and the color discrimination. At the same time, through schools and periodicals, discussions and lectures, he is intellectually quickened and awakened. The soul, long pent up and dwarfed, suddenly expands in new-found freedom. What wonder that every tendency is to excess—radical complaint, radical remedies, bitter denunciation or angry silence.[87]

Notice how the affects of bitterness and anger are now aligned with these "spiritual sons of the Abolitionists." My claim is that it is not an accident that the affects of sorrow, bitterness, and anger occur at this juncture of increased education, relocation northward, and extreme disappointment with the continued impediments to Black men's performance of their masculinity. Rather, the interaction of class displacement, regional disappointments, and problematic gender ideals creates a persistent denial of avenues to become the type of men they wish to be. And the affectual response to this persistent denial has been this tragic constellation of feelings which plagues the "spiritual sons of the Abolitionists." While some of these men will sink beneath their bitterness and resentment, Du Bois notes that the "better classes" will separate themselves from both Blacks and whites.[88] In their separation, they form "an aristocracy, cultured and pessimistic, whose bitter criticism stings while it points no way of escape."[89] Moreover, while neither hypocritical compromise nor radical revolt is acceptable to Du Bois, he is closer to radicalism. I say this given his own recurring bouts of bitterness and resentment. Hurston perceived this when she claimed that Du Bois was "the bitterest opponent of the white race that America has ever known."[90]

The "Sorrow Songs" of Du Bois

Negro spirituals are not only the site of abolitionist transformation in the dialectic of Black religion, but a central motif of *The Souls of Black Folk*. Carefully placed before each chapter, they are the sheet music that guides the reader in the performance of Black life that Du Bois outlines. Du Bois writes:

> Before each chapter, as now printed, stands a bar of the Sorrow Songs,—some echo of haunting melody from the only American music which welled up from black souls in the dark past. And finally, need I add that I who speak here am bone of the bone and flesh of the flesh of them that live within the Veil?[91]

There are two things to note from Du Bois's invocation of "Sorrow Songs" here. First, Du Bois is gesturing toward his audience. His audience is sympathetic (northern) whites who have already been primed with abolitionist readerly expectations. For these readers, Black stories were granted legitimacy when they adhered to the abolitionist script of Black tragedy under slavery. But what happens when the conditions that produced the criteria of legitimacy (i.e., enslavement) have ceased? In *The Souls of Black Folk*, we find Du Bois wrestling with this problem—how to address an audience of sympathetic whites whose capacities for engagement with and whose trust in the testimony of Black folk have largely been shaped by a struggle whose political goal (i.e., the abolition of slavery) has already been met. Second, to meet these readerly demands, Du Bois not only relies upon an abolitionist interpretation of the spirituals (as "sorrow songs") to shore up the lingering abolitionist sentiments of his audience, but he also relies upon the trope of the "sorrow songs" to authenticate his revelation of the inner lives of Black folks.[92] That is, the "sorrow songs" are how he can lay claim to a racial identity ("bone of the bone and flesh of the flesh of them that live within the Veil") to which his sympathetic white audience can readily relate.[93]

This relationship between Black music (i.e., Negro spirituals) and Black authenticity was first forged by Frederick Douglass in his innovative interpretation of Black song-making under slavery. That is, Douglass's abolitionist interpretation of Negro spirituals first made possible these links between racial identity, the experience of racism, and the "sorrow songs." In his alignment of Negro spirituals with the abolitionist message, Douglass introduced a shift in the terms of legitimacy concerning Black testimony: from the bloody Blacks of the enslaved to their sorrowful songs. For in Douglass's abolitionist interpretation of the spirituals, the "sorrow songs" came to be seen as "a window on the inner lives" of Blacks.[94] Du Bois, in turn, draws upon this abolitionist meaning, equating Blackness with the suffering in the "sorrow songs" throughout *The Souls of Black Folk*.[95] This move enables Du Bois to lay claim to a common history of oppression, even though enslavement is far removed from his own experience. Through his attunement to the "sorrow songs," Du Bois can still speak with the authority of "the slave" to an abolitionist audience, even after the abolition of slavery.

The "sorrow songs" also reconcile Du Bois to Black southern culture, to which he is foreign.[96] Several scholars have noted Du Bois's ambivalence toward southern Black culture due to his New England roots.[97] This is significant, given that southern Blacks are by and large those whom Du Bois means by those "within the Veil."[98] However, as Cheryl Wall observes, "at every destination" in Du Bois's travels further South, he "encounters a community more unfamiliar to him than the last, more distant from northern customs and mores, and more steeped in the southern expressive traditions honed during slavery."[99] This seems to create anxiety for Du Bois—anxiety that is quelled by his connection to the "sorrow songs," whereby he appropriates the culture of the previously enslaved.[100] By way of Douglass's connection between racial identity and the "sorrow songs," Du Bois can claim that he "knew of [the 'sorrow songs'] as of me and of mine" even though the "[the 'sorrow songs'] came out of the South unknown to me, one by one."[101] Just as Douglass unveiled the "noise" of Negro spirituals by interpreting them as "sorrow songs" for his abolitionist audience, Du Bois unveils the "unknown" lifeworld of Black southerners through the "sorrow songs" for his abolitionist-descended audience.

In other words, Du Bois's attempt to peel back the Veil for his audience is cast primarily in abolitionist terms. For instance, he continues in the abolitionist tradition of using sorrow as a lens by which to interpret the spiritual and political dimensions of Black southern life in "Of the Sorrow Songs." Du Bois writes:

> What are these songs, and what do they mean? I know little of music and can say nothing in technical phrase, but I know something of men, and knowing them, I know that these songs are the articulate message of the slave to the world. They tell us in these eager days that life was joyous to the black slave, careless and happy. I can easily believe this of some, of many. But not all the past South, though it rose from the dead, can gainsay the heart-touching witness of these songs. They are the music of an unhappy people, of the children of disappointment; they tell of death and suffering and unvoiced longing toward a truer world, of misty wanderings and hidden ways.[102]

Drawing upon Douglass and straining against the minstrel tradition, Du Bois asserts that these songs are primarily a witness to the evils of slavery, the ultimate "unhappiness" and "suffering" of "the slave."[103] While there are aspects of the "sorrow songs" that are "naturally veiled and half-articulate," what *is* rendered articulate, comprehensible, and meaningful is the sorrow of Black life under slavery.[104] This sorrow, due to the injustice of slavery, also confirms the sense of justice found in abolitionist discourse. "Through all the sorrow of the Sorrow Songs there breathes a hope," writes Du Bois, "a faith in the ultimate justice of things."[105] This view of justice concurs with the goals of liberalism in its hope that "sometime, somewhere, men will judge men by their souls and not by their skins."[106] In this way, Du Bois not only draws upon abolitionist discourse to weaponize the sorrow of the spirituals for his political message, but he expands the meaning of the "sorrow songs" beyond the immediate abolitionist target of emancipation. Now, the "sorrow songs" stand as a model of racial justice to meet the demands of the Reconstruction era, where Blacks are still not "judged" by their "souls," but rather by their "skins."

But what does this model of racial politics leave out? Similar to Douglass, Du Bois also must disavow Black joy in the South, especially at the site of Negro spirituals.[107] Against the specter of minstrelsy, Du Bois must insist that even what appears to be joy is really suffering in southern Black life.[108] This disavowal of Black joy is intimately tied to the wedding of Christianity to the abolitionist cause. For instance, secular songs are either left out or dismissed from Du Bois's analysis in this essay.[109] "Purely secular songs are few in number," Du Bois claims, "partly because many of them were turned into hymns by a change of words, partly because frolics were seldom heard by the stranger, and the music less often caught."[110] The removal of "purely secular songs" (by their conversion to Christian hymns or lack of witnesses) allows him to confirm that "of nearly all the songs, however, the music is distinctly sorrowful."[111] Moreover, what is "African" in these songs is relegated to "noise" or incomprehensibility beyond the main message of abolitionism.[112] That is to say, it is the "African" aspect that veils or makes the songs half, rather than wholly, articulate to white, abolitionist audiences.[113] Although Du Bois may have embraced a glorious "African" past, he displayed deep ambivalence toward certain expressions of "African" religiosity in Negro spirituals, such as "shouting," a practice of root work.[114]

By drawing upon Douglass's innovative interpretation of Negro spirituals, I take Du Bois's "recovery" of the "sorrow songs" as an example of the development of neo-abolitionism. This tendency to equate sorrow and tragedy with Blackness, or to call upon the sympathy of whites by drawing attention to Black pain, lingers in our political imaginary. For example, in his recent *Hope Draped in Black: Race, Melancholy, and the Agony of Progress*, Joseph Winters mobilizes Du Bois's "sorrow songs" as a political resource for our time. He argues that Du Bois enlisted the "sorrow songs" to resist illusions of racial progress "that hastily reconcile and explain away past and present forms of suffering and injustice."[115] All the same, this view does not take into account how the "sorrow songs" functioned as a *medium* of racial progress and racial recognition for Du Bois.[116] Most importantly, this view misses the context of abolitionism that originally directed Du Bois to emphasize the "sorrow" of the spirituals. As a result, Winters's analysis reinforces the abolitionist message; that is, he also approaches Negro spirituals as "a kind of witness" to the evils of slavery.[117] And by bringing Black pain near through such witnessing, Winters writes that the sympathetic white listener is "potentially render[ed]. . . . more attuned and sensitive to the ways race-inflected formations of power have caused pain and suffering for Black subjects."[118] Although Winters wants to avoid the claim that "sadness and melancholic hope define some authentic Black self," I argue that the baggage of abolitionist discourse still ensnares him.[119] For the resources of "melancholy" that Winters discerns within Negro spirituals were first forged within Douglass's abolitionist interpretation of Black song-making.[120] Without addressing the originating context of abolitionist discourse, we fall prey to normalizing the abolitionist message, thus taking for granted that Negro spirituals are *indeed* "sorrow songs."

On "Spirituals and Neo-Spirituals"

Against the backdrop of neo-abolitionism, Hurston's criticism of Du Bois in her 1934 essay "Spirituals and Neo-Spirituals" becomes much more than just a matter of authenticity or accuracy. In my reading, Hurston's criticism of Du Bois can be seen as a refusal of the neo-abolitionist mandate that we reduce southern Black life to tragedy and sorrow. While Douglass and Du Bois both infuse the spirituals with abolitionist significance (i.e., the "true" meaning of the spirituals lies in their protest against slavery), Hurston challenges the

centrality of slavery in the formation of Negro spirituals. At the opening of
"Spirituals and Neo-Spirituals," Hurston writes:

> The real spirituals are not really just songs. They are unceasing varia-
> tions around a theme. Contrary to popular belief their creation is not
> confined to the slavery period. Like the folk-tales the spirituals are
> being made and forgotten every day.[121]

In this passage, Hurston both extends the life of the spirituals beyond slavery
and renders them commonplace, ordinary enough to be forgotten. While Du
Bois and Douglass "emphasized the singularity of sorrow" in the spirituals
to shore up abolitionist sentiment, Hurston decenters sorrow by widening
the range of topics covered by them.[122] "The idea that the whole body of
spirituals are 'sorrow songs' is ridiculous," Hurston asserts. "They cover a
wide range of subjects from a peeve at gossiper to Death and Judgement."[123]

Hurston's displacement of the abolitionist context enables her to focus on
the continued cultural and spiritual significance of Negro spirituals within
southern Black communities.[124] This shift in focus points to different modes
of performance. In these southern Black communities, their participation in
Negro spirituals is not about resistance to and protest against the racism of
whites. Instead, it is about how we relate to each other.[125] And it is a mode
of performance that Hurston seems to privilege toward the end of her 1938
essay "Art and Such," which has more explicit criticisms of neo-abolitionism.
She writes of her own work:

> Here at last is a Negro story without bias. The characters live and
> move. The story is about Negroes but it could be anybody. It is the
> first time that a Negro story has been offered without special plead-
> ing. The characters in the story are seen in relation to themselves
> and not in relation to the whites as has been the rule. To watch these
> people one would conclude that there were no white people in the
> world. The author is an artist that will go far.[126]

If we keep in mind these different modes of performance (protest vs. self-
relation), we can read Hurston's criticism of the Fisk Jubilee Singers as more
than just an attribution of inauthenticity. Rather, the performance of the Fisk
Jubilee Singers confirms and continues the project of abolitionism, a message directed primarily at white folk. In contrast, as Hurston notes in her
1934 "Characteristics of Negro Expression," the spirituals sung in some
"unfashionable Negro church," such as the Sanctified Church, are about
Black communal religious expression.[127] As such, "true" Negro spirituals are
about our relationship to each other, one that Hurston describes as a "jagged
harmony."[128] Perhaps this is why Hurston also remarks in "Characteristics
of Negro Expression" that there is no "genuine presentation of Negro songs

to white audiences."[129] The tradition of Negro spirituals found in southern Black churches is primarily about communal religious worship and artistic showmanship which are not addressed to whites. By privileging contemporary Black southern churches (over the tragic past of slavery) as the site of the spirituals, Hurston also brings regional and class differences to the fore. As Wall observes, "geography is always a factor in Hurston's analysis as well: some of her observations are clearly specific to rural Black southerners."[130] Hurston's criticisms of the label "sorrow songs" thus included a "defense of the unappreciated aesthetic complexities" of Black southern churches.[131] To this end, her focus on these forgotten Black southern churches evinced her "primary concern . . . for the anonymous musicians who kept other traditions of Black sacred music alive in their communities rather than on the stage."[132] Moreover, Hurston was aware of how class chiseled a divide between the Fisk Jubilee Singers and the anonymous participants of Negro spirituals in these churches. "The spirituals that have been sung around the world are Negroid to be sure," Hurston admits, "but so full of musicians' tricks that Negro congregations are highly entertained when they hear their old songs so changed."[133] However, people in the Sanctified Church never sing spirituals like the Fisk Jubilee Singers unless "some daughter or son has been off to college and returns with one of the old songs with its face lifted, so to speak."[134] In tying liberal arts education to the Fisk Jubilee Singers, Hurston's remarks touch upon how these singers modeled Du Bois's early programs of racial uplift.[135]

Written four years after "Spirituals and Neo-Spirituals," Hurston's 1938 essay "The Sanctified Church" also foregrounds these regional and class distinctions between the Fisk Jubilee Singers and Black southern churches. "The mode and mood of the concert artists who do the spirituals is absolutely foreign to the Negro churches," Hurston observes. "It is a conservatory concept that has nothing to do with the actual rendition in the congregation who make the songs."[136] Written for the Florida Federal Writers' Project alongside "Art and Such," this essay shares similar themes. Noting that *the whole movement of the Sanctified church is a rebirth of song-making,* Hurston claims that the Sanctified Church has *brought in a new era of spiritual-making.*[137] Hurston's appraisal of the spirituals within the contemporary Sanctified Church enables her to reject the mandate of sorrow in neo-abolitionism:

> So that it is ridiculous to say that the spirituals are the Negro's "sorrow songs." For just as many are being made in this post-slavery period as ever were made in slavery as far as anyone can find. At any rate the people who are now making spirituals are the same as those who made them in the past and not the self-conscious propogandists that our latter-day pity men would have us believe.[138]

"Pity-men" being those who continue the "indoctrination" started by abolitionism which renders us "object[s] of pity," as stated in the epigraph of this chapter. Not only are the spirituals not confined to the slavery period, but even their "sorrow" is stripped of its abolitionist context for Hurston. "They sang sorrowful phrases then as now," asserts Hurston, "because they sounded well, and not because of the thought-content."[139]

"The Sanctified Church" also rejects a narrative of cultural assimilation that neo-abolitionism often harbors by way of Christian conversion. As argued earlier, Du Bois displaces the cosmology of root work (such as the "shout") in Negro spirituals through his neo-abolitionist interpretations found in "Of the Faith of the Fathers" and "The Sorrow Songs."[140] However, Hurston reemphasizes those "elements which were brought over from Africa" and are present in Negro spirituals.[141] Indeed, Hurston asserts that "the Negro has not been Christianized as extensively as is generally believed."[142] Rather, we are "still standing before [our] pagan altars and calling old gods by new names."[143] Her evidence for this claim is the "drum-like rhythm of *all* Negro Spirituals" and "shouting," which is "a continuation of the African 'Possession' by the gods," both practices of root work.[144] Although the abolitionist story moves us toward Christian conversion, Hurston uses a staple of abolitionist discourse (the spirituals) to turn us back toward the "Negro elements" in African American religion.[145] Put another way, the Christian impulses in abolitionism turned elements of Black song-making that were not Christian into "noise" or "inarticulate," as we saw in Du Bois's analysis. What meaning does Hurston bring to these elements of Black song-making that fell out of the Christian-abolitionist schema? She *mobilizes* them as resources for refusing assimilation. The music and religious practices of the Sanctified Church were "putting back into Negro religion those elements which were brought over from Africa and grafted onto Christianity as soon as the Negro came into contact with [it]," Hurston observes, "but which are being rooted out as the American Negro approaches white concepts."[146]

If we piece together Hurston's various commentaries on the spirituals within the context of neo-abolitionism, we can see that her criticism of Du Bois in "Spirituals and Neo-Spirituals" goes far beyond concerns of authenticity or accuracy. Instead, Hurston's criticism of the "sorrow songs" limns a refusal of a neo-abolitionist mandate concerning representations of Black southern life: the reduction of Black folk to an "object of pity" in abolitionist discourse. This neo-abolitionist mandate can be traced back to Du Bois's undertaking of Douglass's abolitionist interpretation of the spirituals, whereby he was able to extend and refashion abolitionism beyond the abolition of slavery. Moreover, this undertaking, especially in Du Bois's discussion of Black religion, has significant class, gender, and regional dimensions. In the following chapter, I will offer an extended account of refusal in Hurston's stance toward abolitionist discourse by analyzing her *Barracoon: The Story of the Last "Black Cargo,"* a slave narrative of sorts.

Scene 3

✦

"She Don't Gotta Give It Up, She Professional"

For many, the song "6 Inch" is an exemplar of how Beyoncé's *Lemonade* recalls the blueswoman tradition. The aesthetic of this piece is reminiscent of the notorious Storyville district of New Orleans which, during the Reconstruction period, was home to both brothels and blues clubs.[1] Not only does the dress of Beyoncé and her cast recall this period, but the piece is also shot under red light, perhaps signaling Storyville's "red-light" status as a district. The song's themes of financial independence ("she got them commas and them decimals"), the high valuation of work ("she don't mind, she loves the grind"), sexual empowerment ("she walked in the club like nobody's business"), rivalry ("she murdered everybody and I was her witness"), and self-esteem ("she worth every dollar, and she worth every minute") are readily known themes in the blueswoman tradition.[2] Moreover, the song "6 Inch" is preceded in the album by references to Yoruba traditions that informed the root work or conjure with which blueswomen were associated.[3] For example, there are references to the orisha Oshun in the interlude before, dressed in a wine-red gown surrounded by fire.[4]

I also read "6 Inch" in the long tradition of dissemblance that many Black women have wielded in the public sphere.[5] While the poignant line in the song, "she don't gotta give it up, she professional," may be read as referring to sexual prostitution, I also think it can be read much more broadly in terms of our public persona. On the outside, in her workplace or on the street, the protagonist is impressive and well put together. She "slangs" and "murders" everyone by her magnetic presence. But when she is at home, it is a different story. She "cries and she sweats those sleepless nights." And her dissemblance is rooted in a sense of value and esteem that is not reliant upon the dominant world. She is "too smart to crave material things" even as she stays "stacking her paper." Like the blueswomen before her, and the enslaved women before them, her sense of self-worth is also rooted in the material conditions of the work she knows she is capable of doing.[6] This is why "she don't mind" the "sleepless nights"—she "loves the grind." Read more broadly, the dissemblance at the heart of the song raises questions about racial politics and Black suffering. That is, Black suffering is not only mandated for racial recognition in the public sphere, but it is also often consumed for white entertainment. Concerning this pressure to put Black suffering on display, the song seems to refuse to "go there" with its audience. For instance, the song is interrupted at the beginning with a scene that could be read as an artistic rendering of the "*mafaa*," a "Ki-Swahili term that means disaster and the human response to it."[7] Standing in the bawdy house, dressed in prostitution garb, Beyoncé swings a red light round and round above her head. She says while swinging the red light, "every fear, every nightmare, anyone has ever had." These fears and nightmares are meant to be read across generations, for when the red light falls on various parts of the room, we see different shots of Black folk from slavery and the Reconstruction era. I read this interruption as foregrounding the *mafaa* in the piece. That is, this strategy of dissemblance, this emotional boundary of not "giving it up," is the protagonist's response to the pressure to perform or disclose the "*mafaa*" for her audience. In this way, what the protagonist is refusing to "give up" through her dissemblance is not just sex for her client's entertainment, but also access to her Black pain.

Hurston was also well known for her many performances of dissemblance in her writing. Many scholars note that this was, in part, a strategy to navigate the social world of the Reconstruction period as a southern Black woman.[8] In the chapter that follows, I explore how Hurston's strategy of dissemblance, when it comes to portrayals of Black suffering, may have also been influenced by her interviews with Kossola, an ex-slave. She records these interviews in *Barracoon: The Story of the Last "Black Cargo,"* written at the beginning of her career. Hurston noticed that when Kossola came close to disclosing his experience of the "*mafaa*," he would often draw an emotional boundary and refuse to "go there," even with her, in the interview. Moreover, Hurston observed that drawing this emotional boundary made Kossola's life in the present livable. Like the protagonist in "6 Inch," we find that Kossola often doesn't "give it up," though not because he's professional. Rather, because it is his way of gaining emotional dominion over his trauma. I argue that Hurston learns crucial lessons from Kossola that shaped her racial politics throughout her career, especially her refusal of the neo-abolitionist mandate to make a show of Black suffering.

Chapter 3

"Tak[ing] the Indian Position"

Hurston within and against the Abolitionist Tradition

> The whole matter revolves around the self-respect of my peo-
> ple. How much satisfaction can I get from a court order for
> somebody to associate with me who does not wish me near
> them? The American Indian has never been spoken of as a
> minority and chiefly because there is no whine in the Indian.
> Certainly he fought, and valiantly for his lands, and rightfully
> so, but it is inconceivable of an Indian to seek forcible asso-
> ciation with anyone. His well-known pride and self-respect
> would save him from that. I take the Indian position.
>
> —Zora Neale Hurston, "Court Order Can't Make Races Mix"

So far, I have argued that some of Hurston's controversial stances with regard
to racial politics can be read as a refusal of neo-abolitionism. In this chapter,
I consider the methodological form of this refusal.[1] Namely, I analyze how
Hurston's approach to self-revelation often thwarted the neo-abolitionist
presumption of access to Black interior life. This presumption can be traced
back to abolitionism's prior attempt to weaponize Black affect (i.e., sorrow) for its political cause. For example, through slave narratives, northern
whites thought they could not only grasp the shocking, foreign world of the
enslaved, but also weaponize this world as part of the "symbolic arsenal of
the abolitionist movement."[2] In other words, through slave narratives, white
abolitionists assumed that they had grasped the "inner meaning" of the experiences of "the slave"—perhaps even better than the enslaved themselves.[3]
As a result, abolitionist discourse cultivated a keen interest in our "inner
lives" *in order to confirm what whites already presumed to "know" about
us*. Although fashioned within abolitionist discourse, this desire for epistemic
access to Black interior life, if only to confirm what was already "known"
about us, continued long after emancipation, especially in the development
of Hurston's disciplinary field of ethnography.[4]

Hurston was well aware that white curiosity about our interior life is more about confirming what they presume to already know about us than about truly learning about us.[5] However, as an ethnographer, her work was to report on both her Black self and Black lifeworlds. I compare Hurston's navigation of this contradictory task—revealing the "self" against the backdrop of what others presume to already "know" about you—with what the Indigenous anthropologist Audra Simpson calls "ethnographic refusal." As Simpson writes in *Mohawk Interruptus*, ethnographic refusal "involves an ethnographic calculus of what you need to know and what [she] refuse[s] to write."[6] I bring Hurston's various refusals into conversation with Simpson's work on Indigenous peoples in North America because of the striking formulation that Hurston offers in the epigraph concerning her approach to race relations: "tak[ing] the Indian position." Hurston often contrasted the approaches that African Americans and Indigenous peoples of North America took in navigating US race relations.[7] And when contrasting these, Hurston often privileged "the Indian position," as in the epigraph above.[8] This contrast also seems to be operating in the background of Hurston's 1928 "How It Feels to Be Colored Me," one of her more famous essays aimed at self-revelation. For instance, in a letter to Alain Locke disclosing how this essay came to be published, Hurston writes as an aside: "I said that white people could not be trusted to collect the lore of others and that the Indians were right."[9] The task of this chapter is to imagine *what* Hurston thought "the Indians" were right about, as well as *how* this could figure into her views on race found in "How It Feels to Be Colored Me."

An essay of singing lyricism and stinging flippancy, "How It Feels to Be Colored Me" continues to be a challenging read for scholars and lay readers alike. Instead of providing a straightforward disclosure of Hurston's racial experiences, the essay leaves us riled up and riddled out. And its controversial statements on slavery exemplify the polemical racial views found throughout Hurston's body of work. For instance, Hurston writes in the essay:

> Someone is always at my elbow reminding me that I am the granddaughter of slaves. It fails to register depression with me. Slavery is sixty years in the past. The operation was successful and the patient is doing well, thank you. The terrible struggle that made me an American out of a potential slave said, "On the line!" The Reconstruction said "Get set!"; and the generation before said "Go!" I am off to a flying start and I must not halt in the stretch to look behind and weep. Slavery is the price I paid for civilization, and the choice was not with me. It is a bully adventure and worth all that I have paid through my ancestors for it.[10]

How do we square Hurston's seemingly cavalier attitude toward slavery in this passage with her firm commitment to our self-respect in this chapter's epigraph? These apparently contradictory stances are what caused Ann duCille, in musing on Hurston's career, to remark: "Hurston was, on the one hand, a fierce cultural nationalist who championed the Black folk at every turn of the page, and on the other a political conservative who declared in print that slavery was the price she paid for civilization."[11] Similarly, Carla Kaplan notes that "passionate individualism and passionate racial pride are both consistent hallmarks of Hurston's writing and her politics, however contradictory the mix may seem."[12]

Hurston's recently released *Barracoon: The Story of the Last "Black Cargo"* may give us some insight on how to hold these two things together. "How It Feels to Be Colored Me" was written alongside *Barracoon*, which is a slave narrative of sorts.[13] Pairing these two texts not only helps us grasp what Hurston might have learned from the ethnographic refusals of the ex-slave Kossola (Cudjo Lewis), whom she interviewed in *Barracoon*, but it also enables us to trace Hurston own ethnographic refusals of personal racial tragedy in "How It Feels to Be Colored Me." I maintain that Hurston's "joyful tendencies" and contradictory turns in "How It Feels to Be Colored Me" can be read as an ethnographic refusal of the mandates of neo-abolitionism that are found in the norms of ethnography.[14] That is, I interpret these "joyful tendencies" as Hurston's engaging in the delicate "ethnographic calculus" that Simpson describes. In turning to ethnographic refusal, I build upon feminist scholarship on Hurston that has noted various refusals in her body of work.[15] I deepen these feminist observations of Hurston's refusals by situating them within an Indigenous context and against the mandates of neo-abolitionism.

When It's "Too Hard to Reveal One's Inner Self"

At the end of *Mohawk Interruptus*, Simpson raises a question that can serve as an entryway into the comparative work at hand.[16] Namely, "How to stop a story that is always being told? Or how to change a story that is always being told?"[17] That story, for Indigenous peoples in North America, speaks of their foretold death and the "just" victory of settler colonialism.[18] The story, for African Americans, stands in stark contrast. This story, for Hurston, is rooted in abolitionist discourse, which renders African Americans an "object of pity" for northern white liberals' sympathy and alliance. The discrepancies between these two stories point to two different machinations of settler colonialism.[19] For settler colonialism to be successful, one population (Native) needed to be eliminated; the other (slaves) needed to be considered an abundant source of labor. Although the contexts for Hurston and Simpson's ethnographic work differ in this way, I want to draw a parallel in their responses to the "story that is always being told" about their peoples using what Simpson terms "ethnographic refusal."

As a cultural anthropologist, Simpson is acutely aware that the norms of her academic discipline require that she perpetuate settler colonialism's "story."[20] Anthropology has worked "to contain, to fetishize and entrap and distill Indigenous discourses into memorizable, repeatable rituals for preservation."[21] This is due to anthropology's acceptance of settler colonialism's "story" of the inevitable "social and political death" of Indigenous peoples in North America.[22] That is to say, anthropological research on Indigenous peoples prioritized cultural preservation because it assumed that the cultural death of these people was inevitable. However, this assumption of inevitability also normalized and made innocuous the violence and dispossession that settler colonialism wrought. In this way, such adherence to settler colonialism's "story" marks anthropology's complicity in the "political project of dispossession and containment."[23] Given this complicity of her discipline, Simpson often finds herself involved in a "discursive wrestling" when producing studies of her people. She "wrestles" to produce work that interrupts, rather than continues, this story that is "always being told" about them.[24]

Simpson's response is a strategy that comes out of her own cultural milieu, as modeled by her respondents. Unlike the terms we often use for critical political projects, such as resistance or recognition, Simpson realized that the responses modeled in her interviews marked a different political domain. She writes:

> Suddenly, I had something else, and that something was no easy answer. In fact, before me was a study in difficulty, a study of constraint, of contradictions, and I had no way to describe or theorize what was crucial. What was crucial were the very deliberate, willful, intentional actions that people were making in the face of the expectation that they consent to their own elimination as a people, that they consent to having their land taken, their lives controlled, and their stories told for them.[25]

Simpson marks these responses as refusal, and she argues that these refusals function as "an ongoing interruption in the story of settlement."[26] Although settler colonialism continues to persist, these refusals remind settlers that they have also *failed* in their efforts to "eliminate Indigenous people; take all their land; absorb them into a white, property-owning politic."[27]

Simpson advances three closely knit arguments to develop refusal as an interruption. First, she argues that "sovereignty may exist within sovereignty."[28] Highlighting the conflict over membership status due to the Indian Act, Simpson shows how refusal challenges the authority of the state.[29] When Indigenous peoples assert their own standards for membership and reject political recognition from the state, they are affirming the legitimacy of their own sovereignty against that of the state. Second, Simpson argues that refusal is a "political alternative to 'recognition,' the much sought-after and presumed 'good' of multicultural politics."[30] In other words, refusal is contrasted with cultural recognition from the state, which evades an Indigenous claim to political sovereignty. Simpson writes:

> [Indigenous peoples in North America] deploy [refusal] as a political and ethical stance that stands in stark contrast to the desire to have one's distinctiveness as a culture, as a people, recognized. Refusal comes with the requirement of having one's *political* sovereignty acknowledged and upheld, and raises the question of legitimacy for those who are usually in the position of recognizing. What is their authority to do so? Where does it come from? Who are they to do so?[31]

The state's political legitimacy is especially challenged when Indigenous peoples refuse the means of political recognition issued by the state, such as passports or various other "gifts" of citizenship. This is because the state's attempt to create political "affiliations" with Indigenous peoples through the apparatuses of citizenship simultaneously "produces the conditions for . . . 'distantiations,' 'disaffiliations,' or outright refusals—a willful distancing from state-driven forms of recognition and sociability in favor of others."[32] (For example, the ritual of showing allegiance to the United States by standing for the national anthem also makes possible the refusal of such allegiance, as Colin Kaepernick has demonstrated.)

Simpson argues that these refusals are "key to Kahnawá:ke's enunciation of self under conditions under which they would have to disappear."[33] That is, citizenship is conditioned upon accepting the state's story of settlement, the justice of the state's origins, and who the state thinks "the Indigenous" are. In contrast, refusal of citizenship constantly reminds the state of its history of violence, the injustice of its settlement, and its own precarity.[34] Given the first two claims, Simpson argues that the life of Indigenous peoples in North America would require "an accounting that neither anthropology nor political science has done robustly."[35] Put another way, to refuse in these circumstances is to put forth a political contradiction—to live under the rule of settler colonialism all the while insisting upon the sovereignty of one's own people. In this way, refusals in the public sphere take up a range of positionings, a host of strategies, that would appear illogical or irrational to liberal discourse.[36] How would things appear, however, if we take Indigenous peoples' claim to sovereignty seriously? And how does this claim to sovereignty complicate Simpson's task as an anthropologist? How might negotiating this tension between her people's sovereignty and anthropology's racist complicity force Simpson to alter her ethnographic goals?

Simpson insists that "sovereignty matters, and such mattering also engenders other ethnographic forms; in this case, one of refusal."[37] Taking up a notion of "literary sovereignty," Simpson describes "ethnographic refusal" as "a mode of sovereignty over the presentation of ethnographic data, and so does not present 'everything.'"[38] Rather, ethnographic refusal respects an "ethnographic limit" put forth by respondents, something that Simpson experienced herself when collecting data.[39] For instance, there were times when her respondents would evade questions, pretend not to know, or request that she shut off the recorder. Simpson writes:

> "Enough," I realized, was when I reached the limit of my own return and our collective arrival. Can I do this and still come home; what am I revealing here and why? Where will this get us? Who benefits and why? And "enough" was when they shut down (or told me to turn off the recorder), or told me outright funny things like "nobody seems to know"—when everybody *does* know and talks about it *all the time*. Dominion then had to be exercised over these representations, and that was determined when enough was said. The ethnographic limit then, was reached not just when it would cause harm (or extreme discomfort)—the limit was arrived at when the representation would bite all of us and compromise the *representational* territory that we have gained for ourselves in the past 100 years.[40]

Simpson's response, both to her respondents and us, as an audience, was to respect such limits drawn. To "not 'get into it' with [her respondents]" and to refuse to "get into it" with her readers. To "exercise dominion" over representations of herself and her people, Simpson performs "an ethnographic calculus of what you need to know and what I refuse to write in."[41] This "calculus" acknowledges that there are "asymmetrical power relations that inform the research and writing about native lives and politics."[42] I argue that it is this acknowledgment of "[un]equal footing" that shifts Simpson's ethnographic goals away from "truth" and "self-revelation" to "how much do you, the reader, need to know?"[43]

This question, "how much do you, the reader, need to know?" seems to haunt Hurston's work as well.[44] Hurston's tendency was often to dissemble rather than reveal, which created much controversy in gauging her racial politics.[45] Many scholars who are sympathetic to Hurston's politics have done important work in identifying the various restraints of her social position that may have produced the impulse of dissemblance.[46] Other Hurston scholars have also noted that her dissembling is rooted in the tradition of "lying," a style of storytelling in African American communities.[47] In the introduction to her 1935 *Mules and Men*, Hurston brings up such "lying" in a context relevant for our discussion; namely, when anthropologists attempt to "spy" on another culture.[48] She writes:

> Folk-lore is not as easy to collect as it sounds. The best source is where there are the least outside influences and these people, being

usually under-privileged, are the shyest. They are most reluctant at times to reveal that which the soul lives by. And the Negro, in spite of his open-faced laughter, his seeming acquiescence, is particularly evasive. You see we are a polite people and we do not say to our questioner, "Get out of here!" We smile and tell him or her something that satisfies the white person, because, knowing so little about us, he doesn't know what he is missing. The Indian resists curiosity by a stony silence. The Negro offers a feather-bed resistance. That is, we let the probe enter, but it never comes out. It gets smothered under a lot of laughter and pleasantries.[49]

The conventional interpretation of this passage is to place the response of "the Negro" here into a larger tradition of double-speak and signifying within African American writing and culture.[50] In this way, some argue that Hurston's turn to dissemblance could be seen as a practice of resistance grounded in the customs of her community.[51]

However, we can develop a different account of "the Negro" response if we take seriously the point of comparison at the heart of this passage: that of "the Indian," who refuses curious whites outright. The response of "the Negro" and "the Indian" are not opposites for Hurston; rather, they are on a continuum of refusals in response to the nosiness of white folks. Both African Americans and Indigenous peoples had to deal with nosy (white) anthropologists at this time. Anthropologists who had their own stories about the people they were studying. These stories prophesied either cultural death (for Indigenous peoples) or (southern) racial tragedy for African Americans (according to neo-abolitionism). In light of these stories that were "always being told," both groups were reluctant to answer the questions of these anthropologists. Although the methods are different ("stony silences" vs. "laughter and pleasantries"), the end goal is still the same: to *not* reveal to these nosy anthropologists "that which the soul lives by." Or, in other words, to maintain some sense of sovereignty over their representations by drawing an "ethnographic limit."

An ethnographic calculus is performed by Hurston's respondents due to an acute awareness that they are *not* on an equal footing when being interviewed by whites. Hurston writes of the motivations behind their "feather-bedded" response: "the white man is always trying to know someone else's business. All right, I'll set something outside the door of my mind for him to play with and handle."[52] Rather than tell the "truth" to someone who doesn't have ears to hear it, they/we lie. Rather than pursue recognition from whites, this response relies upon *maintaining the misrecognition of whites* (i.e., relying upon whites *not* "knowing what they are missing").[53] Respondents "put this play toy in [their] hand" (read "lie") so that whites will "seize it and go away."[54] Because only then can we "say [our] say and sing [our] song."[55] Although Hurston uses the language of "resistance" in this passage, we should note that a failure of epistemic exchange or a gain in epistemic friction is sought by the respondents (through "stony silences" or "laughter and pleasantries"), for they desire to be left alone rather than be known, to be misrecognized rather than recognized by whites.[56] Given the privileging of misrecognition in both "the Indian" and "the Negro" response, I maintain that ethnographic refusal is the spirit of the comparison drawn in this passage.

It is Hurston's own experience of being refused by her respondents (while using the methods of her mentor, Franz Boas) that brought this dynamic of refusal to her awareness.[57] Hurston discusses this experience of ethnographic refusal not only in *Mules and Men* but also in *Dust Tracks on a Road*, her autobiography. "My first six months were disappointing," Hurston admits. "I found out later that it was not because I had no talents for research, but because I did not have the right approach."[58] It is significant that Hurston foregrounds this story of ethnographic refusal in her autobiography, another place where she manages to thwart the imperative to reveal her "inner self."[59] This story of ethnographic refusal also invites us to consider how Hurston's interactions with her respondents informed her entire career—not only in *Mules and Men*, but across the whole body of her ethnographic work. How might these kinds of experiences have influenced Hurston's mode of representing both herself and her people? How might the ethnographic refusals of Hurston's respondents have offered her tools to handle when it became "too hard to reveal one's inner self"? And to what extent did neo-abolitionism make it "too hard" for her to tell her own story? To answer these questions, I propose that we go back to the beginning of her career with *Barracoon*.

Ethnographic Refusals in *Barracoon*

Barracoon comes off as a strange text when compared with other books of its genre: fugitive slave narratives. In some ways, it does fit within the genre of these narratives.[60] It follows the general arc of stories in this genre, sharing Kossola's journey from harrowing enslavement to legal emancipation. But it also departs from the genre of slave narratives in several ways. For instance, fugitive slave narratives advanced the political aims of abolitionism. However, as Deborah Plant observes, *Barracoon* "does not articulate an explicit political agenda."[61] In recounting his story of freedom to Hurston, Kossola even questions whether the abolition of slavery was really why the North waged war in the first place.[62] *Barracoon* also thwarts the typical progressions mapped in fugitive slave narratives, such as those from slavery to freedom, from South to North, and from "pagan" to Christian. For example, there is no epic struggle for or heroic escape to freedom in the narrative, as in the *Narrative of Frederick Douglass, an American Slave*.[63] Instead, upon hearing news of the Emancipation Proclamation, Kossola waits for someone to "come tell us we free."[64] Moreover, Kossola's journey begins in Africa, unlike many slave narratives that begin several generations into captivity in the South. And Kossola not only becomes "free" in the South, but he *stays* in the South instead of migrating to the North. Following fugitive slave narrative conventions, Kossola's story does include his conversion to Christianity. However, even that conversion seems incomplete when we consider the ways that West African spirituality continued to inform and shape Kossola's daily life, especially his social relations. As such, *Barracoon* "is a kind of slave narrative in reverse."[65] Given its departure from various norms of the fugitive slave narrative genre, *Barracoon* is a perfect text by which to explore Hurston's ethnographic refusals of the norms of neo-abolitionism. I will develop these refusals at two levels. First, there are ethnographic refusals at the discursive level. This includes the ways that Hurston frames the narrative of her respondent, Kossola, as well as the ways that Kossola responds to Hurston's questioning. The second level is Kossola's own story, those things he tells us about his experiences of slavery and freedom.

Discursive Refusals

At the discursive level, Hurston staged several interventions in framing Kossola's story. For instance, Hurston strove to carefully preserve Kossola's dialect in composing this text. Her refusal to alter his dialect in the manuscript resulted in the text's original failure of publication.[66] Hurston's refusal was partly based upon a defense of and commitment to Kossola being able to tell his story "in his own way."[67] Hurston also seemed to refuse certain standards of objectivity that her discipline (as a science) imposed upon her research.[68] In her introduction, Hurston asserts that this text "makes no attempt to be a scientific document."[69] This doesn't mean that she is absolving Kossola's story of truth. Rather, "the thought of the back of the act," Hurston discloses, "was to set down the essential truth rather than the fact of detail, which is so often misleading."[70] Over fifty years later, Toni Morrison makes a similar distinction in her discussion of fugitive slave narratives in "The Site of Memory." Observing that fugitive slave narratives don't allow us to "access the interior life" of enslaved Blacks, Morrison proposes a method of "literary archeology" that would enable us to "reconstruct" their world.[71] Although this method employs fiction, Morrison insists that this does not cede the veracity of its results. That is, the important distinction to consider is not between "fact and fiction," Morrison tells us, "but the distinction between fact and truth."[72] Like Hurston, what drives the distinction for Morrison is a deep mistrust of the "facts" issued or "stories always being told" by our oppressors.[73] Given the over-determination of the abolitionist message in fugitive slave narratives, it is interesting that both writers attempt to carve a space between "fact" and "truth" when tasked with revealing the inner lives of enslaved Blacks. I argue that this marks an ethnographic refusal of the "truth" of abolitionist discourse (i.e., Black sorrow and suffering) by privileging instead "the revelation of a kind of truth" that respects the sovereignty of inner Black life.[74]

Region also figures prominently in Hurston's discursive ethnographic refusals. In *Barracoon*, Hurston subtly remakes the South into a site of joy and pleasure. For instance, in many of the vignettes that structure the text, Hurston frames her interactions with Kossola by signaling the pleasure of Black southern food-ways. Food is a significant component in fashioning a Black southern identity.[75] So it is no surprise that we find references to Georgia peaches and Virginia hams and rain-barrels of Gulf Coast blue crabs, all while conversations are passed between Hurston and Kossola on his porch.[76] Even watermelon is mentioned, which was (and perhaps still is) a touchy topic for African Americans, given its role in racist stereotypes during the Reconstruction period.[77] Alice Walker grounds these moments in *Barracoon* within the context of rural, Black southern norms. "From moment to moment, we watch our beans and our watermelons grow. We plant. We hoe. We harvest. We share with our neighbors," Walker observes, and "if a young anthropologist appears with two hams and gives us one, we look forward to enjoying it."[78] While sharing food rituals with her respondent might have been important for her research methods, we should also consider the implications of Hurston's inclusion of such moments in light of the slave narrative genre.[79] As Walker indicates, Hurston's inclusion of pleasurable Black southern food-ways went against certain norms of representation of Black life at the time. "[Hurston] shares peaches and watermelon," Walker writes, and "(imagine how many generations of Black people would never admit to eating watermelon!)."[80] And yet, Hurston not only admits to eating watermelon but deeply affirms its delights.[81] Why highlight these tiny, explicitly Black, decidedly southern moments of pleasure in a slave narrative? I argue that we can sketch a kind of ethnographic refusal here as well. That is, Hurston refuses a depiction of Black life in the South that arises from abolitionist discourse—one wholly of Black sorrow and tragedy due to slavery.

Hurston also complicates the religious progression from "pagan" to Christian found in conventional fugitive slave narratives. For example, an insistence upon Kossola's retention of "paganism" (i.e., West African spirituality) opens and closes *Barracoon*. In the introduction, Hurston indicates that Kossola's "paganism" is a central research question that motivates her project. "How does a pagan live with a Christian God? How has this Nigerian 'heathen' borne up under the process of civilization?" Hurston asks.[82] And she closes *Barracoon* by affirming Kossola's "paganism." "I am sure that [Kossola] does not fear death. In spite of his long Christian fellowship, he is too deeply pagan to fear death."[83] We can also find this antipathy toward Christianity developed in later places of Hurston's work. For instance, in her 1938 "The Sanctified Church," she insists that particular sects of African American Protestants have retained their "paganism" by their continued use of root work. "In fact, the Negro has not been Christianized as extensively as is generally believed," Hurston asserts; "the great masses are still standing before their pagan altars and calling old gods by a new name."[84] As some scholars have noted, Hurston's antipathy toward Christianity is also rooted in a critique of imperialism. For instance, in the excised chapters from *Dust Tracks on a Road*, she criticizes the violent imperialist tendencies of Western forms of Christianity.[85] In this way, Hurston's interest in Kossola's retention of "paganism" is not only a refusal of the cultural assimilation (i.e., conversion to Christianity) that abolitionist discourse encourages, but is also a precursor of her later discussions of African American root work.

And perhaps most controversially, Hurston also refuses the victimization that abolitionist discourse assigns to "the slave," albeit in a way that continues to rankle us. Walker notes that Hurston dislodges a myth that has long shaped our understanding of slavery, "that Africans were only victims of the slave trade, not participants."[86] Disclosing how deeply this revelation shook her, Hurston writes in *Dust Tracks on a Road*:

> One thing impressed me strongly from this three months of association with Cudjo Lewis. The white people had held my people in slavery here in America. They had bought us, it is true and exploited us. But the inescapable fact that stuck in my craw, was: my people had *sold* me and the white people had bought me. That did away with the folklore I had been brought up on—that the white people had gone to Africa, waved a red handkerchief at the Africans and lured them aboard ship and sailed away. I know that civilized money stirred up African greed. That wars between tribes were often stirred up by white traders to provide more slaves in the barracoons and all that. But, if the African princes had been as pure and innocent as I would like to think, it could not have happened.[87]

Against the "folklore" of abolitionist discourse which views Blacks as tragic victims in want of white saviors, Hurston shifts the conversation by highlighting our agency—even if that agency is shown through our ability to commit heinous wrongs against each other. To be clear, this is an intervention that many of us, myself included, cringe upon hearing. However, addressing the ways that abolitionist discourse denies Black agency both hurts and heals. And part of that healing involves introducing more complex stories of Black life.

In addition to Hurston's own discursive refusals, Kossola himself refuses Hurston at times during her interviews. For example, when she encourages Kossola to discuss religion in Africa, Kossola insists upon his conversion to Christianity.[88] Similarly, when Hurston asks him about "juju" (or root work), he pretends not to know.[89] Since he was persecuted by his fellow African Americans for displays of "African" religiosity, it is not surprising that Kossola would veil his response in this way to Hurston.[90] Also, Kossola sometimes refuses Hurston's method of interviewing. For instance, when Hurston asks him about his life in Africa, he insists upon telling her his family line first. Viewing this as "tangent" information, Hurston interrupts Kossola to redirect the interview.[91] However, Kossola chides her: "Where is de house where de mouse is de leader? In de Affica soil I cain tellee you 'bout de son before I telle you 'bout de father."[92] And at times, Kossola outright refuses Hurston's visits, saying "Didn't I tellee you not to come bother me on Sat'day?" or specifying long breaks before she can repeat a visit.[93]

What I find most interesting is how often Hurston's interviews become laced with Kossola's "muted silences" when broaching the topic of slavery.[94] There are times when the trauma of enslavement, what Plant refers to as the "*mafaa*," causes the conversation to dissolve into silence.[95] However, there are other kinds of silences in the text as well: silences that demonstrate an active reluctance to answer further questions about slavery or a decision to abruptly end the interview.[96] For instance, during one of their interview sessions, Kossola begins to retreat into the "*mafaa*." At that moment, Hurston observes that something important happens:

> Kossula sat silent for a moment. I saw the old sorrow seep away from his eyes and the present take its place. He looked about him for a moment and then said bluntly, "I tired talking now. You go home and come back. If I talkeed wid you all de time I cain makee no garden. You want know too much. You astee too many questions. Dat do, dat do (that will do, etc.), go on home."[97]

"Dat do." Enough. He has reached an ethnographic limit. And Hurston, like Simpson, respects that limit. She does not "get into it" with her readers. Her response, in this passage, is to be "far from offended" at his wanting to stop.[98] When Hurston observes that he has drawn this limit, she often slips away quietly to let him be, rather than press him for more.[99] She seems to understand that Kossola's willingness to disclose the *fact* of slavery's horror is quite distinct from a willingness to divulge or *relive* that experience of horror for our readerly consumption.

Kossola's Narrative Refusals

Within his narrative, Kossola weaves together several moments that bear striking similarities to the types of refusals that Simpson catalogs in *Mohawk Interruptus*. I would like to focus on two clusters: the range of refusals that mark membership problems (via racial betrayal) and the refusals that expose disaffiliations with the state (i.e., the US government). There are many ways in which Kossola, along with the other *Clotilda* survivors, were betrayed by the very people that the state designates as "Black." The problem of racial

solidarity is flagged early on in Kossola's story when he is sold by his own people to white slavers. In a cruel turn of events, Kossola and the other *Clotilda*
survivors also experience strife with African Americans once they arrive in the
United States. African Americans viewed and treated them as "savages" rather
than as racial allies.[100] For instance, upon learning that they were free (after
the Emancipation), Kossola and the other *Clotilda* survivors worshipped on
Sunday in an "African" style. However, Kossola reports that "de American
colored folks, you unnerstand me, dey say we savage and den dey laugh at
us and doan come say nothin' to us."[101] Only Free George, a free Black man,
bothered to explain the religious (Christian) norms of African Americans to
the *Clotilda* survivors. When Kossola and the other *Clotilda* survivors later
establish their own town (Africatown), they refuse to worship with the African Americans who had mocked them before. While they take the advice
of Free George to "gittee de religion and join de church," they simply will
not worship with the "colored folks" who "pick at us all de time and call us
ig'nant savage."[102] Kossola explains: "We doan want to be mixee wid de other
folks what laught at us so we say we got plenty land and derefo' we kin build
our own church."[103] The painful prejudice of these African Americans caused
their relationship with Kossola and the other *Clotilda* survivors to be severed.

These racial divisions highlight what Simpson describes as a membership
issue for Iroquois peoples as well. By way of the Indian Act, the state prescribes
who is a member of their tribal groups, regardless of their own histories and
traditions. When the Iroquois peoples contest the Indian Act, they call upon
an alternative understanding of their political order and group affiliation—an
alternative understanding which affirms their own political sovereignty. For
African Americans, the "one-drop rule" was/is the state's determination of
who is considered "Black" or in our group. As Morrison puts it in her novel
A Mercy, the slave trade made it so that "I was not a person from my country,
nor from my families. I was negrita. Everything. Language, dress, gods, dance,
habits, decoration, song—all of it cooked together in the color of my skin."[104]
However, Kossola's navigation of racial solidarity in the United States shifts
how the determination of group membership is assessed. That is, the refusals
of Kossola and the other *Clotilda* survivors indicate different standards or
an alternative "genealogic" than that of the state by which to assess who is a
member, who is a friend, or who is a foe.[105]

Although according to the one-drop rule, Kossola and the African Americans he encountered are all "Black," his refusal to include them in his worship
practices signals that group membership requires *more* than skin tone (or
"one drop" of African blood). Kossola and the other *Clotilda* survivors also
recall an "archive" that slavery sought to erase through the very construction
of the concept of race, for their various refusals preserve the distinctiveness
and complexity of all those things that were "cooked together." This can be
seen not only in their relationship to African Americans but in their relationship to Gumpa, a nobleman from the kingdom of Dahomey which sold them

to the whites. Instead of throwing Gumpa away for his people's (the Daho-
means) betrayal, the *Clotilda* survivors decide to preserve his African noble
status in the New World.[106] They do so by installing Gumpa as the chief of
Africatown, the settlement they developed to "embod[y] the ethos and traditions of their homelands."[107] Kossola explains: "We ain' mad wid him 'cause
de king of Dahomey 'stroy our king and sell us to de white man. He didn't
do nothin' 'ginst us."[108] And so they decide upon Gumpa to preserve their
understanding of political order from their homelands.

Another cluster of refusals pertains to recognition from the state. Kossola and the other *Clotilda* survivors could not afford to go back to Africa,
so they decided to "make de Affica where dey fetch [them]."[109] With the
establishment of Africatown, I argue that we can see some of the "normative
challenges" that come with experiences of "nested sovereignty." For instance,
consider the dispute over Kossola's marital status due to his lack of a marriage license. By administering the marriage license, the church facilitates the
recognition of Kossola's familial relationships by the state. However, Kossola
complains to Hurston:

> Derefo', you unnerstand me, after me and my wife 'gree 'tween our-
> selves, we seekee religion and got converted. Den in de church dey
> tell us dat ain' right. We got to marry by license. In de Afficy soil, you
> unnerstand me, we ain' got no license. De man and de woman dey
> 'gree 'tween deyselves, den dey married and live together. We doan
> know nothin' 'bout dey have license over here in dis place. So den we
> gittee married by de license, but I doan love my wife no mo' wid de
> license than I love her befo' de license. She a good woman and I love
> her all de time.[110]

Within this passage, there is a dispute over the very legitimacy of Kossola's
marriage. In his homeland, his marriage would have been recognized as legitimate simply because of the agreement he and his wife had made between
each other. While he does end up getting a marriage license, Kossola still
challenges the authority of the state's license to legitimate his marriage. They
got the license, but Kossola insists that he "doan love [his] wife no mo' wid
de license." Similarly, when Kossola buries one of his children, he complies
with the rituals of church and state. "We Christian people now, so we put
our baby in de coffin and dey take her in de church, and everybody come
look down in her face," Kossola informs us.[111] And yet, he refuses to sing the
hymn of the church when they bury his baby. He admits that he does know
the song ("Shall We Meet Beyond de River"), for he has "been a member of
de church a long time now."[112] But he does not sing along. Instead, he sings a
song from his homeland. "I know de words of de song wid my mouth," Kossola confesses, "but my heart it doan know dat. Derefo' I sing inside me 'O
todo ah wah n-law yah-lee, owrran k-nee ra ra k-nee ro ro.' "[113]

I argue that the distance between Kossola's "mouth" and his "heart" maps those possibilities of disaffiliation that the state creates *through* its very attempts to produce citizens. Simpson calls these disaffiliations "feelings citizenships": "alternative citizenships to the state that are structured in the present space of intracommunity recognition, affection, and care outside of the logics of colonial and imperial rule."[114] This type of recognition is not "juridical" or based upon the state's law, but is "home-grown and dignified by local history and knowledge."[115] And refusals based upon these "feeling citizenships" highlight the fact that "different forms of recognition are at play" in cases of nested sovereignty.[116] We can find these different and contradictory forms of recognition at play even in the naming of Kossola and Abila's children. "So you unnerstand me, we give our chillum two names," Kossola informs us. "One name because we not furgit our home; den another name for de Americky soil so it won't be too crooked to call."[117] From refusals of the one-drop rule to various refusals of state recognition, I want to consider the possible effects that Kossola's ethnographic refusals may have had upon Hurston throughout her career, before turning to a close reading of her essay "How It Feels to Be Colored Me." How might Kossola's disaffiliations with the state and his creation of "feeling citizenships" in Africatown have shaped the development of Hurston's own racial politics?

What Got "Stuck" in Hurston's "Craw"

One important lesson that Hurston may have learned from Kossola's refusals is the importance of a kind of emotional sovereignty when it comes to the trauma of racism. For instance, a major theme in her interpretation of Kossola's story is how much the trauma of slavery intrudes upon the present. Indeed, at the outset of her investigation, Hurston tells us that part of her quest is to find out "how does one sleep with such memories beneath the pillow?"[118] During her interviews, Hurston witnesses Kossola reliving traumatic experiences as he tells her his story. Bearing witness to his suffering surely caused her to remark, at the end of the book, that Kossola is "full of trembling awe before the altar of the past."[119] As such, I argue that Hurston learns the importance of drawing limits when poked and prodded by others to relive Black traumatic experiences. That is, she seems to link Kossola's refusals to talk with her about the pain of slavery with his being able to live in the present. "Sometimes we just talked," Hurston writes. "At other times neither was possible, he just chased me away. He wanted to work in his garden or fix his fences. He couldn't be bothered. *The present was too urgent to let the past intrude.*"[120] When Kossola draws an "ethnographic limit" in her interviews, saying "dat do," Hurston brings up his past sorrow in relationship to his livable present. "I saw the old sorrow seep away from his eyes," Hurston interprets, "and the present take its place."[121] In her body of work,

I maintain that Hurston translates this struggle for emotional dominion over the trauma of slavery (such as in Kossola's narrative) into a struggle for literary sovereignty over representations of Black life, especially when it concerns Black enslaved life.[122]

This struggle over literary sovereignty runs counter to the mandate of neo-abolitionism that we contort ourselves into an "object of pity" in order to garner white liberal empathy. And this insight lays the groundwork for Hurston's own refusals of the pains and pity of slavery in her later work. For instance, in "Seeing the World as It Is," an excised chapter from *Dust Tracks on a Road*, Hurston writes: "I turn my back upon the past. I see no reason to keep my eyes fixed on the dark years of slavery and the Reconstruction."[123] Perhaps remembering how starkly her experiences of oppression differ from Kossola's, Hurston notes that "I am three generations removed from [slavery], and therefore have no experience of the thing. From what I can learn, it was sad. No doubt America would have been better off if it had never been."[124] I argue that she is not being naive about race relations here. Rather, she is drawing an ethnographic limit with her readers in the way that Kossola drew limits with her. Kossola sometimes refused to relive the trauma of slavery in interviews with Hurston, in an attempt to make his present livable. Likewise, Hurston also shores up the present in this passage: "I want to get on with the business in hand. Since I cannot pry loose the clutching hand of time, I will settle for some influence on the present."[125] In other words, to make her present serviceable, she is refusing to "get into it" with her readers in the way they would expect, such as "gazing backward over [her] shoulder and buking the grave of some white man who has been dead too long to talk about."[126] Nor does she "see any use in button-holing his grandson about it."[127]

Her refusal to even enter into a discussion with her primarily white audience over slavery may be due to her awareness of the impossibility of an equal footing in such a conversation.[128] That is, we can see Hurston refusing to entertain the conversation with her usual flippancy. "But the old man is dead," Hurston writes, "my old folks are dead. Let them wrestle all over Hell about it if they want to. That is their business."[129] However, what seems like abstained judgment may be an acknowledgment of a lack of "equal footing" with her imaginary white counterpart. "The old [white] man probably did cut some capers back there," Hurston writes, "and I'll bet you anything my old folks didn't like it."[130] In the "game" of racial politics in America, Hurston is well aware that "some in there are dealing from the bottom and cheating like hell in other ways."[131] And Hurston also suggests that "the idea of human slavery is so deeply ground in [white folks] that the pink-toes can't get it out of their system. It has just been decided to move the slave quarters farther away from the house."[132] Rather than barter for the recognition you could never win in these circumstances, might it not be better to refuse to "get into it" in the first place? These ethnographic refusals may have been one way that Hurston got through writing a book that she didn't even want to write in the first place.[133] As many Hurston scholars have pointed out, *Dust Tracks on a Road* is one of the least self-revealing autobiographies in the genre due to Hurston's constant evasions, dissemblances, and refusals.[134]

Another lasting influence of Kossola on Hurston's work may have been the complexity of race relations that his story evokes. As Plant notes, the racial tensions of Kossola's story may have influenced later themes in Hurston's work on race, for "this elder, an Isha Yoruba in America, had schooled her in the sociopolitical and cultural complexities of 'My People.'"[135] In this quote, Plant references Hurston's discussion of race in "My People, My People," another chapter in *Dust Tracks on a Road*. In this chapter, Hurston refuses to answer an imaginary white interviewer asking her "who are your people?"[136] Instead, Hurston undermines conventional notions of racial solidarity based upon "race pride" by pointing to the fault lines along class and gender in Black communities.[137] These fault lines produce painful strife and "varied interests" that "run counter to race lines."[138] And too often, these differences are how we oppress each other within Black communities, such as privileging lighter-skinned, middle-class women.[139] Instead of a "race pride" that is automatically engineered by skin tone, Hurston advocates a more complex notion of racial solidarity that is captured in a folk-saying: "my skin-folks, but not my kinfolks; my race but not my taste."[140] The playful distancing captured in the folk-saying captures the range of divisive interests, stinging betrayals, and varied moral and political stances that Blacks hold in relation to each other. It also emphasizes that racial solidarity is a political choice (and achievement) rather than a guaranteed given. Concerning the struggle for racial solidarity, Hurston writes, "so I sensed early, that the Negro race was not one band of heavenly love."[141] Rather, "there was stress and strain inside as well as out. Being Black was not enough. It took more than a community of skin color to make your love come down on you."[142] In fact, at the end of the chapter, Hurston even refuses the terms of the question, "who are your people?" Addressing the imaginary white interviewer, Hurston answers: "still, if you have received no clear cut impression of what the Negro in America is like, then you are in the same place with me. There is no *The Negro* here."[143]

At the heart of this refusal is a contestation of the state's definition of Blackness and the terms of membership: one drop of African blood, a biological conception of race.[144] Hurston seems to refuse the state's definition of Blackness in favor of one that is evidenced through our own cultural practices. In this way, instead of relying upon state recognition, Hurston may be signaling a "genealogic" of membership similar to what Simpson describes.[145] Indeed, at the opening of *Dust Tracks on a Road*, Hurston seems to compare these two different ways of defining racial identification and group membership. In describing the origins of her hometown, the "memories within" the "dead-seeming, cold rocks" that made her, Hurston highlights Indigenous struggles against settler colonialism.[146] One source of contention between the

Indigenous peoples and white settlers was the question of escaped Blacks. Hurston writes:

> The sore point of returning escaped Negroes could not be settled sat-
> isfactorily to either side. Who was an Indian and who was a Negro?
> The whites contended all who had negro blood. The Indians con-
> tended all who spoke their language belonged to the tribe. Since it
> was an easy matter to teach a slave to speak enough of the language
> to pass in a short time, the question could never be settled. So the
> wars went on.[147]

In this quote, the one-drop rule of the white settlers (or the emerging state) is put in juxtaposition to the language and/or cultural membership require-ments of Indigenous peoples.

While it is clear that enslaved Blacks could not abide by either defini-tion ("the question could never be settled"), throughout *Dust Tracks on a Road* Hurston seems to prefer the "Indian position." For instance, in the appendixed chapter of "My People! My People!" Hurston explicitly shifts the classification of "her people" away from skin tone: "still and all, you can't just point out my people by skin color."[148] To specify "who her people are," Hurston turns to the folklore of her people, laying out vignettes of cultural practices by which "her people" are identified. These practices themselves are complex and contradictory as well, defying the easy classification that the imaginary white reader seeks. In this move, from skin tone to cultural tradi-tions, Hurston exemplifies the "feelings citizenships" that Simpson discusses, the "'feeling side' of recognition, one that is not juridical, is home-grown, and dignified by local history and knowledge," in a word, folklore.[149]

These moves also enable Hurston to refuse the *meaning* of Blackness that lies within neo-abolitionism. Namely, that we are an "object of pity." For this neo-abolitionist meaning is also premised upon the state's definition of Black-ness. The one drop of African blood signifies enslavement and prophesies a lifetime of tragedy. However, Hurston shifts this meaning with a folktale in the appendixed version of "My People! My People!" This folktale describes how humans got divided into races. Blacks, in this folktale, got their skin tone by accident.[150] I suspect that part of the appeal of this folktale is that it neutralizes the loaded meanings of Blackness that abolitionist discourse provided. Under neo-abolitionism, Blackness continues to be loaded with sorrow and suffering. In this folktale, Black skin is a contingent feature, not a prophetic sign. In this way, Hurston refuses the "prophesied" tragedy of Blackness due to slavery by recasting Blackness as something accidental. To the imaginary white interviewer, Hurston confides:

> But maybe, after all the Negro doesn't really exist. What we think is
> a race is detached moods and phases of other people walking around.

What we have been talking about might not exist at all. Could be the
shade patterns of something else thrown on the ground—other folks,
seen in shadow. And even if we do exist it's all an accident anyway.
God made everybody else's color. We took ours by mistake.[151]

The folktale trappings take the sting out of what Hurston may be saying
to her white, neo-abolitionist audience: "Blackness, as you think of it, dear
white reader, may not truly exist."[152] Instead, it "could be the shade patterns
[read discourse] of something else thrown on the ground—other folks, seen
in shadow [read, white projections]." As such, Hurston refuses both the bless-
ing ("race pride") and the curse (the tragedy of neo-abolitionism) that are
often ascribed to Blackness in public discourse.

On Refusing the "Problem" of Blackness

I argue that we can also see Kossola's lessons of ethnographic refusal at play
in Hurston's essay "How It Feels to Be Colored Me," which was written at
the same time as *Barracoon*. There are four points of refusal that I want to
analyze in the essay. First, the title, which I take to be a rejection of the Du
Boisian question that opens *The Souls of Black Folk*: "How does it feel to
be a problem?"[153] Second, the "joyful tendencies" that tend to crop up in the
essay at precisely those moments when a northern white liberal would expect
confirmations of racial tragedy. Third, the stinging rejection of the pity and
pain of slavery that forms the crux of the essay. And finally, the jazz club
scene that ends the essay. In this scene, Hurston performs a reversal of racial
pity concerning her northern white liberal counterpart.

The title "How It Feels to Be Colored Me" may be posing a pithy reformulation of the question posed by Du Bois's white readers: "How does it feel
to be a problem?"[154] While Du Bois often refuses to answer this question in
face-to-face encounters with whites, he chooses to answer the question in
the opening essay of *The Souls of Black Folk*, "Of Our Spiritual Strivings."
In this essay, Du Bois tells us "how it feels" with a childhood story of racial-
ization.[155] As a young boy in a racially integrated school in New England,
Du Bois participated in an exchange of "gorgeous visiting-cards" between
the boys and the girls.[156] All went well until one white girl refused his card,
"peremptorily, with a glance."[157] Her refusal marked him as different from
the others because of his race. "Then it dawned upon me with a certain sud-
denness," Du Bois informs us, "that I was different from the others; or, like
mayhap, in heart and life and longing, but shut out from their world by a vast
veil."[158] Many Black intellectuals have depicted similar first experiences of
racial awareness as primarily negative.[159] In Du Bois's experience here, Blackness was the basis upon which he could be denied recognition by a fellow
human being. The metaphor of the "Veil" captures the unjust racial division

that Blacks face in the US context. That is, the "Veil" is a symbol of lack, of the ultimate denial of equal goods and opportunities for Blacks.

It is within the context of the "Veil" that Du Bois introduces the concept of "double-consciousness." Blacks are born, claims Du Bois, as "a sort of seventh son with a veil and gifted with second-sight in this American world."[160] The white American world, for Du Bois, is a world that does not allow our true self-consciousness (or perception of ourselves). Rather, it "only lets [us] see [ourselves] through the revelation of the other world."[161] And this "revelation" through the other world renders us an object of pity. "It is a peculiar sensation, this double-consciousness," Du Bois says, "this sense of always looking at one's self through the eyes of others, of measuring one's soul by the tape of a world that looks on in amused contempt and pity."[162] This view of ourselves from the American world can lead to self-doubt, a desire to prove ourselves, and internalized self-hatred. Throughout *The Souls of Black Folk* we encounter a constellation of affects arising from double-consciousness: shame, pride, joy, hope, sorrow, tragedy, bitterness, contempt, pity. The dominant affect, however, is the sorrow of Black life.[163] Given the despair, the bitterness, the shame, the pity that come from these aspects of our experiences of oppression, it is not hard to see how sorrow can become the prevailing emotional response. However, under neo-abolitionism, these negative affects come to bear the weight of the "truth" or meaning of Black life. They come to signify what we mean by "Blackness." What would happen, however, if our depiction of African American life started in a different place?

One alternative starting point is refusal. In her analysis of refusal, Simpson argues that refusal does not easily fit into some of our models of critical engagement with oppression. The model she has in mind is postcolonial studies, which stresses a duality or double-ness in the consciousness of the oppressed, following Du Bois.[164] Consciousness, in this model, becomes doubled through its attempt to gain recognition from the Other. But what happens if you refuse the very terms of the Other's recognition, and instead, disengage?[165] Simpson argues that in this case, refusal enables a different sort of subject formation. Instead of double-consciousness, there seems to be "a tripleness, a quadrupleness, to consciousness and an endless play" that marks such acts of refusal.[166] Simpson relays the "endless play" of refusals to us like this: "I am me, I am what you think I am and I am who this person to the right of me thinks I am and you are full of shit and then maybe I will tell you to your face."[167] Simpson's point is that the kind of "play" that refusal invokes stands in stark contrast to models of double-consciousness. This is because such "play" seems to be issued from a *self*-consciousness or a "definite core" that reveals "a stance, a principle, a historical narrative, and an *enjoyment*" in its very refusal of the Other's gaze.[168] Hurston also seemed to be privy to this kind of "play."[169] Recall the tactics of ethnographic refusal that Hurston describes in *Mules and Men*:

> The theory behind our tactics: "The white man is always trying to know into somebody else's business. All right, I'll set something outside the door of my mind for him to play with and handle. He can read my writing but he sho' can't read my mind. I'll put this play toy in his hand, and he will seize it and go away. Then I'll say my say and sing my song."[170]

In this passage, there is the "play" that Simpson describes, where we put "a play toy" in the hands of whites for them to handle. But there is also a "definite core" from which this playful performance emanates, as suggested by the "white man" being placed "*outside* the door of my mind." The space signaled between "read[ing] my writing" and "read[ing] my mind." Moreover, as discussed earlier, the point in this passage is not to achieve the recognition of whites, but to continue to evade their recognition so that we can "say [our] say and sing [our] song" in peace.[171]

Hurston also seems to signal this turn away from double-consciousness by the subtle shift in the point of view posed by the title of the essay, "How It Feels to Be Colored Me." Indeed, one recurring motif of the essay seems to be the rejection of the Du Boisian notion of double-consciousness as a model of racialized experience.[172] Under this model, double-consciousness makes us constantly aware of how America sees our Blackness as "a problem." But whereas Du Bois claims that we live our lives under this shadow of the "Negro problem," and we lead a "double life" as "a Negro and an American," Hurston asserts that she has "no separate feeling about being an American citizen and colored."[173] Perhaps her experiences interviewing Kossola made her aware of just *how* Americanized African Americans already are, and so opting out of citizenship is not a live option. At any rate, the United States is "[her] country, right or wrong."[174] Although Hurston's reformulation of Du Bois's question in the title (from "how it feels to be a problem" to "how it feels to be colored me") is often taken as characteristic of her emphasis on individuality, I want to consider this reformulation against the backdrop of neo-abolitionism. Recalling our earlier discussion of *Barracoon*, the lessons Hurston learns from Kossola's story shatter the foundation of neo-abolitionism—from notions of collective racial identity to the tragic victimizations of enslaved Blacks.

For instance, with her seemingly simple reformulation of Du Bois's question, Hurston refuses a mandate of neo-abolitionism, to be a representative or "tragic unit of the Race."[175] To this end, Hurston not only emphasizes how her *personal* experience does not represent the whole, but she also neutralizes the neo-abolitionist *meaning* of her skin color. "I am colored," Hurston begins the essay, "but I offer nothing in the way of extenuating circumstances except the fact that I am the only Negro in the United States whose grandfather on the mother's side was *not* an Indian chief."[176] In other words, sure, she is Black, but her Blackness does not require an apology or an explanation.

While neo-abolitionism equates Blackness with tragedy, Hurston refuses this equation at the heart of the essay. "But I am not tragically colored," Hurston assures us, "there is no great sorrow dammed up in my soul, nor lurking behind my eyes. I do not mind at all."[177]

In addition, toward the end of the essay, Hurston uses a metaphor that makes skin tone an accidental feature rather than the determining, tragic feature in neo-abolitionism. She is like a bundle of items tucked into a "brown bag." "In your hand is the brown bag," Hurston writes, "on the ground before you is the jumble it held," and the bag-jumbles are so similar that all the bags could be emptied and re-stuffed "without altering the content of any greatly."[178] Although I think this metaphor breaks down rather quickly, I am interested in the rhetorical effect of this metaphor. Race, in this metaphor, is an accidental feature; it is not constitutive of what lies within. As I have argued earlier, Hurston developed a sensitivity to racial divisions and betrayal through interviewing Kossola for *Barracoon*. Skin color is no indication of loyalty, nor is it an assurance of ethical principles.[179] In this light, it makes sense that Hurston would reject an essentialized notion of Blackness as in the "Great Bag Stuffer" metaphor.

The second point of refusal recounts the "joyful tendencies" of Hurston as a child in Eatonville, an "exclusively colored town."[180] In contrast to Du Bois's story of childhood racial rejection in New England, Hurston informs us that her childhood was marked by "joyful tendencies," such as singing and dancing for all who came through her Florida hometown.[181] Hurston notes that such "joyful tendencies" were often "deplored" by the older Black folks who witnessed them.[182] To them, to have such displays of Black joy in the South might confirm the assumption that "life was joyous to the Black slave, careless and happy."[183] Against the figure of the "happy darky," neo-abolitionism advocated that we stress the sorrow and tragedy of southern Black life. However, Hurston almost taunts her white liberal (neo-abolitionist) audience by describing her childhood adventures in terms reminiscent of minstrel shows.[184] "My favorite place was atop the gate-post. Proscenium box for a born first-nighter," Hurston confides. "Not only did I enjoy the show, but I didn't mind the actors knowing that I liked it. I actually spoke to them in passing."[185] She also happily takes money from strangers for performing songs and dances. Rather than conform to the neo-abolitionist mandate of racial tragedy in the South, Hurston highlights such "joyful tendencies" as these.

I mark Hurston's "joyful tendencies" in the South as ethnographic refusal instead of racial naivete because they can be read as instances of the "endless play" that Simpson observed concerning refusals. Rather than give us a tale of double-consciousness and despair over the racial rejection by whites, Hurston violates the readerly expectations formed by neo-abolitionism. She "plays" with us by confirming that she is a minstrel, even as she rejects the terms upon which the minstrel tradition proceeds (i.e., a racial essence of

Blackness that minstrels can imitate). And this "endless play" is made possible by a "definite core" from which Hurston's "joyful tendencies" issue. Consider, for instance, Hurston's altercation with her grandmother over her "shows," as discussed in *Dust Tracks on a Road*. When her grandmother catches her during one of her "shows" for the white folks, she yells at her to "git down offa dat gate post! You li'l sow, you! Git down! Setting up dere looking dem white folks right in de face! They's gowine to lynch you, yet."[186] Hurston explains her grandmother's behavior in terms of her experiences of slavery. "My grandmother worried about my forward ways a great deal," Hurston writes. "She had known slavery and to her, my brazenness was unthinkable."[187]

This generational divide was a source of recurring tension between Hurston and her grandmother. While her mother always defended her "joyful tendencies," Hurston's grandmother would often "foam at the mouth" to discipline her.[188] Hurston's response to her grandmother's attempts to discipline her reveals her "definite core." "I knew that I did not have to pay too much attention to the old lady and so I didn't," Hurston confides. "Furthermore, how was she going to tell what I was doing inside? I could keep my inventions to myself, which was what I did most of the time."[189] She can refuse her grandmother's orders because there is something else she is "doing inside." This is not double-consciousness, but a firm *self*-consciousness. I argue that this is the core from which her "joyful tendencies" issued, making the worries of how whites would perceive her irrelevant. Moreover, these "joyful tendencies" were considered to be "brazen" precisely because they violated neo-abolitionist norms. It is her "joyful tendencies" that cause her to refuse the tragedy of Black life that abolitionism prophesied. She not only does not "mind" her Blackness, but she also refuses to "weep at the world."[190] She is "too busy sharpening [her] oyster knife."[191] Perhaps the lessons learned in *Barracoon*—such as the betrayal by fellow Africans and the gumption by which Kossola and the other *Clotilda* survivors established Africatown— equipped Hurston to neither succumb to victimhood (i.e., the "sobbing school of Negrohood") nor to absolve herself of agency (i.e., the "world is to the strong regardless of a little pigmentation").[192]

There is a parallel between the "joyful tendencies" found in this essay and those in *Barracoon*. In the essay, Hurston's resurrection of minstrel imagery, I argue, "playfully" violates the neo-abolitionist mandate of representations of Black southern life as tragic. Similarly, in *Barracoon* we also see these "joyful tendencies" disrupt the norms of abolitionist discourse embedded in the genre of fugitive slave narratives. Recalling our discussion earlier, food is often the medium of these joyful eruptions, such as Hurston's bold insertion of the enjoyment of watermelon, a key component of "happy darky" imagery in the Jim Crow era. For Alice Walker, these "joyful tendencies" correspond to the healing, or positive, aspect of Hurston's project in *Barracoon*. Exposing the participation of fellow Africans in the transatlantic slave trade breaks

with our preconceived notions of slavery to "show us the [racial] wound."[193]
However, underscoring the joy in Black life via southern food-ways, showing
that "though the heart is breaking, happiness can exist in a moment, too," is
a type of "medicine."[194]

A third, and perhaps most controversial, point of refusal is when Hurston
refuses the pain and pity of slavery. She writes:

> Someone is always at my elbow reminding me that I am the grand-
> daughter of slaves. It fails to register depression with me. Slavery is
> sixty years in the past. The operation was successful and the patient is
> doing well, thank you. The terrible struggle that made me an Ameri-
> can out of a potential slave said "On the line!" The Reconstruction
> said "Get set!"; and the generation before said "Go!" I am off to a
> flying start and I must not halt in the stretch to look behind and weep.
> Slavery is the price I paid for civilization, and the choice was not
> with me. It is a bully adventure and worth all I have paid through my
> ancestors for it. No one on earth ever had a better chance for glory.[195]

Hurston here is refusing to contort herself into an "object of pity" as neo-
abolitionism mandates. Instead, she pivots to highlight the agency of her
ancestors: "[Slavery] is a bully adventure *and* worth all I have paid through
my ancestors for it." And if we take into account that she was writing this
while composing *Barracoon*, another layer of refusal presents itself. Might
she also be drawing an ethnographic limit with her readers? As we discussed
in the previous section, Hurston may have learned an important lesson in
emotional sovereignty from Kossola—when to say "dat do" or "enough" in
response to someone "at [your] elbow" demanding tales of Black sorrow and
trauma. Perhaps she did not want to "get into it" with her readers here. So
rather than discuss the pain of slavery, Hurston turns to compare her situation to that of whites. "The position of my white neighbor is much more
difficult," Hurston observes. "No brown specter pulls up a chair beside me
when I sit down to eat."[196] The implication is that shame and pity over slavery do not belong to African Americans. They belong to whites.

This reversal of pity is also present in the fourth and final point of refusal
for our analysis. Toward the end of the essay, Hurston recounts an experience
at a jazz club, the New World Cabaret. She is seated next to a white person
and notices immediately that "her color comes."[197] As they sit through the
music, Hurston is moved by that African American cultural expression. She
participates in the performance as part of the audience:

> I follow these heathen—follow them exultingly. I dance wildly inside
> myself; I yell within, I whoop; I shake my assegai above my head,
> I hurl it true to the mark *yeeeeooww!* I am in the jungle and living
> in the jungle way. My face is painted red and yellow, and my body

is painted blue. My pulse is throbbing like a war drum. I want to slaughter something—give pain, give death to what, I do not know. But the piece ends. The men of the orchestra wipe their lips and rest their fingers. I creep back slowly to the veneer we call civilization with the last tone and find the white friend sitting motionless in his seat, smoking calmly.[198]

We can again see the "endless play" here. On the one hand, she seems to confirm the "savagery" that her white counterpart may assume of her—she "dance[s] wildly," she "yell[s]" and "whoops," being "in the jungle and living in the jungle way." On the other hand, she also refuses the ascription of civilization to the West. What the West calls "civilization" is simply a "veneer."

And then, perhaps taking a leaf from Kossola's book, Hurston calls into question the assumption of African savagery and Western civilization by reversing the terms.[199] For example, the fact that her white counterpart could remain unmoved (i.e., "sitting motionless" and "smoking calmly") by such art could be taken as symptomatic of the brutishness historically assigned to "savages." Appreciation of the arts was often considered reserved for the upper class, the more "civilized" of us. And yet, Hurston remarks of her white associate: "The great blobs of purple and red emotion have not touched him. He has only heard what I felt."[200] And what has "civilized" her, what has enabled her to be sensitive to the art that is this music, is her connection to Africa. "[My white companion] is far away," Hurston observes, "and I see him but dimly across the ocean and the continent that have fallen between us."[201] It is not the descendant of slaves who is to be pitied here, but he who is "so pale with his whiteness."[202] In refusal of neo-abolitionism's equation of Blackness with tragedy, Hurston asserts her Blackness here with glee instead of sorrow: "I am so colored."[203]

This tendency to revel in her culture, to gleefully exclaim that she is "so colored," or to profess her deep love for both her "skinfolks" and her "kinfolks" at the close of *Dust Tracks on a Road*, is part of what prompts some to assert that "passionate racial pride" is a determining feature of Hurston's politics.[204] In this chapter, I have argued that the concept of ethnographic refusal may help us make sense of the other, seemingly contradictory feature of Hurston's racial politics, her "passionate individualism."[205] In reading *Barracoon* against "How It Feels to Be Colored Me," I interpret Hurston's turns to individualism, "joyous tendencies," and controversial comments on slavery as an ethnographic refusal of the mandates of neo-abolitionism. By layering her tactics with those of Kossola in *Barracoon*, I have interpreted Hurston's refusals in light of the neo-abolitionist demand that we lay bare our inner lives for white folks who already presume to know all about us. In this way, Hurston's evasions and dissemblances in her self-revelatory texts can be interpreted as an "ethnographic calculus" of how much her audiences need to know and what she could live with telling them. While Hurston's refusals in this chapter took on a methodological form, we turn, in the next chapter, to a different form of refusal that the politics of joy takes. Hurston's tendency to revel in her culture also goaded her refusal of the imperatives of cultural assimilation embedded in neo-abolitionist narratives of Black liberation. This polemic takes place in Hurston's discussion of the Sanctified Church, where she defies the assumption that we have been fully Christianized. In her contestation of the neo-abolitionist story of our Christian conversion, Hurston's refusal takes the form of an important "historical possibility."[206]

Scene 4

✦

"Slay Trick, or You Get Eliminated"

For those looking for explicit references to anti-Black racism and resistance in *Lemonade*, the song "Formation" is an apt place to look. Draped on a police car in the waters of Lake Pontchartrain that overflowed during Hurricane Katrina, Beyoncé indicts America for its treatment of Black and brown peoples in one fell swoop.[1] Because of these explicit connections to social protest, we might be tempted to read "Formation" through the lens of resistance. However, I want to recall an important distinction that Angela Davis makes when analyzing the presence of protest in the blueswoman tradition, in which *Lemonade* participates. Davis argues that these songs do not constitute social protest; rather, they may help to "create the emotional conditions for protest."[2] As such, while these songs may be intimately connected to protest (and indeed, enable protest to arise), they are not protest in and of themselves. Rather, they are something else.

With this distinction in mind, we may wonder what type of agency practices of "formation" *do* exhibit. A closer look at "slaying" may provide a clue. Some may read "slaying" as a violent response to our oppressors, where we strive to annihilate them. However, throughout the song, an attitude of staying "above the fray" is conveyed when it comes to our enemies, such as "twirl on them haters" and "always stay gracious, best revenge is your paper [i.e., your success]."[3] The main action of the song, instead, focuses on how we relate to ourselves. For example, the protagonist describes slaying as: "I see it/I want it/I stunt/yellow bone it/I dream it, I work hard/I grind 'til I own it." The protagonist pushes herself, "go[ing] hard" in trust that she can "get what's [hers], take what's [hers]."[4] This is because of the value she places on herself as "a star." And her focus on excellence, satisfaction, pleasure, and even joy resonates with Audre Lorde's discussion of the erotic, "an internal sense of satisfaction to which, once we have experienced it, we know we can aspire."[5] For Lorde, the erotic within ourselves is a source of self-determination and self-definition, for it provides an internal, positive standard by which to assess our social environment.[6] Put another way, the erotic is that "*yes* within ourselves, our deepest cravings" that we have been taught to fear by dominant culture.[7] And paying attention to that "*yes* within ourselves" can help us define ourselves amid all the counter-messages dominant culture sends our way. We can see this when the protagonist gleefully says "yes" to the joys of southern Black culture ("when he fuck me good I take his ass to Red Lobster"). This "yes" grounds her affirmation of a working-class southern Black identity amidst the pressures to assimilate to the middle class ("earned all this money but they never take the country out me").[8]

In "Formation," many of the sources of "slaying" are found in practices of root work. For example, the song alludes to the practice of "shouting" in the southern Sanctified Church, the figure Maman Brigette in Haitian Vodou, and Mardi Gras Indians who are associated with Louisiana Voodoo.[9] It is as if Beyoncé suggests that the way we get "in formation" is by "seeking the spirits for self-liberation."[10] In this final chapter, I will examine what type of agency root work practices exhibit. I do so to move away from the oppressor/ oppressed relations that neo-abolitionism privileges (by exposing the suffering of Black folk due to white folks' racism). Similar to Beyoncé's "slaying" and Lorde's "erotic," Hurston's analysis of root work also seemed to privilege the relation of the self to the self. Instead of focusing on resistance, Hurston highlighted how root work practices helped the enslaved "win [their] war from within."[11] And like "slaying," "winning within" is more about determining the self ("winning with the soul of the Black man whole and free") than about waging war with our oppressors.[12] For Hurston, what is at stake in paying attention to this register of agency is no less than our own sense of self. This is why, for Hurston as well as Beyoncé, we must strive to "slay"—else we will be "eliminated" by the forces of the dominant culture.

Chapter 4

"Winning [Our] War from Within"
Moving beyond Resistance

> And all the time, there was High John de Conquer playing his
> tricks of making a way out of no-way. Hitting a straight lick
> with a crooked stick. Winning the jack pot with no other stake
> but a laugh. Fighting a mighty battle without outside-showing
> force, and winning his war from within. Really winning in a
> permanent way, for he was winning with the soul of the black
> man whole and free. So he could use it afterwards.
>
> —Zora Neale Hurston, "High John de Conquer"

In this final chapter, I analyze how Hurston's account of root work exhibits
the politics of joy by privileging self-determination (or encouraging us to
"win within") over resistance to racism. By focusing on self-determination
rather than resistance, not only does Hurston's account of root work challenge the neo-abolitionist mandate of representations of southern Black
tragedy, but it also refuses the cultural assimilation that neo-abolitionism
encourages for racial progress. That is, sometimes a narrow focus on resisting our oppressors can actually cause us to emulate them. We can begin to
see some of these insights come into play if we contrast Hurston's account of
root work in her 1938 "The Sanctified Church" with Du Bois's discussion of
root work (i.e., "voodooism") in his "Of the Faith of the Fathers." Du Bois's
discussion of African American religion shares several points of comparison
with Hurston. In some ways, Hurston picks up where Du Bois left off, since
many of the practices Du Bois describes in "Of the Faith of the Fathers" later
became part and parcel of the Sanctified Church. Both Du Bois and Hurston
pay special attention to the "preacher, the music, and the frenzy" involved
in southern religious revivals.[1] However, their accounts of African American
religious expression differ when it comes down to the persistence of root
work. The "frenzy" which Du Bois bemoans is the ring shout that Hurston
celebrates.[2] What Du Bois describes as "a pythian madness, a demoniac possession," Hurston describes as "'shouting' which is nothing more than a

continuation of the African 'Possession' by the gods."[3] And while Du Bois asserts that "after the lapse of many generations the Negro church became Christian," Hurston points to the persistence of root work in the Sanctified Church to contend that "the Negro has not been Christianized as extensively as is generally believed."[4]

Their differences in approach to and interpretation of root work highlight the political tensions in their thought. For instance, Du Bois disparages the retention of "voodooism" as "the vein vague of superstition" that the lower class (i.e., "unlettered Negro") stubbornly hold on to.[5] However, Hurston commends the presence of root work in the Sanctified Church as a site of internal class struggle, or "a protest against the highbrow tendency in Negro Protestant congregations as the Negroes gain more education and wealth."[6] Du Bois maps a regional evolution of Black churches that moves us away from the southern "Gold Coast" and toward the "institutional Negro church of Chicago."[7] In contrast, Hurston pivots back to the South, where the old is being reborn such that "older forms of Negro religious expression" are "asserting themselves against the new."[8] As such, the Sanctified Church is

> a revitalizing element in Negro music and religion. It is putting back into Negro religion those elements which were brought over from Africa and grafted onto Christianity as soon as the Negro came into contact with it, but which are being rooted out as the American Negro approaches white concepts.[9]

Put another way, the model of the Sanctified Church can provide a warning of how visions of Black liberation can sometimes encourage cultural assimilation by mirroring white establishments. While Du Bois denounces southern Black churches for their participation in the ring shout, members of the Sanctified Church mock Black churches that mimic whites in manner and worship.[10] These more "orderly" New England churches strove to resist the racist narrative that Blacks were wild and savage.[11] While the decorum of these New England churches may have gained approval from their white equivalents, members of the Sanctified Church seemed to grasp a significant relationship between the pursuit of such recognition and cultural emulation. Namely, if we focus too much on gaining political recognition from our white counterparts, we may fail to develop an independent sense of self.

Hurston also mobilizes the "Negro elements" found in root work to refuse neo-abolitionist mandates concerning representations of southern Black life. For example, she contests the narrative of cultural assimilation found within abolitionist discourse, such as the Christian conversion of the enslaved. Hurston asserts that "the Negro has not been Christianized as extensively as is generally believed. The great masses are still standing before their pagan altars and calling old gods by a new name."[12] In her discussion of Negro spirituals in this essay, Hurston also uses the root work practices of the Sanctified

Church to further contest the abolitionist context of Du Bois's "sorrow songs." For instance, Hurston displaces Christianity by introducing the ring shout and spirit possession into the context of the spirituals performed in the Sanctified Church.[13] This move also enables Hurston to decenter slavery and its sorrow in defining the spirituals as well:

> So it is ridiculous to say that the spirituals are the Negro's "sorrow songs." For just as many are being made in this post-slavery period as were ever made in slavery as far as anyone can find. At any rate the people who are now making spirituals are the same as those who made them in the past and not the self-conscious propogandists that our latter-day pity men would have us believe. They sang sorrowful phrases then as they do now because they sounded well, and not because of the thought-content.[14]

Not only are Negro spirituals not confined to slavery, but they are also not restricted to sorrow. I argue that at the heart of Hurston's dispute with Du Bois, and neo-abolitionism at large, is the modes of agency that we privilege in our discussions of Black life. That is to say, Hurston's account of root work has important implications for how we interpret the practices of the oppressed. In our discussions of agency under oppression, do we privilege resistance, and thus the relation of the oppressed to oppressors? Or do we foreground, as the epigraph suggests, the mode of self-relation or "winning within"?

The Limitations of Resistance

As discussed in "An Object of Pity," Du Bois advances an interpretation of Black religiosity that aligns root work (i.e., "voodooism") with revolt and resistance.[15] The willful, rebellious spirit of the enslaved, as exemplified in the revolts spawned by "voodooism," later fueled various strains of the abolitionist movement. Or so goes Du Bois's argument. At the time, it was important for Du Bois to emphasize revolt and rebellion against the pro-slavers who argued that the enslaved were docile and "happy" with their lot in life. Similarly, scholarship on Black religious expression has often emphasized resistance in discussions of the religious practices of those who were enslaved.[16] Against those who claim that we merely accepted the religion of our masters, race scholars have advanced decades' worth of arguments detailing how we have wielded such religious expression for our own purposes.[17] Race scholars have also rejected the abolitionist assumption that we were merely victims during slavery, and have rightfully shown that we were active participants in ensuring our own liberation. However, race scholars often maintain ties with abolitionist discourse by reducing our expressions of agency (including Black religiosity) to a testimony against the evils of slavery.[18] This is done by privileging resistance to domination in our narratives of enslaved life over and above other types of relations formed under slavery. This focus on resistance is tempting because it is taken to be one way of showing our own will and identifying the true expressions of our agency. Unfortunately, the emphasis on resistance to slavery has overdetermined our accounts of Black religiosity by centering our relation to white supremacy over and above other facets of Black life. But we don't always think about white people, and our spirituality may be so precious precisely because we center the divine over whites.

Against this trend, several scholars have noted the limitations of the term "resistance" when attempting to address the fullness of the lives of those who are oppressed. There are two main concerns that are relevant to our discussion.[19] The first concern refers to the flattening aspect of the category of "resistance." That is, the category of "resistance" can often flatten the complexity of the lives of the oppressed (especially intragroup relations) by privileging the relationship between oppressed and oppressor. For example, the anthropologist Sherry Otner argues that the way we ascribe "resistance" to the practices of the oppressed may result in "ethnographical thinness": "thin on the internal politics of dominated groups, thin on the cultural richness of those groups, thin on the subjectivity—the intentions, desires, fears, projects—of the actors engaged in these dramas."[20] In foregrounding the relationship of oppressed to oppressors, Ortner argues that "resistance studies" often bypasses the "intentions, desires, fears, projects" of the oppressed.[21] This is done, for instance, when we understand resistance to be taking place regardless of the "intentions of the actors or of the presence of very mixed emotions."[22] Such bypassing also ignores the *intragroup* tensions and politics that make such acts of "resistance" ambiguous to those within the group.[23] In a group of racially oppressed people, there is often an array of divisions and differences, such as gender dynamics, age gaps, varying sexual orientations, class stratifications, regional disparities, and so on. These divisions and differences are often a "ground of ambivalence" regarding the oppressed/ oppressor relation, which results in "different, even opposed, but still legitimate positions" that members of the group may express regarding their racial oppression.[24] In other words, we do not all respond the same way to our oppression. And to categorize all of our responses as "resistance" glosses over the differences within our internal group politics.

Ortner surmises that this ethnographic "thinness" is produced out of fear of delving too deeply into our internal politics or the messiness of our lives. This is partly due to a concern that acknowledgment of the ways that we oppress each other will justify the dominant group's violence toward us.[25] In studies of African American life, we can observe this fear when it comes to discussions of African participation in the transatlantic slave trade. However, I agree with Ortner's assertion that this concern is unfounded. No matter how we treat each other, it does not justify somebody *else* doing us harm.[26] There is also a very real fear that looking too closely into our lives will yield moments of complicity with or acceptance of our domination.[27] We can see this in the neo-abolitionist anxiety over public expressions of Black joy. In these cases, there is pressure to limit the expression of Black joy, lest our oppressors come to believe that we are content with the injustice they sow in our lives. Both fears contribute to ethnographic thinness concerning how we study the cultures of the oppressed. Moreover, these fears suppress the insight that the oppressed are often "doing more than simply opposing domination, more than simply producing a virtually *re*-action" to their oppression.[28] When we read these practices primarily through the lens of resistance, we run the risk of viewing "subaltern responses to domination as ad hoc and incoherent, springing not from [our] own senses of order, justice, meaning . . . but only from some set of ideas called into being by the situation of domination itself."[29] However, Ortner reminds us that oppressed peoples have a "prior and ongoing" culture that is not wholly subsumed by the "situation of domination."[30]

The second concern refers to how the resistance discourses can obscure other modes of agency. That is, the quick and ready attribution of "resistance" to the actions of the oppressed can cover over other modes of agency that the oppressed exhibit.[31] For instance, Eddie Glaude notes that there is a tendency to reduce agency to resistance in analyses of African American Christianity. This tendency is partly motivated by the enduring pro-slavery narratives that diminished our humanity. "Too often American history has denied the active presence of African Americans," Glaude writes, "whom slavery supposedly reduced to 'sambos.' Freedom and agency—so the story went—was the possession of white folks."[32] Our conversion to Christianity, in this light, was taken to be "an accommodation to slavery."[33] To trouble this claim, we have spent decades trying to show how our conversion to Christianity was more complicated and may even be seen as resistant to white supremacy. However, buried in these accounts is often the assumption that any expression of agency exhibited by the oppressed is inherently resistant as well as emancipatory. This not only ignores that "there is much more to our living than simply white supremacy," but it also renders our analyses of "resistance" inadequate and incomplete.[34] "Too often an unproblematized invocation of agency as political resistance stands in for any detailed account of that resistance or what we might mean by this elusive term," Glaude points out.[35] Within discussions of Black Christianity, linking agency to "emancipatory politics has often blocked . . . a more nuanced understanding of the role and function of African American Christianity in the context of slavery."[36] As a corrective, Glaude urges us to develop a "thicker account of the 'religious meanings' of the slaves' conversion."[37] Drawing upon insights from Albert Raboteau's *Slave Religion*, Glaude attempts to draft a story of African American Christianity that takes seriously the enslaved's own religious experiences. Glaude argues that accounts of agency that privilege resistance will miss the profound effects of conversion upon the enslaved, for the terms of conversion itself cannot be read as resistance. Put another way, the terms of their conversion experience did not consist in the overthrow of the current regime of oppression, but in their "submission to divine agency."[38] In this way, those who claim that the Christian conversion of the enslaved was "resistance" fail to "show us *how* the embrace of Christian doctrine might have substantially aided the slave in negotiating her subordination."[39] Yes, Christian conversion may have afforded the enslaved some agency. And yes, it may even have "precipitated a form of rebelliousness."[40] But Glaude is careful to point out that, within Christian conversion, the terms of that agency itself was not "rebelliousness."[41] Unlike in the mode of resistance, the relationship that was central here, for the enslaved, was that of them to God, not them to their slave masters. This is how, as Glaude rightly argues, "God's presence in the slaves' lives. . . . short-circuited the ultimate power of the master-slave relationship. The slave was now beholden to a master who was no respecter of persons."[42]

How are we to capture the range of relationships and paradoxes that this type of agency entails? A form of agency whose investment in "otherworldliness" ultimately makes the state's rule irrelevant? A form of agency where the free expression of the will is demonstrated by submission rather than insurgence, deference rather than subversion? A form of agency where the actor conceives of herself as merely a vessel of divine agency? If we approach this type of agency through the lens of resistance, not only do we obscure the mode of agency exhibited (i.e., submission), but we are in danger of rendering the very machinations of resistance and the conditions of its emergence mysterious.[43] Perhaps it is Hurston's sensitivity to these complexities in Black religious expression as an anthropologist that caused her to describe her approach as writing "from the middle of the Negro out—not the reverse."[44] Rather than "solve any problems," in her work she "tried to deal with life as we actually live it—not as the Sociologists imagine it."[45]

While there are now many accounts of African American Christianity that do not focus primarily on resistance, the same cannot be said for accounts of root work. There is still a trend in scholarship that follows Du Bois's lead in reading root work (or conjure) through the lens of resistance—even if there is no direct mention of oppression or any expressed intention against whites.[46] This trend has also influenced Hurston scholarship. For instance, the root work practices described in Hurston's popular 1943 essay "High John de Conquer" often get interpreted as practices of resistance.[47] There is, of course, much work that points to the correlation of root work and slave rebellions.[48] And yet, with its prioritization of resistance, much of this work reproduces the ethnological thinness critiqued in this section. Although we are good at tracking the correlation between spirit work and slave rebellions, we are not so good at showing *how* or *why* participation in these practices could support and prompt rebellion. Moreover, a closer look at the cosmology of some of these spiritual traditions may, paradoxically, move us further away from resistance rather than confirm our presumption of it. Although I agree that our religious expression often bore the seeds of something powerful enough to challenge our oppression, I want to expand our catalog of modes of agency beyond resistance.

Conjuring Agency

My entryway into root work is Hurston's "High John de Conquer," a funny little piece written in 1943 for the *American Mercury*. I say funny because the essay conceals even as it reveals. Perhaps this is because Hurston's practitioner status meant that she was bound to secrecy concerning what she actually could tell us about these practices. During her time, hoodoo practices were aggressively prohibited not only by churches but by the law itself.[49] Also, Hurston was under pressure from her editor to "sugar up" the piece to offer support for the current World War II efforts.[50] As a result, there are depths to the essay's content that Hurston did not probe in print. As she writes in a letter to Alaine Locke, this essay "is a mere scratch on the surface . . . all that mass of stuff which is yet unwritten."[51] In her classic charming way, Hurston also invites Locke to work on this material with her, for she "think[s] that [they] can do something enduring for the world" with this material, "when it is all worked out and correlated."[52] Her "scratch" at the surface also invites us to delve deeper into the practices she references, to see their meaning when they are "all worked out and correlated."

John de Conquer is the center of the essay, linking together multiple hoodoo practices, such as specific kinds of folktales, ancestor reverence, and the creation of mojo bags, a magical bundle or charm. I want to focus on Hurston's veiled reference to mojo bags, since it draws upon several basic beliefs found in root work or hoodoo, such as spirit possession, ritual water immersion, ancestor reverence, and herbal medicine.[53] Hurston writes:

> The thousands upon thousands of humble people who still believe in him, that is, in the power of love and laughter to win by their subtle power, do John reverence by getting the root of the plant in which he has taken up his secret dwelling, and "dressing" it with perfume, and keeping it on their person, or in their houses in a secret place. It is there to help them overcome things they feel they could not beat otherwise, and to bring them the laugh of the day. John will never forsake the weak and the helpless, nor fail to bring hope to the hopeless.[54]

In this passage, we not only find that the spirit of John de Conquer inhabits or "possesses" a root, but he is also woven into a mojo bag that practitioners wear on their persons or store in a "secret place" of their house.[55] Several scholars have also noted how mojo bags are derived from the Kongo word *nkisi* (plural *minkisi*), meaning "medicines of the gods."[56] These mojo bags were "dressed" or imbued with a liquid the spirit is taken to like, in keeping with sacred rituals of water immersion.[57] And practitioners do this out of their reverence for or worship of the spirit (or in this case, John de Conquer, who also symbolizes ties to their enslaved ancestors through the land or "soil of the South").[58] Overall, mojo bags were used to "direct spirits, diagnose, protect, and foretell."[59] In this way, they were involved in what anthropologists call "luck management."[60] In "High John de Conquer," we can see John de Conquer being used in similar ways. For instance, one of John de Conquer's functions is protective—he is the means by which the enslaved "pulled the covers up over their souls," thus "ke[eping] them from all hurt, harm, and danger."[61] When worn upon the person, mojo bags allowed practitioners to maintain contact with the spirits of the charms, to touch or physically carry their spiritual help with them. But the bags were also sometimes stored, as Hurston observes in this passage, in other places. As the anthropologist Katrina Hazzard-Donald notes, hoodoo had "its sacred locations and power sites such as the crossroads, the cemetery, the threshold, railroad tracks, and special clearings in the woods."[62]

When placed in these "power sites," these bundles were also sometimes arranged in the shape of a cosmogram, a cross or X enclosed within a circle.[63] Anthropologists report that this circle "represents the path the human soul voyages from birth to full maturity, to decline, to life as a spirit in the underworld where one is still powerful enough to influence life on earth."[64] Some note that the ring shout's sacred, counterclockwise dancing also traces the circle of the cosmogram on the ground.[65] Regarding the two lines that intersect in the circle, "one line of the X is the horizontal axis that divides the world of humans here on earth, from the world of spirits, the world above and below."[66] The other line of the X, the vertical line, "represents the life line running between the living and dead."[67] The symbol of the cross in the center has signified several convergences throughout centuries of Black religiosity: the meeting of the living and the dead, the meeting of the physical and supernatural realms, and even the meeting of Christianity and West African religious traditions.[68]

The importance of incorporating the spiritual meanings of these practices into our analyses is underscored in the remarks above. To an average observer, these objects may appear to be yard debris or the accumulation of trash. What distinguished these objects for anthropologists was the self-reported accounts of hoodoo in folklore and ex-slave interviews.[69] That is, "the origins, decorations, and form" of these objects "proved to be important only in so far as these attributes referenced a world of Hoodoo meanings."[70] In other words, what distinguishes these objects from trash is the intention, and the intention is bound up in *the spiritual terms of the practice.* One entryway into the terms of the practice is the image of the cosmogram. The use of the cosmogram in the arrangement of these magical bundles is taken to be representative of what anthropologists call "crossroads thinking," where crossroads signify "the meeting place of heaven and earth, the living with the dead, the beginning and the end of life, and a place of magic where life's problems can obtain supernatural solutions."[71] Moreover, through the use of sacred rituals, these crossroads can "occur, and be found, almost anywhere."[72]

This is because the practitioners held that the world of the dead is always "imminent," always present, in this one.[73] As such, it was possible, through rituals, to create a space where the dead and the living could meet.[74] As such, "crossroads thinking is directly related to a representation of a threshold between this world and the next."[75] Out of this cosmology, in which the dead can be called upon through the creation of these sacred spaces, "grew ways of building yards, using crossroads, recognizing that the world was filled with 'altars' to the gods."[76] In "High John de Conquer," mojo bags also invoke the realm of spirits intermediate between human and divine beings, especially our ancestors. When we wear John de Conquer "on our persons" or place the root in some secret space in our homes, we maintain links to those who also called upon High John before us—those who came across the Atlantic and those who toiled on the plantations long after.[77] And in this meeting between the living and the dead, we find the help that we need. Indeed, this preoccupation with the dead marks Black religious expression through and through, across various religious traditions in the African diaspora.[78]

How might crossroads thinking, especially its prioritization of our relationship to the dead, may trouble our narratives of resistance? For instance, in *Rituals of Resistance*, Jason R. Young argues that the creation of mojo bags was a practice of resistance under slavery. Drawing upon James Scott's work on "hidden transcripts," Young writes that these practices were not only defensive (i.e., protective and healing) but also "offensive, enabling them to attack directly the ideological underpinnings of slavery."[79] As such, Young takes these religious practices to be "immanently political in nature."[80] That is, he extends the category of resistance to include "any tactic that slaves undertook" to disrupt the "forced extraction" of slave labor, whether it be "slowdowns, feigned illness, and/or destruction of tools."[81] This extensive definition is how Young also bypasses the intentions of the enslaved using these practices—even if the enslaved were using conjure primarily against another enslaved person rather than the slave master.[82] Part of his claim of extensive resistance seems to rely on the fact that slave owners (and the state) sensed a threat in conjure. Because of this perceived threat, Young claims that slave owners (and the state) understood these practices as resistance.[83] Not only does this account neglect the range of relationships that slave owners held to conjure (from the exploitation of midwives, to the fearful respect of the conjurer, to exorcizing root work from the plantation altogether), but we are left with an account of agency wherein the attribution of resistance relies upon the perception of those being "resisted" rather than upon the terms the actors themselves have used to describe their own actions.[84] In this way, the oppressor rather than the oppressed gets the final word on what our actions are.

This is not to disagree with Young's rightful observation that conjure did, in fact, enable some of the enslaved to rebel against their slave owners and slavery itself. The correlation between rebellion and conjure seems strong enough to support this claim. However, I want to push against the thinness of his account of the agency of the enslaved here. While conjure may have endowed the enslaved with power, the *means* of securing such power was not resistant in itself. For instance, in Young's discussion of *minkisi* and their derivation, the mojo bag, he notes that the *nkisi* is possessed by a powerful spirit:

> Although *minkisi* are fabricated objects, they have a will of their own that they exert in the world. Indeed, they could be very jealous and so temperamental that one attributed both success and failure in an endeavor to the proper observance or regrettable neglect of their demands. As living entities, they might be considered superior to human beings in that they regularly moved between this world and the land of the dead and were active in both worlds in ways that exceed human capabilities.[85]

Harnessing the power of the spirit that inhabits the *nkisi* is an intimate negotiation of a relationship that has nothing to do with the oppressor. In this relationship, the *nkisi* demands authority and respect, deference and submission.[86] Their dual role as both person and item causes Young to argue that *minkisi* challenge a basic distinction of Western metaphysics, that of subject and object. These "Kongolese ritual objects blur the distinction between things and persons," Young observes, "and alter the way we commonly conceive of agency such that some 'objects' [namely, *minkisi*] could be conceived as agents."[87]

If this is the case, then these spiritual practices should also alter the way we commonly think of modes of agency as well. Young's discussion of *minkisi* and mojo bags touches upon the phenomenon of spirit possession, which is present in so many iterations of Black religiosity. Spirit possession suggests a sense of self that is porous, where blurred boundaries are *constitutive* of the range of agency available. How are we to understand the agency of people who, in their own terms, attribute their actions to the agency of another?[88] Whose will are they expressing in these moments? And in what ways can we understand their actions as "resistance" if the very source of the action is ambiguous? And, even further, what if the very terms of the agency displayed are submission (to the spirit) instead of rebellion (against the slave master)?

I argue that these questions point to a confusion of effect and cause in Young's account of conjure. That is to say, resistance or friction may be an *effect* of the practices. This does not mean, however, that these practices are necessarily resistant or even political. Resistance in some cases may be, as Ortner puts it, "the [analytic] by-product" of an action rather than the "form" of agency displayed.[89] In other words, conjure may be responsible for providing the "emotional conditions" of resistance without being a practice of resistance itself.[90] One such emotional condition for resistance may be what Angela Davis describes in her "Lectures on Liberation" as "an independent means of judging the world."[91] Under slavery, what may be needed for resistance to occur at all is "a refusal to accept the definitions of the slave master . . . a rejection of the institution of slavery, its standards, its morality."[92] Root work can provide that. The recognition of "powers" (other than our oppressors) to whom we owe reverence could, in effect, instill within us a system of valuation that is independent of our oppressors, whereby we could pronounce judgment upon and condemn our oppression.[93] But root work offers this by privileging the relationship to the dead over our relation to the slave owner or oppressor—by, for example, securing the power from *minkisi*, which center our relationship to the spirit world. The oppressor's authority is demoted in this transaction, for our power resides in proper deference to the spirit inhabiting the *nkisi*. In this instance, root work offers an "independent means" of evaluating the world not by reacting to (or directly challenging) the views of the dominant world, but by proactively offering values through the observation of specific forms of piety toward the prior and ongoing religious beliefs of our ancestors.[94]

"Claiming Ownership of That Freed Self"

So if practices of root work cannot straightforwardly be categorized as "resistance," what form of agency do they exhibit? A useful distinction from Toni Morrison's *Beloved* will help situate our analysis of the various types of agency that root work invokes and models. Set in the Reconstruction period, this novel follows the struggle of newly emancipated Blacks for their inner liberation or their coming to terms with the trauma endured under slavery. The story revolves around Sethe, a character figured after the real-life case of Margaret Garner. The sexual and racial trauma that Sethe suffered under her slave master, Schoolteacher, as well as her performance of infanticide, haunts her even in her newfound "free" status.[95] As Sethe begins to cope with these horrific events, she realizes that "bit by bit, at 124 and in the Clearing, along with the others, she had claimed herself. Freeing yourself was one thing; claiming ownership of that freed self was another."[96] In Sethe's escape from slavery, crossing the Ohio River into free territory, she had "freed herself." She became formally (or legally) free. But there was still a sense in which Sethe was not free, even after setting foot upon northern soil. Until she found the means to process her trauma, she remained imprisoned by her past. As such, I gather that, for Morrison, "freeing the self" is not enough for full-fledged emancipation. Another task in emancipatory work is highlighted in the quote above: "*claiming ownership* of that freed self."[97] I say that this is a different task because "claiming the ownership of that freed self" had nothing to do with ending slavery, for Sethe had already successfully escaped.[98] As we progress through the novel, as we watch Sethe come to terms with her past, we gain a glimpse of what "claiming ownership" of the "freed" self might look like.

In our scholarly accounts of root work, we tend to focus on its role in "freeing the self" or bringing about the abolition of slavery, whether directly in rebellions or indirectly in some sly, secret undermining of the system. But in *Beloved*, Morrison shows us how root work can be used for this other dimension of emancipatory work as well. The one that concerns what you do with yourself after abolition. One crucial aspect of Sethe's healing, or how she came to "claim ownership" over her "freed self," was the communal gatherings in "the Clearing," a space cleared of trees, deep in the woods.[99] Morrison hints in several ways that the Clearing is also a space of root work. For instance, the description of the space marks the Clearing as one of the innumerable sacred dancing spaces all over the African diaspora.[100] Closed off and largely unknown to outsiders, the Clearing was located "at the end of a path known only to deer and whoever cleared off the land in the first place."[101] Cleared of trees except those that section the space off, the area was a ready place for dancing. And out there in the Clearing, the previously enslaved met to dance. They all danced until "exhausted and riven, all lay about the Clearing damp and gasping for breath."[102] Morrison also hints at sacred rituals of root work performed in this space. For instance, Sethe remembers that, out there in the Clearing, there were "thunderous feet and the shouts that ripped pods off the chestnuts."[103] The references to shouts and dancing call to mind the ring shout, a sacred dancing ritual in hoodoo.[104] Due to the union of dance and divine through the ring shout, the Clearing is considered spiritually potent by the community.[105] For long after the meetings there have ceased, members of the community still imagine that the dead go there to roam.[106]

Several scholars have also noted that Baby Suggs, the mother-in-law of Sethe, is a conjure woman and the spiritual leader of these gatherings in the Clearing.[107] She has spiritual authority both "in the pulpit" and in her "dance in the Clearing."[108] Emblematic of the blended faith of many Black women, both Christian and conjured, Baby Suggs preaches in churches during the winter and leads the people out into the woods when it is warm.[109] And it is she who initiates the ring shout. Morrison writes: "after situating herself on a huge flat-sided rock, Baby Suggs bowed her head and prayed silently. The company watched her from the trees. They knew she was ready when she put her stick down."[110] It is important to note that sticks like these were "used to beat out the rhythm of the ring shout" in such spiritual gatherings.[111] As the elder in the novel, Baby Suggs is also the symbol of the type of "cosmology" that Morrison points to in "Rootedness: The Ancestor as Foundation."[112] This cosmology is a blending of "two worlds," one of "practicality" and one of (what is called) "superstition and magic," which yields "a different way of knowing things."[113] Put another way, Baby Suggs's presence transforms the Clearing into a meeting place of these "two worlds."[114] And in this meeting, a crucial task of emancipatory work is revealed to the newly freed who gathered—"imagining grace." In the Clearing, Baby Suggs taught them that "the only grace they could have was the grace they could *imagine*. That if they could not see it, they would not have it."[115] By "grace," I take Morrison to mean something like relief from the effects and burdens of slavery on the soul. To "imagine grace" is to reorder their present according to a future state they have yet to achieve, a state that is determined by the tenor of their own imagination.[116]

The connection between communal capacities to "imagine grace" and root work is dramatized by Sethe's development in the novel. When the meetings in the Clearing cease upon Baby Suggs's death, Sethe loses a space to confront and come to terms with the trauma of her past under slavery. This leaves her brain "loaded with the past and hungry for more . . . lea[ving] her no room to imagine, let alone plan for, the next day."[117] As a result, Sethe remains "shut up" in her past, without relief from her trauma and without future possibilities. Sethe herself seems to be aware that it was what they did there in the Clearing, those practices of root work such as the ring shout, that produced the ability to "imagine grace."[118] This is because the performances of African American dances during slavery "proclaimed, with the sovereignty of the body, the vibrant intensity of one's imagining power."[119] I want to emphasize here that the ability to imagine grace was engendered within this communal conjure space. I emphasize this point not only to delineate a task of emancipatory work beyond the abolition of the institution of slavery (i.e., "claiming ownership of that freed self" or "imagining grace"), but also to draw a relationship between accessing this dimension of emancipation and root work.

I draw two insights from Morrison's depiction of root work in *Beloved*. First, these practices are a possible reservoir of alternative values to that of the dominant culture. And that possibility is grounded in the spiritual meaning of these practices, which imbued the body with an alternative value to that garnered under oppression. In other words, through these practices, the body is transformed—from an instrument of oppression into a dearly loved "prize" won back by the newly freed. In her widely quoted speech, Baby Suggs tells the newly freed that "here . . . in this place, we flesh; flesh that weeps, laughs; flesh that dances on bare feet in grass. Love it. Love it hard."[120] Why? Because "yonder they do not love your flesh."[121] Because, under slavery, our flesh is flayed, bound, chopped off, broken, starved, unheeded.[122] Through these acts under slavery, our bodies are turned into vehicles of oppression, disciplined to sport the profit of our slave masters. Baby Suggs instructs the various people under her charge to do certain things with their bodies in this space. This is similar to "calling the numbers," a practice common in secret, sacred dance meetings of the enslaved at that time.[123] Through "calling the numbers" in the Clearing, Baby Suggs instructs them to re-discipline their bodies. For instance, to dance, to "raise up [their hands] and kiss them," to caress their face and shoulders.[124] Her instructions for their bodily movements in this space represent a new type of subjugation, whereby they come to love the flesh they were disciplined, under slavery, to despise. And they alone are responsible for loving the flesh that has been so devalued.

Put another way, this speech whereby Baby Suggs "calls the numbers" outlines the terrain over which ownership is to be "claimed"—the racialized body itself. Glaude refers to this as the "sanctification" of the Black body, highlighting the bevy of spiritual meanings that transformed our bodies during conversion.[125] The imagination of grace begins with the body, because the capacity to imagine a different future—a different future they would not have unless they could first imagine it—is itself procured through these sacred bodily rituals. I stress the tactile element of these practices. The practice of crafting spaces where we can "touch" our ancestors can cultivate an attentiveness to multiple layers of reality in our current state of living. It staves off the kind of fatalism that chronic oppression encourages by cultivating an attentiveness to the possibilities of life-altering, radical change within our present. Such an attentiveness is the scaffold upon which the hope and confidence that "things will come out right tomorrow" is built.[126] It is the means by which we "imagine grace."[127] This insight is crucial for how I analyze practices of root work. Namely, I argue that the submission of the body through highly specific, concrete tasks within the context of root work cultivated capacities within the oppressed that might not otherwise have been possible under oppression.

Moreover, this bodily submission through spiritual dance in *Beloved* can cultivate these capacities precisely because it recalls the "prior and ongoing culture" that slavery attempted to destroy.[128] We can see this in how the ring shout featured in *Beloved*, a foundational dance for hoodoo, was also "a vessel for the retention of foundational African spiritual values" that were "embedded in dance, and which informed both individual and community relations" such as "sharing, secrecy, community obligation in work and spiritual assistance."[129] Although we may have lost the gods and the oral languages of our ancestors, there seems to be a lingering "codes" into which dance may tap.[130] Put another way, certain elements of African American dance form a kind of grammar.[131] And, as we all know, grammar is to be learned within particular communities; it is not biologically inherited.

Some have gone so far as to argue that the prevalence of the ring shout (and by extension, hoodoo or conjure) in African American religious expression makes it constitutive in the formation of African American identity and culture.[132] While I worry that such claims flatten out and erase the ambivalence that conjure often provoked for African Americans, it does speak to the possibility of conjure (its habits and orientations toward the spiritual and physical world) as one source of self-definition (beyond the dominant culture) for Black peoples.[133] Conjure, on the one hand, bears the fissures and gaps between African Americans and their African ancestors. With the loss of certain gods, languages, and ties to the land, it does not make sense to describe these traditions of conjure in the New World as untainted African retentions or unbroken continuities. (That ship has sailed.) On the other hand, traditions of conjure are the result of experimentation in the New World that reaches back to the world prior to our enslavement in its orientation and approaches.[134] As such, practices of root work may be precisely the place to turn if we want to develop thicker ethnographic accounts of Black liberation that emphasize self-definition over mere reactions to whites. Indeed, Morrison's implicit references to the practices of hoodoo in *Beloved* reflect an awareness of the place that root work occupied in African Americans' conception of their own lives during slavery and the Reconstruction period.[135]

The second important insight I draw from this novel is that "claiming ownership of that freed self" suggests there may be dimensions of Black emancipation that require other modes of agency besides resistance. For instance, we might (and perhaps should) resist internalizing the values of white supremacy in American culture. But sometimes the attempt to resist these values may only serve to further entrench them. In *Beloved*, Morrison describes this dynamic as the "jungle" that white people planted inside of Black folks. Whites believed that something animal and jungle-like lurked inside us. And our attempts to dissuade whites of this belief had unintended, devastating effects upon us. Morrison writes:

> The more colored people spent their strength trying to convince [whites] how gentle they were, how clever and loving, how human, the more they used themselves up to persuade whites of something Negros believed could not be questioned, the deeper and more tangled the jungle grew inside. But it wasn't the jungle Blacks brought with them to this place from the other (livable) place. It was the jungle whitefolks planted in them. And it grew. It spread. In, through and after life, it spread, until it invaded the whites who had made it. Touched them every one. Changed and altered them. Made them bloody, silly, worse than even they wanted to be, so scared they were of the jungle they had made. The screaming baboon lived under their own white skin; the red gums were their own.[136]

The "jungle" that whites had attributed to us was projected upon or "placed" within us by them. Yet, to address this jungle head-on is only to enmesh us deeper. Why? Because the address *itself* puts us on the racist whites' terms.

Or, as Morrison puts it, the contradictory address to white supremacist values moves us to question what, at first, we "believed could not be questioned."[137] In this way, the "jungle" dynamic highlights certain limits to the mode of resistance. Because resistance is a negative reaction, it gains its terms (or character) from those we are resisting.[138] Moreover, the reactive nature of resistance closely aligns it with a desire for recognition from our oppressor— even if that recognition is simply and rightfully, "I am human and what you are doing is unjust, so stop." When we are dealing with people who refuse (or are perhaps unable) to grant us that, who instead gleefully plant a "jungle" within us, we may need other modes of agency so that we can protect and heal ourselves in the meantime.

"How You Gonna Win, When You Ain't Right Within?"

Closely associated with Brer Rabbit, John de Conquer is not only a root used in hoodoo, but a prominent trickster figure in African American folktales.[139] His (usually humorous) stories of "getting over" on "Ole Massa" have often caused us to read this figure as inherently resistant and subversive.[140] So Hurston's focus on this figure in her discussion of hoodoo in "High John de Conquer" would seem to support the trend of reading hoodoo practices through the lens of resistance. However, Hurston's John de Conquer departs from common narratives of outwitting, revenge, or subversion.[141] In contrast to rebellion, Deborah Plant observes that there is a "reconciling sentiment" that characterizes John de Conquer's actions in this essay.[142] "John had numerous scrapes and tight squeezes, but he usually came out like Brer Rabbit," Hurston writes, and sometimes even "Old Massa won the hand."[143] This does not, however, lead to "bitter tragic tales" because "the thing ended up in a laugh just the same."[144] This was due to "a sort of recognition that life is not one-sided."[145] In this way, the trickery of John de Conquer seems to be more about a game (i.e., "winning the jackpot") than getting back at the master.[146] As Cheryl Wall observes, the invocation of games for Hurston "creates a discursive space in which politics can be held at bay. The tone is at once ebullient and arch."[147] For these reasons, I do not view the trickster figure as necessarily normative or political. Perhaps what we like about tricksters is that they harbor *capacities* for resistance in their ability to "shape an untenable reality," to cast what appears not to be as if it were.[148] I have argued that this capacity, the ability to "imagine grace," is informed by the spiritual meanings of root work practices, which attune us to the merging of the worlds of the living and the dead.

Like Morrison's contrast between "freeing the self" and "claiming ownership of that freed self," Hurston also draws distinctions in the modes of agency that the oppressed exhibit. For instance, in the third section of the essay, Hurston tells us a story "of how the Negro got his freedom through

High John de Conquer."[149] What ensues is a story of how the enslaved take an inward spiritual journey while working in the fields. In search of a "song," John de Conquer leads them eventually to heaven, where God ("the Old Maker") "made them a tune and put it in their mouths."[150] But the story ends with them still on the plantation, singing this "tune" while they go back to work.[151] In what sense, then, are they free? The answer, I argue, can be found in the first section of the essay, in what Hurston calls "winning within." This type of freedom is not legal emancipation or freedom from the external effects of oppression. On the contrary, this type of freedom has nothing to do with our oppressors. Hurston writes:

> And all the time, there was High John de Conquer playing his tricks of making away out of no way. Hitting a straight lick with a crooked stick. Winning the jack pot with no other stake but a laugh. Fighting a mighty battle without outside-showing force, and winning his war from within. Really winning in a permanent way, for he was winning with the soul of the black man whole and free. So he could use it afterwards. For what shall it profit a man if he gain the whole world, and lose his own soul? You would have nothing but a cruel, vengeful, grasping monster come to power.[152]

I argue that this mode is distinguished from resistance because it is more closely aligned with Morrison's "claiming ownership of that freed self." That is, this mode of agency concerns the self beyond abolition, how we use our soul "afterwards," or outside the situation of domination. It is about living or "winning" in a way that does not turn us into our oppressors, or "cruel, vengeful, grasping monster[s]" that have "come to power."[153] (Put another way, it is to answer the question that Lauryn Hill posed in her album *The Miseducation of Lauryn Hill*, "how you gonna win, when you ain't right within?")

We would be in danger of becoming "cruel, vengeful, grasping monster[s]" because resistance has no prescriptive power—it takes its direction from those we are opposing. However, by providing the enslaved with an "inside thing to live by," John de Conquer offered an internal standard by which to measure their lives.[154] In this way, practices of root work like John de Conquer functioned similarly to Audre Lorde's discussion of the power of the "erotic," that "measure between the beginnings of our sense of self and the chaos of our strongest feelings."[155] Refusing to separate the spiritual (as well as the political) from the erotic, Lorde draws a connection between the erotic and joy.[156] "Another important way in which the erotic connection functions," Lorde informs us, "is the open and fearless underlining of my capacity for joy."[157] That experience of joy via the erotic places a demand on her as well. "And that deep and irreplaceable knowledge of my capacity for joy," Lorde warns, "comes to demand from all of my life that it be lived within the knowledge that such satisfaction is possible."[158] In other words, being in touch with the erotic provides "an internal sense of satisfaction to which, once we have experienced it, we know we can aspire," Lorde observes, "for having experienced the fullness of this depth of feeling and recognizing its power, in honor and self-respect we can require no less of ourselves."[159] Because the erotic makes these demands upon us, such that we perpetually evaluate the quality of our doings and our lives, it is also a means of self-definition for Lorde.[160] Hurston anticipates these connections among self-definition, the erotic, spirituality, and liberation when she identifies that John de Conquer is not only the help of the enslaved but also a source of their "pleasure."[161]

By turning to that "inside thing to live by," Hurston also shifts the focus of our energies in navigating oppression—from the war we wage in resisting our oppressors to the struggle to define ourselves.[162] This is what it means to "really" win "in a permanent way."[163] Unlike resistance, this type of "winning" has no "outside-showing force" or message to deliver to our oppressors. This type of "winning" is not characterized by the terms of resistance and rebellion, such as "the sword."[164] "Heaven arms with laughter and love those it does not wish to see destroyed," Hurston warns, and "he who carries his heart in his sword must perish. So says the ultimate law."[165] That is, if *all* we do is resist, we are in danger of becoming defined by the very thing that we oppose. In contrast, by offering the enslaved an "inside thing to live by," John de Conquer provided an alternative set of values that offer the enslaved an independent means of evaluating themselves, their oppressors, the world, and the quality of their liberation. This is how John de Conquer enables us to "win within" and become part of the "Be" class, those whose self-determination is drawn from a sense of the prior and ongoing culture that their oppressors sought to destroy (but which will even outlast them). "*Be* here when the ruthless man comes," Hurston remarks, "and *be* here when he is gone."[166]

Instead of reading "High John de Conquer" as a tale of resistance and subversion, I suggest we read it as a meta-hoodoo tale.[167] Reading the essay as a meta-hoodoo tale moves us away from interpreting its root work practices as resistance and also highlights Hurston's strains against neo-abolitionism. On one level, Hurston's interaction with Aunt Shady can be read as a literal, traditional hoodoo tale. Hurston can be viewed as a client in search of a conjurer.[168] Aunt Shady, a previously enslaved respondent and conjurer, treats Hurston as a wayward client during the interview. When Hurston begins the interview, Aunt Shady is at first reluctant to give her information, assuming that Hurston is ailed by the pangs of "progress."[169] Aunt Shady retorts:

> I hope you ain't one of these here smart colored folks that done got so they don't believe nothing, and come here questionizing me so you can have something to poke fun at. Done got shamed of the things that brought us through. Make out 'tain't no such thing no more.[170]

Aunt Shady steps into the role of the conjurer in hoodoo tales by recounting for Hurston the knowledge gained through her use of John de Conquer. This knowledge of "things that got us through" was passed down by the ancestors—in this case, Aunt Shady's own mother who "wouldn't mislead [her]."[171] Additionally, Hurston (a client seeking knowledge) cannot have access to this information without first assuring Aunt Shady (the conjure woman) that she is open to the knowledge to be given. Similarly, at the heart of hoodoo tales is the submission of the troubled member of the community to the instructions of the conjurer or hoodoo doctor. And the very future of these troubled members relies upon their success or failure in following the conjurer's instruction.[172]

On a meta-level, the essay itself can be read as Hurston's own conjuring, weaving a tale of diagnosis and warning for the neo-abolitionists in her audience. For example, by devising her own folktale of Negro spirituals in the third section of the essay, Hurston provides an origin story that is an alternative to Du Bois's (and Douglass's) "sorrow songs."[173] This folktale is significant because it strikes at three major points of neo-abolitionism: the mandate of sorrow, the narrative of cultural assimilation, and the presumed access to our interior lives. Hurston writes of the enslaved on this journey:

> [High] John and his party had a very good time at that and other things. Finally, by the way they acted and did, Old Maker called them up before His great workbench, and made them a tune and put it in their mouths. It had no words. It was a tune that you could bend and shape in most any way you wanted to fit the words and feelings that you had. They learned it and began to sing.[174]

In this story, Negro spirituals are born out of joyous religious expression, not simply sorrow. Moreover, placing John de Conquer at the center of this origin story emphasizes the West African religious elements that remained in the spirituals, despite Christian conversion. As Hurston writes early in the essay, John de Conquer "came from Africa" and trekked along the Middle Passage with us.[175] Finally, this story contests the access of whites to our interior lives. Aunt Diskie, one of those who went on this inward "journey" with John de Conquer, remarks afterward on the slave master's ignorance: "Ain't that funny? Us got all that, and he don't know nothing about it. Don't tell him nothing. Nobody don't have to know where us gets our pleasure from."[176] The pleasure invoked here is not an endorsement of the pro-slavery claim that we were "happy darkies," since Huston also attests to the cruelty of slavery in this essay.[177] Instead, it is an indication that root work cultivated an "inside thing to live by" within the enslaved that neither the abolitionist nor the minstrel had access to, for it is beyond both frameworks.

Imitating a conjurer herself, through the figure of John de Conquer Hurston disavows the "whole mess of sorrow" or "bitter tragic tales" that were mandated in portrayals of Black enslaved life within abolitionist discourse.[178] And while Hurston has revealed some things about hoodoo in this essay, she also reports that the essay is actually "a mere scratch on the surface."[179] Although whites are curious about our interior life, if only to confirm what they already "know" about us, John de Conquer "has evaded the ears of white people," for "they were not supposed to know."[180] And some might argue that, by the end of the essay, the white folks still do not know. Because all Hurston gave them were funny trickster tales. She does not give them very much about hoodoo practices themselves, "the inside thing to live by" or "where us gets our pleasure from." Instead, we have to surmise when she is talking to us and read those things in. Hurston also warns us about the resources we might lose in the effort to culturally assimilate. When legal emancipation came, John de Conquer seems to have disappeared. "His people had their freedom, their laugh and their song," Hurston writes, and "they have traded it to the other Americans for things they could use like education and property, and acceptance [read, political recognition]."[181] But she also gives us a healing prescription for the blues that often come with the projects of integration. John de Conquer has sunk into the "soil of the South," where they still "do [him] reverence."[182] In fashioning the politics of joy in Black southern life, Huston not only rejects the neo-abolitionist assumption of tragedy, but she anticipates the return of many Black millennials to the South and to those old and ancient forms of spirituality, in search of the help their ancestors once obtained.

Conclusion

✦

The Politics of Joy in the Time
of the Coronavirus

In *The Politics of Black Joy*, I have provided an interpretation of Zora Neale Hurston's views on race as the politics of joy. This reading shows how Hurston's pivot to Black southern joy is informed by a deep pessimism concerning racial relations in the United States. Not only was Hurston wary that racism is much too deep-seated in her white counterparts for true recognition to arise, but she was also concerned that the terms of political recognition in the public sphere were conditioned by shows of Black suffering, thereby undermining our self-respect. I have traced this requirement of shows of Black suffering back to abolitionist discourse, which weaponized Black sorrow in service of a political cause. In this way, Hurston's emphasis on joy in representations of Black southern life can also be read as a refusal of the presumption of Black southern tragedy by abolitionists and their "spiritual sons" (northern liberals), such as W. E. B. Du Bois. We can also see a dramatization of Hurston's refusals of neo-abolitionist mandates in her ethnographic work, such as *Barracoon* and "How It Feels to Be Colored Me." That is, when I read those texts together, I showed how some of Hurston's most controversial comments on race and slavery could be read as an "ethnographic refusal" that draws an "ethnographic limit" to the (imperialist) nosiness of whites.[1] This nosiness was encouraged in abolitionist discourse, for white abolitionists wanted a report of our inner lives in order to confirm what they already presumed to "know" about us. Moreover, I have argued, contrary to the abolitionist presumption that our lives revolve around white folk, that Hurston's analysis of root work privileges Black self-determination. Put another way, root work is one site where Hurston can fashion a sense of agency (i.e., "winning within") that emphasizes our inward struggle for joy rather than our resistance against white supremacy.

While my development of the politics of joy has largely occurred within the context of Hurston's racial politics, I have also connected the politics of joy to our own period by providing interludes on Beyoncé's visual album, *Lemonade*. These interludes offer an example of what a Black southern aesthetic that centers Black joy looks like. As such, *Lemonade* is an alternative to the tragic representations of southern Black life that neo-abolitionism often mandates. As I conclude *The Politics of Black Joy* from my home in Memphis, Tennessee, there is another national crisis that would lend itself well to exploring the politics of joy and the legacy of neo-abolitionism in our public discourse. The arrival of the coronavirus (COVID-19), a global pandemic, has caused many of us to seriously reflect on our lives in new ways. Although it is much too soon to say many definitive things about the coronavirus and its impact on our nation, there are a few preliminary lines of inquiry that might be fruitful once the dust settles. These lines of inquiry refer to the larger public narratives that shape how the South, and in particular Black New Orleans, have been covered in the news during this crisis.

"This Ain't Nothin' like Hurricane Katrina"

That this national crisis has revealed racial disparities is perhaps not a surprise to many.[2] Reports have now shown that African Americans are dying at a rate much, much higher than their white counterparts. One of the ways that we can trace the legacy of neo-abolitionism in our public discourse is to consider how this fact has been reported in the news. Consider, for instance, the report by David Benoit, titled "Coronavirus Devastates Black New Orleans: 'This Is Bigger Than Katrina' ":

> New Orleans and Louisiana are taking a direct hit from the coronavirus pandemic. More people in the state are currently on unemployment rolls—300,000—and more have died—2,500—than when Hurricane Katrina slammed the shores 15 years ago. The New Orleans area at one point had the worst coronavirus death rate in the U.S. As with Katrina, the burden is falling disproportionately on Black Louisianians. Black residents make up 32% of the state's population but 55% of its deaths from Covid-19, the disease caused by the novel coronavirus. The numbers are similar in New York, Chicago, and across the country.[3]

There are many things to wonder about from this passage, even though the report is factual. For instance, why make the "devastation" of Black New Orleans a singular phenomenon (i.e., "a direct hit") if the rates of Black death are similar across the nation, even in the North (i.e., New York and Chicago)? Moreover, what is the rhetorical effect of framing this crisis in terms of Hurricane Katrina? To raise these questions is to consider how region is discussed in our national discourse. As some have noted, national coverage has upheld the image of the South as socially and politically "backward," as if we are unable to grasp the proper social distancing measures needed to slow the spread of the virus.[4]

We can spot neo-abolitionist impulses in the framing some have used to explain why we are dying at such a horrible rate compared to our white counterparts. For instance, some are reaching back to slavery and Jim Crow to frame their political intervention.[5] Hurston criticized this tendency as part of the political tradition that neo-abolitionism enforced, whereby Black life is always discussed in terms of the tragedy of slavery. It is this political tradition that causes our leaders "in the very face of a situation as different from the 1880s as chalk is from cheese," to still use abolitionist rhetoric in their political platforms, or to "stand around and mouth the same trite phrases, and try their practiced-best to look sad."[6] To rehearse current crises in terms of slavery and Reconstruction not only upholds the narrative of southern Black tragedy that abolitionist discourse first produced, but it also obscures the specificity of racism during this particular crisis. While it is true that the legacy of institutional racism can be traced back to slavery, we are not undergoing the same problems in the same way at this present moment. How might framing things in this way forfeit the diligent research needed to distinguish what is indeed inherited from slavery from what is truly novel about our current crisis?

Hurston's criticism also suggests that certain kinds of framing of Black life get uptake in public discourse. I argue that a similar thing is happening with the impulse to frame this current crisis in New Orleans in terms of Hurricane Katrina. That is, Hurricane Katrina summons images of Black devastation. And some use these images to stir our national conscience into action. For example, Katy Reckdahl, Campbell Robertson, and Richard Fausset write in "New Orleans Faces a Virus Nightmare, and Mardi Gras May Be Why":

> The feeling is at once familiar and distinct for a city whose history is punctuated with epic disasters, including the deadly yellow fever outbreaks of 1853 and 1905, and Hurricane Katrina a century later in 2005. Once again, New Orleanians are afraid they could be neglected by national leaders, only this time because the coronavirus is a worldwide calamity. "This hurricane's coming for everybody," said Boderick Bagert, an organizer with the community organizing group Together Louisiana.[7]

Recalling Hurricane Katrina in this way reminds the state of its neglect of Black lives in New Orleans. And it positions the authors to make a plea for us not to be neglected again this time. Sometimes this method is quite effective. My point, however, is that this political mobilization of images of Black suffering (via Hurricane Katrina) inherited its political efficacy from abolitionist discourse. And, as Hurston noted, this method means positioning us as an "object of pity" in the public sphere.[8] And so, in this quote, we are presented as a people who are dependent upon and "afraid" of being neglected by a powerful state.

The impact of neo-abolitionism can also be found in the difficulty of pars-
ing out what it means to say that racism is a "pre-existing" condition, like
diabetes or severe asthma, that makes us more susceptible to the coronavirus.
Consider, for instance, Surgeon General Jerome Adams's recent controversial
remarks on the coronavirus. To be fair, in his address to the nation, Adams
is clear that it is not Blackness itself, per se, that makes us more susceptible.
There is nothing "biologically" wrong with us.[9] Rather, we have a "social
predisposition" to the coronavirus.[10] While many agree with the distinction
Adams has made, pointing to institutional racism as the cause of this "social
predisposition," many took issue with Adams's subsequent "advice" to African Americans in his speech.[11] Zeeshan Aleem writes:

> So Adams's remarks *did* acknowledge that there are structural socio-
> economic factors like housing and job conditions contributing to the
> acute vulnerabilities of communities of color. But he didn't get into
> why they exist and how much of it doesn't come down to individual
> behavior. Instead, his talk of personal responsibility—a familiar trope
> that's often used to blame communities of color for their suffering—
> obscured the fact that a lot of these issues stem from a history of
> institutional racism.[12]

However, we fail to see how these two things are connected in Adams's
remarks—the turn away from a biological conception of Blackness and the
turn toward social uplift and personal responsibility—if we ignore the legacy
of abolitionist discourse within the public sphere. That is to say, abolitionists indeed strove to show that slavery was not "natural" as the pro-slavers
argued.[13] But this point was emphasized not only for the abolition of slavery
but also for the possibility of southern reform.[14] To say that slavery was
not by "Nature's" design made room for arguments that the South could
assimilate to Northern virtues.[15] Similarly, to say that race, and thus our predisposition to the coronavirus, is not biological makes room for arguments
that our social disposition could be assimilated to middle-class respectability.
Adams is clearly right to insist that our predisposition to the coronavirus
is not due to biology. However, his rhetorical use of this fact, his pivot to
respectability politics, is due to the legacy of abolitionist discourse.

"Expression of Joy" or "Epidemiologists' Nightmare"?

The cultural assimilation embedded in discussions of our "social predisposition" is intimately tied to the neo-abolitionist disavowal of Black joy. For
instance, many have blamed the accelerated spread of the coronavirus in
New Orleans on the Mardi Gras cultural celebration. As Reckdahl, Robertson, and Fausset write:

> In a grim irony, there is a rising suspicion among medical experts that
> the crisis may have been accelerated by Mardi Gras—the weeklong
> citywide celebration that unfolds in crowded living rooms, ballrooms
> and city streets—which this year culminated on Feb. 25. It is the city's
> trademark expression of joy—and an epidemiologist's nightmare.[16]

This is not to dispute that large gatherings do, in fact, lead to the spread
of COVID-19. Rather, it is to question the language of tragedy that marks
this particular holiday in our public discourse.[17] In this quote, it is as if our
southern Black joy, expressed in a celebration that is specific to the Gulf
Coast region, is taken to be the source of our undoing during this crisis. That
is, Mardi Gras is rendered not only as a health nightmare in the news, but
as an example of the South's "backward" culture that "socially predisposes"
African Americans to devastation down here.

This in spite of the fact that no one was shutting down large gatherings
in the nation at this time.[18] And if we compare New Orleans to New York,
also a virus hot spot during this period, the neo-abolitionist impulse becomes
even more conspicuous. Health experts point to the influx of tourists during Mardi Gras as leading to the accelerated spread of the virus. But at that
point, New York had also failed to stop domestic travel, thus also increasing
the spread of the virus. In fact, some health experts claim that the traces of
the virus from the New Orleans outbreak after Mardi Gras can be traced
back to the strains previously found in New York.[19] So why is our focus on
the cultural expression of Black southern joy, Mardi Gras, and not on the
New York tourists who flooded our streets to "have a good time"? I argue
that this is due to the legacy of abolitionist discourse—the political disavowal
of Black southern joy—within our public sphere. Rather than critically inves-
tigate the problematic racial dynamics that draw northerners to the South for
the "safe" consumption of Black culture, we are encouraged to focus on how
"problematic" it is to express Black joy amid a national crisis.[20]

Moreover, the language used in the description of Mardi Gras in the news
profoundly misrepresents this holiday. For example, in some news outlets,
Mardi Gras has been rendered as a frivolous party for tourists.[21] But this
misses what the holiday means to the people who live here. It is not a week-
long party. It is part of Carnival, an international cultural celebration held
across the African diaspora that is steeped in West African religious traditions. To reduce it to a "party" strips it of its social, political, and cultural
specificity. For instance, consider central practices of Mardi Gras festivities,
such as the "second line." As Richard Brent Turner writes:

> For some participants, a second line was "nothing but a party goin'
> on" (also the title of a famous second-line brass band song); for
> others, however, it was a profound expression of New Orleans' Afri-
> can diaspora past, an experience of communal meditation or even

trance that re-created the historic nineteenth-century performances in Congo Square, where Black New Orleanians had reinterpreted the sacred music and dances of Vodou in weekly public African festivals every Sunday until the Civil War.[22]

This turn toward what it means to us, Black southerners, is part of the work that the politics of joy does. Through the politics of joy, we can capture the social and political insights that neo-abolitionism misses.

"Show Me 'Dat Footwork"

An example of the politics of joy during this crisis can be found in the You-Tube video composed by Shamarr Allen, "Quarantine and Chill." In the video, Allen encourages fellow (Black) New Orleanians to "show him 'dat footwork" or to "second line" right where they are quarantined. While public discourse paints the South as static in its preservation of cultural traditions, this video is an example of how living traditions are always malleable to the current situation. Here, Allen is adhering to the spirit of the "second line," even though the form has to be altered given this crisis. Moreover, in contrast to the assumptions of southern rebellion against social distancing, Allen encourages us to follow the Centers for Disease Control's guidelines while we engage in this virtual "second line." He sings, "stay away from me, and that goes for everybody" as he "shows us 'dat footwork." And there are several images of masks, gloves, and disinfectant throughout the video to encourage changes in our hygiene habits. As this video suggests, our joyous cultural traditions are not to blame for the spread of the coronavirus. In fact, with proper information, these joyous cultural traditions can be adapted to the crisis at hand. "Since you can't go to second-line," Allen sings, "I'ma bring that bish to you." And, perhaps most striking, the video is full of images of Black New Orleanians dancing in joyous ecstasy within the same neighborhoods that news outlets have pronounced as "devastated" by the coronavirus.

Perhaps in response to this pronouncement of Black southern tragedy, we find this example of southern Black joy performed at the heart of the video:

> Don't you wish you was at the line right now? Get your ass up off the couch right now. I don't want to hear your mouth right now. It's the cards that we got dealt. You can play your hand or you can play yourself. Cause I'm gonna go with my moves. I'ma make it do what it do. *Laissez les bon temps les beaucoup.* I'ma get me, hope you get you. I brought a second line to your living room. I'm trying to get it in your system. Cause those second line Sundays, I miss them. Oh those second line Sundays, I live for, so let me see your footwork.

In this quote, there is the principled indifference that we saw so often in Hurston's work. While there's an admission that times are bad, there is also the insistence upon choosing not to "study" it: "I don't want to hear your mouth right now." Instead, there is a pivot to our agency. "It's the cards we got dealt. You can play your hand or you can play yourself." And that agency is found within the context of "dat footwork," which has roots in the ring shout about which Hurston wrote so often.[23] Like Hurston's High John de Conquer, "dat footwork" is not only a source of healing; it is the terms by which the joy so often needed at this moment is conceived.[24] Allen recognizes that the mandate to quarantine, while necessary, is wreaking havoc with the social order as we know it. And by trying to "put the second line in our system," by bringing the "second line to [our] living room," he is reminding us of the tools our ancestors used to also get through social upheaval and trying times. He is reminding us of the "second line Sundays" that we "live for." Or, as Hurston would put it, of that "inside thing to live by."[25]

Part of why Hurston is both beloved and despised is because she was constantly attentive to this joyous dimension of our lives, that "inside thing to live by," in her fiction. In this book, I have tried to show how her nonfiction work, especially her essays, did a lot of the critical work needed to make room for these joyous depictions of southern Black life. That is, they did the critical work of identifying and refusing the tradition of neo-abolitionism that insists upon shows of Black suffering for political recognition. While this tradition has been effective for some goals of Black liberation, it has and continues to obscure Black southern agency. Our current crisis provides another occasion for us to consider how Hurston's interventions can provide an alternative political tradition that undermines this tendency. For the power of this alternative political tradition, the politics of joy, is that it offers a bevy of responses that highlight the dynamics of Black southern agency. Or, as Allen put it, if you want to grasp the politics of Black southerners, as well as Hurston's own racial politics, you have to be willing to embrace Black joy and "show [us] 'dat footwork."

NOTES

Introduction

1. The novelist Jesmyn Ward describes an experience that brings this issue to the fore in her essay "My True South: Why I Decided to Return Home." When asked why she chose to return to Mississippi to live, Ward informs us that "it is difficult for [those who are asking] to understand why a successful Black woman would choose to return to the South and, worse yet, to Mississippi, which looms large in the public's imagination for its racist depredations, and rightfully so." It is an experience to which I can heartily relate. I often met with such bafflement when I informed my northern friends of my intentions to move back to the South after earning my degree. See Jesmyn Ward, "My True South: Why I Decided to Return Home," *Time*, July 26, 2018, https://time.com/5349517/jesmyn-ward-my -true-south/.

2. My use of the term "agency" is not a naive embrace of the term. As many scholars have argued, the term "agency," especially in the discipline of philosophy, is bound up with notions of liberal, Western subjectivity and personhood. I heartily agree with these critiques. However, I use the term to track how Black southerners get excluded from narratives of agency already found within Black political discourse.

3. Lynell L. Thomas, *Desire and Disaster in New Orleans: Tourism, Race, and Historical Memory* (Durham, NC: Duke University Press, 2014), 5–6.

4. Thomas, *Desire and Disaster in New Orleans*, 6. See also Zandria Robinson, *This Ain't Chicago: Race, Class, and Regional Identity in the Post-Soul South* (Chapel Hill: University of North Carolina Press, 2014), 31.

5. In the tourism industry, the Black population in New Orleans is presented as a simultaneous site of disaster *and* desire. Thomas rightfully criticizes the portrayals of Black communities in New Orleans as dangerous, lawless, and completely devastated. Alongside portrayals of current Black communities as tragic, Thomas notes that there are also static, historical representations of Black New Orleans culture that have been carefully curated for consumption by visiting tourists. See Thomas, *Desire and Disaster*, 5–6, 15–16, 35, 39–44, 47–48.

6. For examples of this type of critique, see Maris Jones, "Dear Beyoncé, Katrina Is Not Your Story," *Black Girl Dangerous*, February 10, 2016, https://www .google.com/search?q=dear+beyonce+katrina&rlz=1C1GGRV_enUS793US793 &oq=dear+beyonce+katrina&aqs=chrome.0.69i59.4779j0j7&sourceid=chrome &ie=UTF-8. See also bell hooks, "Moving beyond Pain," May 9, 2016, http:// www.bellhooksinstitute.com/blog/2016/5/9/moving-beyond-pain.

7. See also Imani Perry, "As the South Goes, So Goes the Nation," *Harper's Magazine*, July 2018, https://harpers.org/archive/2018/07/as-goes-the-south-so -goes-the-nation/.

8. Cynthia Greenlee, "Just Say No Thanks to #ThanksAlabama and 'Magical Negro' Narratives," Rewire.News, December 14, 2017, https://rewire.news/article/2017/12/14/just-say-no-thanks-alabama-magical-negro/.

9. Greenlee, "Just Say No Thanks."

10. For more on the powerful reception of Hurston in the 1980s and 1990s in our schools, see Ann duCille, "The Mark of Zora: Reading between the Lines of Legend and Legacy," *The Scholar and Feminist Online* 3, no. 2 (Winter 2005), http://sfonline.barnard.edu/hurston/ducille_02.htm.

11. There are, however, numerous essays that have attempted to advance more complex readings of Hurston's views on race. For examples, see Helen Mary Washington, "Zora Neale Hurston's Work," *Black World* 21, no. 10 (1972): 68–75; June Jordan, "Notes toward a Black Balancing of Love and Hatred," in *Some of Us Did NOT Die* (New York: Basic Civitas Books, 2002), 284–89; and Susan Meisenhelder, "Gender, Race, & Class in Zora Neale Hurston's Politics," *Solidarity: A Socialist, Feminist, Anti-Racist Organization* 10, no. 1 (1995), https://www.solidarity-us.org/node/2838. For contemporary examples, see Ernest Julius Mitchell II, "Zora's Politics: A Brief Introduction," *Journal of Transnational American Studies* 5, no. 1 (2013); Lynn Moylan, "'A Child Cannot Be Taught by Anyone Who Despises Him': Hurston versus Court-Ordered School Integration," in *"The Inside Light": New Critical Essays on Zora Neale Hurston*, ed. Deborah G. Plant (Santa Barbara, CA: Praeger, 2010), 215–24; and Olivia Marcucci, "Zora Neale Hurston and the *Brown* Debate: Race, Class, and the Progressive Empire," *Journal of Negro Education* 86, no. 1 (2017): 13–24.

12. See Zora Neale Hurston, "Court Order Can't Make Races Mix," in Hurston, *Zora Neale Hurston: Folklore, Memoirs, and Other Writings*, ed. Cheryl A. Wall (New York: Library of America, 1995), 956.

13. For example, see Alice Walker, "On Refusing to Be Humbled by Second Place in a Contest You Did Not Design: A Tradition by Now," in *I Love Myself When I Am Laughing and Then Again When I Am Looking Mean and Impressive*, ed. Alice Walker (New York: Feminist, 1979), 1.

14. Barbara Smith, "Sexual Politics and the Fiction of Zora Neale Hurston," *Radical Teacher* 8 (1978): 26–27.

15. Smith, "Sexual Politics," 26–27. Moreover, as Barbara Christian writes: "One of the reasons for the surge of Afro-American women's writing during the 1970s and its emphasis on sexism in the Black community is precisely that when the ideologues of the 1960s said *Black*, they meant *Black male*." See Barbara Christian, "The Race for Theory," *Cultural Critique* 6 (1987): 60, https://www.jstor.orga/stable/1354255.

16. For example, see Walker, "On Refusing to Be Humbled," 1–3. Walker writes: "We do not love her for her lack of modesty (that tends to amuse us: an assertive Black person during Hurston's time was considered an anomaly); we do not love her for her unpredictable and occasionally weird politics (they tend to confuse us); we do not, certainly, applaud many of the *mad* things she is alleged to have said and sometimes actually did say; we do not even claim to never dislike her . . . We love Zora Neale Hurston for her work, first, and then again (as she and all Eatonville would say), we love her for herself. For the humor and courage with which she encountered a life she infrequently designed, for her absolute disinterest in becoming either white or bourgeois, and for her *devoted* appreciation

of her own culture, which is an inspiration to us all." Further, Walker writes that "we are better off if we think of Zora Neale Hurston as an artist, period, rather than as the artist/politician most Black writers have been required to be."

17. For instance, Hurston wrote extensively on the blueswoman tradition in her essays, anthropological work, and novels. Hurston's identification with and immersion in the blueswoman tradition has led some scholars, such as Walker, to place Hurston within the tradition itself. Walker writes: "In my mind, Zora Neale Hurston, Billie Holiday, and Bessie Smith form a sort of unholy trinity. Zora *belongs* in the tradition of Black women singers, rather than among 'the literati,' at least to me." See Alice Walker, "Zora Neale Hurston: A Cautionary Tale and a Partisan View," in *In Search of Our Mothers' Gardens: Womanist Prose*, ed. Alice Walker (San Diego, CA: Harcourt Brace, 1983), 91. While Beyoncé is a pop singer, many scholars have also argued that she, too, is a blueswoman, and that *Lemonade* can be read as a neo-blues narrative. For an example of this type of analysis of *Lemonade*, see Kinitra Brooks and Kameelah Martin, "'I Used to Be Your Sweet Mama': Beyoncé at the Crossroads of Blues and Conjure in *Lemonade*," in *The Lemonade Reader*, ed. Kinitra Brooks and Kameelah Martin (New York: Routledge, 2019), 202–14. For analyses of the Black southern aesthetic fashioned in *Lemonade*, see Alexis McGee, "The Language of *Lemonade*: The Sociolinguistic and Rhetorical Strategies of Beyoncé's *Lemonade*," in Brooks and Martin, *The Lemonade Reader*, 55–68; and Tyina Steptoe, "Beyoncé's Western South Serenade," in Brooks and Martin, *The Lemonade Reader*, 183–91.

18. For an extended comparison of Richard Wright's "Between Laughter and Tears" and bell hooks's "Moving beyond Pain," see Lindsey Stewart, "'Something Akin to Freedom': Sexual Love, Political Agency, and *Lemonade*," in Brooks and Martin, *The Lemonade Reader*, 19–20.

19. As Robinson notes concerning such stereotypes about the South: they "ensure that the South functions as the polar opposite to the rest of the nation. As Toni Morrison has argued persuasively about the relationship between Blackness and whiteness in American culture, the South is constructed as a backdrop against which American national identity is formed and without which it cannot exist." These stereotypes include the representational strategies of abolitionism. Robinson writes: "As the nation's region, whose economic, political, and social mores have driven the national consciousness since slavery, the South has often served as a repository for national illness, quarantined, sealed off, and punished in order to maintain a national façade of progress and morality." See Robinson, *This Ain't Chicago*, 31.

20. For more background on Hurston's time working for the Florida Federal Writers' Project, see Pamela Bordelon, "Zora Neale Hurston: A Biographical Essay," in *Go Gator and Muddy the Water*, ed. Pamela Bordelon (New York: W. W. Norton, 1999), 30–32.

21. "'Art and Such' is Hurston's stout defense of her own literary point of view," Bordelon observes, "which by the late 1930s was under vehement attack" by other Black writers who "felt that her focus on the beauty of Black culture ran against the social politics of the day." See Bordelon, "Zora Neale Hurston: A Biographical Essay," 31.

22. Cheryl A. Wall, *On Freedom and the Will to Adorn: The Art of the African American Essay* (Chapel Hill: University of North Carolina Press, 2018), 107.

23. Bordelon also makes conjectures about Hurston's targets within the Harlem Renaissance, such as Sterling Brown and Richard Wright. See Bordelon, "Zora Neale Hurston: A Biographical Essay," 31–32.

24. Wall, *On Freedom*, 107.

25. For examples of this type of analysis, see George B. Hutchinson, *Harlem Renaissance in Black and White* (Cambridge, MA: Harvard University Press, 1995), 1–29; David Levering Lewis, *When Harlem Was in Vogue* (New York: Penguin, 1997), 156–97; and Paul Allen Anderson, *Deep River: Music and Memory in Harlem Renaissance Thought* (Durham, NC: Duke University Press, 2001), 1–13, 167–218.

26. See Saba Mahmood, *The Politics of Piety: The Islamic Revival and the Feminist Subject* (Princeton, NJ: Princeton University Press, 2005), 5–10; Eddie Glaude, *In a Shade of Blue: Pragmatism and the Politics of Black America* (Chicago: University of Chicago Press, 2007), 78–80; and Carole McGranahan, "Theorizing Refusal: An Introduction," *Cultural Anthropology* 31, no. 3 (2016): 319–20, https://journal.culanth.org/index.php/ca/article/view/ca31.3.01.

27. Audre Lorde, "Uses of the Erotic: The Erotic as Power," in *Sister Outsider: Essays and Speeches by Audre Lorde* (Berkeley, CA: Crossing, 2007), 56, 58.

28. As Lorde writes, "in touch with the erotic, I become less willing to accept powerlessness, or those other supplied states of being which are not native to me, such as resignation, despair, self-effacement, depression, self-denial." See Lorde, "Uses of the Erotic," 58.

29. See Lorde, "Uses of the Erotic," 54.

30. See McGranahan, "Theorizing Refusal," 319–20. As Tina Campt writes, refusal is a "generative and capacious rubric for theorizing everyday practices of struggle often obscured by an emphasis on collective acts of resistance." See Tina Campt, "Black Visuality and the Practice of Refusal," *Women and Performance*, February 25, 2019, https://www.womenandperformance.org/ampersand/29–1/campt.

31. See McGranahan, "Theorizing Refusal," 320, 322.

32. See Audra Simpson, *Mohawk Interruptus: Political Life across the Borders of Settler States* (Durham, NC: Duke University Press, 2014), 11–12; and Saidiya Hartman, "Intimate History, Radical Narrative," *Black Perspectives*, May 22, 2020, https://www.aaihs.org/intimate-history-radical-narrative/.

33. See Angela Davis's discussion of the the role of reversal of master and slave in Frederick Douglass's fight with the slave-breaker Mr. Covey. Angela Y. Davis, "Second Lecture on Liberation," in Frederick Douglass, *Narrative of the Life of Frederick Douglass, An American Slave, Written by Himself*, ed. Angela Y. Davis (San Francisco: Open Media Series, 2010), 83.

34. As Campt observes, refusal is "a rejection of the status quo as livable and the creation of possibility in the face of negation, i.e., a refusal to recognize a system that renders you fundamentally illegible and unintelligible; the decision to reject the terms of diminished subjecthood with which one is presented, using negation as a generative and creative source of disorderly power to embrace the possibility of living otherwise." See Campt, "Black Visuality and the Practice of Refusal."

35. As Hurston describes her own fiction work: "The characters in the story are seen in relation to themselves and not in relation to the whites as has been

the rule. To watch these people one would conclude that there were no white people in the world." See Hurston, "Art and Such," in Hurston, *Zora Neale Hurston*, 910.

36. Saidiya Hartman and Fred Moten, "To Refuse That Which Has Been Refused to You," *Chimurenga Chronic*, October 19, 2018, https://chimurengachronic.co .za/to-refuse-that-which-has-been-refused-to-you-2/.

37. Hartman and Moten, "To Refuse That Which Has Been Refused to You."

38. Hartman and Moten, "To Refuse That Which Has Been Refused to You."

39. For examples, see Jared Sexton, "The Social Life of Social Death: On Afro-Pessimism and Black Optimism," *Tensions* 5 (Fall/Winter 2011), https:// www.yorku.ca/intent/issue5/articles/pdfs/jaredsextonarticle.pdf. See also Frank B. Wilderson III, "Afro-Pessimism and the End of Redemption," *Humanities Futures*, March 30, 2016, https://humanitiesfutures.org/papers/afro-pessimism -end-redemption/.

40. Christina Sharpe writes: "We must think about Black flesh, Black optics, and ways of producing enfleshed work; think the ways the hold cannot and does not hold even as the hold remains in the form of the semiotics of the slave ship hold, the prison, the womb, and elsewhere in and as the tension between being and instrumentality that is Black being in the wake. At stake is not recognizing anti-Blackness as total climate. At stake, too, is not recognizing an insistent Black visualsonic resistance to that imposition of non/being." Christina Sharpe, *In the Wake: On Blackness and Being* (Durham, NC: Duke University Press, 2016), 21.

41. Kameelah Martin defines "conjure" as the "syncretic African spirituality practiced in the United States. This includes Louisiana Voodoo and the hoodoo, goopher, or root work traditions associated with the American South." See Kameelah Martin, *Conjuring Moments in African American Literature: Women, Spirit Work, and Other Such Hoodoo* (New York: Palgrave Macmillan, 2012), 137. "Root work," "hoodoo," and "conjure" are terms that Hurston used interchangeably in her own work to describe West African-derived spiritual traditions practiced by southern African Americans. She writes: "'Conjure' is also freely used by the American Negro for these practices. 'Roots' is the Southern Negro's term for folk-doctoring by herbs and prescriptions, and by extension, and because all hoodoo doctors cure by roots, it may be used as a synonym for hoodoo." See Hurston, "Hoodoo in America," *Journal of American Folklore* 44, no. 174 (1931): 317. https://www.jstor.org/stable/535394. In keeping with Hurston, I do the same throughout *The Politics of Black Joy*.

42. See Angela Davis, *Blues Legacies and Black Feminism: Gertrude "Ma" Rainey, Bessie Smith, and Billie Holiday* (New York: First Vintage Books Edition, 1999), 155.

43. See Jeffery E. Anderson, *Conjure in African American Society* (Baton Rouge: Louisiana State University Press, 2005), 50–75.

44. For examples of such refusals in root work, see Davis, *Blues Legacies and Black Feminism*, 141–44, 154–60; and Jenny M. Luke, *Delivered by Midwives: African American Midwifery in the Twentieth-Century South* (Jackson: University Press of Mississippi, 2018), 125–32.

45. Deborah G. Plant, *Every Tub Must Sit on Its Own Bottom: The Philosophy and Politics of Zora Neale Hurston* (Urbana: University of Illinois Press, 1995), 2.

46. Plant, *Every Tub Must Sit on Its Own Bottom*, 4.

47. Susan E. Meisenhelder, *Hitting a Straight Lick with a Crooked Stick: Race and Gender in the Work of Zora Neale Hurston* (Tuscaloosa: University of Alabama Press, 2001), 10.

48. Meisenhelder, *Hitting a Straight Lick*, 5.

49. Meisenhelder, *Hitting a Straight Lick*, 4.

50. In addition, Tiffany Ruby Patterson's *Zora Neale Hurston and a History of Southern Life* contextualizes Hurston's comments on race and gender by drawing upon Hurston's anthropological writings on Black labor in small Black towns (like Eatonville).

51. Wall, *On Freedom*, 6.

52. Wall, *On Freedom*, 85.

53. Regarding the internal complexity of Hurston's essays, Wall suggests that we read them as "jagged harmonies" instead of "consistent and orderly wholes," as "variations around a theme . . . that are as often as not dissonant." See Wall, *On Freedom*, 109.

54. Robinson, *This Ain't Chicago*, 21.

55. Robinson writes: "'Not stud'n 'em white folks,' at the very least, means supplanting emotional reactions to everyday racialized injustice, whether a slight in service during a restaurant visit or a blatantly discriminatory employment outcome, with indifference. Many respondents indicated that they are neither surprised nor regretful when 'good' white folks go bad, nor do they demonstrate or express gratefulness or surprise when 'bad' white folks do good." See Robinson, *This Ain't Chicago*, 94.

56. Robinson, *This Ain't Chicago*, 99.

57. Robinson, *This Ain't Chicago*, 106.

58. Robinson, *This Ain't Chicago*, 106.

59. Robinson, *This Ain't Chicago*, 107.

60. Robinson, *This Ain't Chicago*, 107.

61. Robinson, *This Ain't Chicago*, 119.

62. Robinson, *This Ain't Chicago*, 115–16.

63. Zora Neale Hurston, "How It Feels to Be Colored Me," in Hurston *Zora Neale Hurston*, 827.

64. For example, Hurston writes in the essay: "The North has no interest in the particular Negro, but talks of justice for the whole. The South has no interest, and pretends none, in the mass of Negroes but is very much concerned about the individual." See Hurston, "The 'Pet Negro' System," in Hurston *Zora Neale Hurston*, 915.

65. Hurston, "The 'Pet Negro' System," 917–18.

66. Hurston, "The 'Pet Negro' System," 918.

67. Zora Neale Hurston, *Mules and Men* (1935; New York: Harper Perennial Model Classics, 2008), 10.

68. Hurston, *Mules and Men* 10.

69. Hurston, *Mules and Men*, 10.

70. Hurston, *Mules and Men* 10.

71. Hurston, "Art and Such," 908.

72. Zora Neale Hurston, "Characteristics of Negro Expression," in Hurston-*Zora Neale Hurston*, 831.

73. Like Yogita Goyal, I too am "interested in questions of aesthetic style as epistemology, as grounds for knowledge production, as the site in which questions of power play out." See Goyal, *Romance, Diaspora, and Black Atlantic Literature* (Cambridge: Cambridge University Press, 2010), 11.

74. For some recent examples, see Michelle Alexander, *The New Jim Crow: Mass Incarceration in the Age of Color Blindness* (New York: New Press, 2012); Sharpe, *In the Wake*; Joseph R. Winters, *Hope Drafted in Black: Race, Melancholy, and the Agony of Progress* (Durham, NC: Duke University Press, 2016); Frank B. Wilderson, *Incognegro: A Memoir of Exile and Apartheid* (Durham, NC: Duke University Press, 2015); Jared Sexton, *Black Masculinity and the Cinema of Policing* (New York: Palgrave Macmillan, 2017); and Yogita Goyal, *Runaway Genres: The Global Afterlives of Slavery* (New York: New York University Press, 2019).

75. Zora Neale Hurston, "Negroes without Self-Pity," in Hurston*Zora Neale Hurston*, 933.

76. Simpson, *Mohawk Interruptus*, 177.

77. As Joseph Winters notes, there is often an "underside" to political recognition: "recognition comes with a price. In order to be recognized and affirmed by those in power, one has to accept and consent to the terms and condition of power (even as those terms and conditions might change and shift)." See Winters, *Hope Drafted in Black*, 39.

78. For example, Toni Morrison writes: "Whatever the style and circumstances of these narratives, they were written to say principally two things. (1) 'This is my historical life—my singular, special example that is personal, but that also represents the race.' (2) 'I write this text to persuade other people—you, the reader, who is probably not Black—that we are human beings worthy of God's grace and the immediate abandonment of slavery.' With these two missions in mind, the narratives were clearly pointed." See Toni Morrison, "The Site of Memory," in *The Source of Self-Regard: Selected Essays, Speeches, and Meditations* (New York: Alfred A. Knopf, 2019), 234.

79. Dwight A. McBride, *Impossible Witness: Truth, Abolitionism, and Slave Testimony* (New York: New York University Press, 2001), 3.

80. McBride, *Impossible Witness*, 5.

81. McBride, *Impossible Witness*, 5.

82. This has long been a Black feminist point of complaint. For instance, in her introduction to the *Narrative of the Life of Frederick Douglass, An American Slave*, Deborah McDowell notes that the agency of slaves was masculinized in Douglass's narrative of freedom. That is, Douglass's freedom narrative employs the trope of the collective, tortured slave body in a way that is deeply gendered. "The beatings proliferate," McDowell observes, "and the women, no longer identified by name, become absolutized as a bloody mass of naked Blacks." As a result, "[Douglass's] journey from slavery to freedom," McDowell writes, "leaves women in the logical position of representing the condition of slavery," i.e., Black suffering. This means that "women, especially slave women, remain trapped in the physical, in the body, excluded from language and symbolic activity." See Deborah McDowell, introduction to Frederick Douglass, *The Narrative of Frederick Douglass, An American Slave*, ed. Deborah McDowell (New York:

Oxford University Press, 2009), xx–xxiv. Building upon McDowell's analysis, Angela Davis surmises that "maimed, flogged, abused Black female bodies are the anchors of [Douglass's] description of slavery." As such, not only is there a convention which mobilizes Black suffering to validate the abolitionist cause, but there is also rhetorical purchase in staging Black *female* bodies as victims of extreme violence. See Davis, introduction to Douglass, *Narrative*, 25.

83. Saidiya V. Hartman, *Scenes of Subjection: Terror, Slavery, and Self-Making in Nineteenth-Century America* (New York: Oxford University Press, 1997), 22.

84. Concerning the sentimentalism of the fugitive slave narrative genre, Morrison writes in "The Site of Memory": "As determined as these Black writers were to persuade the reader of the evil of slavery, they also complimented him by assuming his nobility of heart and his high-mindedness. They tried to summon up his finer nature in order to encourage him to employ it. They knew that their readers were the people who could make a difference in terminating slavery. Their stories—of brutality, adversity, and deliverance—had great popularity in spite of critical hostility in many quarters and patronizing sympathy in others." Morrison, "The Site of Memory," 235; see also 237. For a discussion of sentimentalism in *Narrative of the Life of Frederick Douglass*, see McDowell, introduction, xvi–xvii.

85. See McBride, *Impossible Witness*, 4; McDowell, introduction to *Narrative*, xvi, xxii; Davis, introduction to *Narrative*, 26; and Hartman, *Scenes of Subjection*, 18–20 and 27.

86. As Hartman remarks, within abolitionist discourse, pain "provides the common language of humanity," for it "extends humanity to the disposed, and, in turn, remedies the indifference of the callous." To tap into the moral sentiments of their readers, abolitionists encouraged an "identification with the enslaved." The "central terms" of that identification, for Hartman, were Black suffering. See Hartman, *Scenes of Subjection*, 18–22.

87. "If the scene of beating readily lends itself to an identification with the enslaved," Hartman writes, "it does so at the risk of fixing and naturalizing this condition of pained embodiment." To this end, "the endeavor to bring pain close exploits the spectacle of the body in pain and oddly confirms the spectral character of suffering and the inability to witness the captive's pain." See Hartman, *Scenes of Subjection*, 20.

88. See Frederick Douglass, *My Bondage and My Freedom* (New York: Modern Library, 2003), 213–16.

89. Douglass, *My Bondage and My Freedom*, 216.

90. Douglass, *My Bondage and My Freedom*, 215.

91. Douglass, *My Bondage and My Freedom*, 214–15.

92. Douglass, *My Bondage and My Freedom*, 215–16.

93. Douglass, *My Bondage and My Freedom*, 216.

94. See McDowell, introduction to *Narrative*, xiv.

95. Jon Cruz, *Culture on the Margins: The Black Spiritual and the Rise of American Cultural Interpretation* (Princeton, NJ: Princeton University Press, 1999), 3.

96. Frederick Douglass, *Narrative of the Life of Frederick Douglass*, ed. Angela Y. Davis (San Francisco: Open Media Series, 2010), 120–21.

97. Douglass, *Narrative*, 121.

98. Douglass, *Narrative*, 121.

99. Douglass, *Narrative*, 121.

100. McBride, *Impossible Witness*, 6. Cruz makes similar points, albeit from a different approach. Cruz analyzes how notions of authenticity shaped the uptake of Black writing and song-making. For Cruz, an emphasis on Black suffering due to slavery is what marked Black writing and song-making as "authentic" during the antebellum and post-Civil War periods. "Such notions of authenticity," Cruz writes, "were never simply tied to Black subjects, but to Black subjects' credibility to testify to an even greater and graver social problem: slavery and the invidious fate of Blacks who succeeded slavery's demise." In this way, not only is Black suffering the means by which our humanity is elucidated, but it is also the terms upon which Black testimony will possess "credibility" (or be *heard* by sympathetic whites). See Cruz, *Culture on the Margins*, 16.

101. Douglass, *Narrative*, 121.

102. See Cruz, *Culture on the Margins*, 111. See also Shirley Moody-Turner, *Black Folklore and the Politics of Racial Representation* (Jackson: University Press of Mississippi, 2013), 30–32, 36.

103. For instance, Hartman notes that there's a preoccupation with the "enjoyment" of the "slave" that marks both the slave-owners' and the abolitionists' staging of the Black body in the public sphere. This can be seen, for instance, in how the auction block is staged in both pro-slavery and abolitionist discourse, where the "assurance to the buyers about the jollity of the slaves on display" on the part of the slave owner is placed right alongside the "intensity of abolitionist efforts to prove that slaves were neither happy nor indifferent to being sold like cattle and separated from their families." See Hartman, *Scenes of Subjection*, 41–42.

104. Douglass, *Narrative*, 122.

105. Douglass, *Narrative*, 122.

106. Douglass, *My Bondage and My Freedom*, 45–46.

107. Hurston, "Art and Such," 908.

108. Wall, *On Freedom*, 107–8.

109. Hurston, "Art and Such," 906.

110. Hurston, "Art and Such," 906.

111. Hurston, "Art and Such," 906.

112. Hurston, "Art and Such," 906.

113. Hurston, "Art and Such," 908.

114. Hurston, "Art and Such," 908. See also Wall, *On Freedom*, 108.

115. See Bordelon, "Zora Neale Hurston: A Biographical Essay," 30–32; Edwards, *Charisma*, 28; and Wall, *On Freedom*, 107–9.

116. Hurston, "Art and Such," 907.

117. Hurston, "Art and Such," 907.

118. Hurston to Fannie Hurst, December 1933, in Carla Kaplan, ed., *Zora Neale Hurston: A Life in Letters* (New York: Anchor, 2003), 286.

119. Hurston to Fannie Hurst, December 1933, 286. In a letter to Annie Nathan Meyer, Hurston explicitly refers to Du Bois's approach as "propaganda." She writes: "You have followed the writings of Dr. DuBois too carefully and he is a propagandist with all the distorted mind of his kind. He is doing a great service for his race, but he must use propaganda methods and those methods

never follow actual conditions very accurately." See Zora Neale Hurston to Annie
Nathan Meyer, October 7, 1927, in Kaplan, *A Life in Letters*, 108.

120. Goyal, *Romance, Diaspora, and Black Atlantic*, 13.

121. See Goyal, *Romance, Diaspora, and Black Atlantic*, 67. See also Alys Eve
Weinbaum, "Interracial Romance and Black Internationalism," in *Next to the
Color Line: Gender, Sexuality, and W. E. B. Du Bois*, ed. Susan Gillman and Alys
Eve Weinbaum (Minneapolis: University of Minnesota Press, 2007), 97–98, 119.

122. Goyal, *Romance, Diaspora, and Black Atlantic Literature*, 62.

123. Goyal, *Romance, Diaspora, and Black Atlantic Literature*, 79–80. In this
way, romance "provides the glue for a national imagined community of Black
folk" for Du Bois. See Goyal, *Romance, Diaspora, and Black Atlantic Literature*, 75.

124. For more on the connection between romanticism and slave narratives,
see Morrison, "The Site of Memory," 236–38.

125. Goyal, *Romance, Diaspora, and Black Atlantic Literature*, 67. As Cruz
writes, these slave narratives functioned as popular tourist narratives during the
time: "Such cultural production quickly engendered a significant number of easy-
chair readers who could vicariously consume images of pathetic, emaciated slaves
cringing under the whips of cruel masters. In the new antislavery literary field
there was something for the sympathetic book-buying literary highbrow as well
as for the sentimental middlebrow. The South and its enslaved inhabitants could
be known intimately through the representations of a slave culture that became
part of the symbolic arsenal of the abolitionist movement. Those who were not
attracted to antislavery literature, and who did not find slavery offensive, could
always find supportive representations of Blacks, free or enslaved, in the racial
caricature of minstrelsy." See Cruz, *Culture on the Margins*, 111.

126. As Weinbaum notes, "what is all too often unrecognized about Du Bois's
call for propaganda is its elaboration in and through a discourse on interracial
romance—a call, albeit subtle, for the centrality of romance, as both form and
content, to the production of propaganda." For example, in Du Bois's "Criteria of
Negro Art," Weinbaum traces how "Du Bois transforms 'romance'—understood
broadly as a love story, however tragic—into 'Romance'—understood as narrative form and convention, as well as political protest." See Weinbaum, "Interracial
Romance and Black Internationalism," 97, 100.

127. Due to these shifts in priority or what "matters," I move away from scholarly interpretations of root work (especially High John de Conquer) that read
these spiritual practices primarily through the lens of resistance. For examples of
these types of interpretations, see Plant, *Every Tub Must Sit on Its Own Bottom*,
45–46; Bordelon, "Zora Neale Hurston: A Biographical Essay," 27; Meisenhelder,
Hitting a Straight Lick, 4, 18–23; and Katrina Hazzard-Donald, *Mojo Workin':
The Old African American Hoodoo System* (Urbana: University of Illinois Press,
2013), 68–73.

128. Imani Perry, *Vexy Thing: On Gender and Liberation* (Durham, NC: Duke
University Press, 2018), 28–29.

129. This is true especially in the realm of fiction and storytelling. For a
development of the use of conjure in Black feminist fiction, see Barbara Smith,
"Toward a Black Feminist Criticism," *Radical Teacher* 7 (March 1978): 22–23;
Martin, *Conjuring Moments*, 55–88; and Akasha Gloria Hull, *Soul Talk: The*

New Spirituality of African American Women (Rochester, NY: Inner Traditions, 2001), 1–21. See also the anthology *Conjuring: Black Women, Fiction, and Literary Tradition*, ed. Marjorie Pryse and Hortense J. Spillers (Bloomington: Indiana University Press, 1985).

130. Perry, *Vexy Thing*, 174.

131. Perry, *Vexy Thing*, 175.

132. Hazzard-Donald, *Mojo Workin'*, 4, 68–69.

133. Zora Neale Hurston, "High John de Conquer," in Hurston, *Zora Neale Hurston*, 923–24.

134. Hurston, "High John de Conquer," 924.

135. Alexis Pauline Gumbs, *Spill: Scenes of Black Feminist Fugitivity* (Durham, NC: Duke University Press, 2016), 96.

136. Hurston, "High John de Conquer," 924.

137. Hurston, "High John de Conquer," 923.

138. Hurston, "High John de Conquer," 930.

139. See Davis, *Blues Legacies and Black Feminism*, 159. We can see this stance toward root work take shape in Black male abolitionist writing that actively disavowed root work in their journey to freedom. See Martin, *Conjuring Moments*, 56–60; and Walter Rucker, "Conjure, Magic, and Power: The Influence of Afro-Atlantic Religious Practices on Slave Resistance and Rebellion," *Journal of Black Studies* 32, no. 1 (September 2001): 95, https://www-jstor.org.ezproxy.memphis .edu/stable/pdf/2668016.pdf?refreqid=excelsior%3Ab105780530adbdf7d5dde9 6673e72875.

140. Hurston, "High John de Conquer," 930.

141. For example, see Sigal Samuel, "The Witches of Baltimore: Young Black Women Are Leaving Christianity and Embracing African Witchcraft in Digital Covens," *The Atlantic*, November 5, 2018, https://www.theatlantic.com /international/archive/2018/11/Black-millennials-african-witchcraft-christianity /574393/.

142. Simpson, *Mohawk Interruptus*, 11.

143. Perry, *Vexy Thing*, 172.

Scene 1

1. Arranged in chapters, Beyoncé's album recounts the protagonist coming to terms with an intimate betrayal by her husband through stages of grief and reconciliation. The song "Sorry" appears in the "Apathy" chapter, making it an apt place to think through the relationships between principled indifference, southern Black joy, and racial politics.

2. Her response to his half-hearted apology is a refusal to entertain his attempts at reconciliation. "He trying to roll me up," Beyoncé acknowledges, but she "ain't picking up." Having "had enough" of his bad behavior, she is now "headed to the club" instead of "thinking about" (or "studying" him). This response is tied to an immense self-respect that pervades the blueswomen tradition. While her husband may be somewhat sorry and missing her, she refuses to perform any sense of personal devastation regarding their breakup. "Suicide before you see this tear fall down my eyes," Beyoncé asserts. Because of her own self-reliance, like blueswomen before her, she can afford to walk away instead: "me and my baby, we gon' be alright/we gon' live a good life." See Davis, *Blues Legacies and*

Black Feminism, 20–21. See also Brooks and Martin, "'I Used to Be Your Sweet Mama,'" 210.

3. The "you" that Beyoncé is addressing can be read on both a personal and national scale. This is signaled, for instance, by the imagery that she weaves into the storyline, such as Gulf Coast plantations in this chapter. See Daphne A. Brooks, "The Lady Sings Her Legacy: Introduction," in Brooks and Martin, *The Lemonade Reader*, 162–63; Patricia Coloma Peñate, "Beyoncé's Diaspora Heritage and Ancestry in *Lemonade*," in Brooks and Martin, *The Lemonade Reader*, 118; and Steptoe, "Beyoncé's Western South Serenade," 183–84. See also LaKisha Simmons, "Landscapes, Memories, and History in Beyoncé's *Lemonade*," *UNC Press Blog*, April 28, 2016, https://uncpressblog.com/2016/04/28/lakisha-simmons-beyonces-lemonade/.

4. See Brooks, "The Lady Sings Her Legacy," 163.

5. See Brooks, "The Lady Sings Her Legacy," 162.

6. The ironic eulogy that opens the chapter is performed on a bus ride that marks an inward, spiritual journey in the album. Moreover, the women on the bus traveling with Beyoncé are marked with white paint, indicating their participation in the Sacred Art of the Ori, a Yoruba tradition. They are also accompanied by Papa Legba, a devil-like figure who sits at the spiritual crossroads. This figure is also present in several Black religious traditions across the African diaspora, from Gulf Coast hoodoo to Haitian Vodou. See Kameelah Martin and Kinitra Brooks, "Introduction: Beyoncé's *Lemonade* Lexicon—Black Feminism and Spirituality in Theory and Practice," in Brooks and Martin, *The Lemonade Reader*, 2–3; Lauren Highsmith, "Beyoncé Reborn: *Lemonade* as Spiritual Enlightenment," in Brooks and Martin, *The Lemonade Reader*, 137; Steptoe, "Beyoncé's Western South Serenade," 188; Melanie C. Jones, "The *Slay* Factor: Beyoncé Unleashing the Black Feminine Divine in a Blaze of Glory," in Brooks and Martin, *The Lemonade Reader*, 100; Peñate, "Beyoncé's Diaspora Heritage and Ancestry in *Lemonade*," 118–19; and Michele Prettyman Beverly, "To Feel like a 'Natural Woman': Aretha Franklin, Beyoncé, and the Ecological Spirituality of *Lemonade*," in Brooks and Martin, *The Lemonade Reader*, 171.

7. See L. Michael Gipson, "Interlude E: From Destiny's Child to Coachella—On Embracing Then Resisting Others' Respectability Politics," in Brooks and Martin, *The Lemonade Reader*, 144.

Chapter 1

1. This review was in response to Richard Wright's earlier and harsh review of her *Their Eyes Were Watching God*, entitled "Between Laughter and Tears." In this review, Wright complains that Hurston's novel has no theme, message, or thought, which reveals that she had no desire to write "serious fiction." Invoking Phyllis Wheatley, Wright claims that Hurston wrote with a "facile sensuality that has dogged Negro expression." While Hurston did capture something true about "folk psychology," she also created characters that "swing like a pendulum eternally in that safe and narrow orbit in which America likes to see the Negro live: between laughter and tears." By simplifying her characters—who "eat and laugh and cry and work and kill"—in order to give "white folks a laugh," Wright concludes that she continues in the minstrel tradition. In fact, his language suggests that she has performed a kind of artistic "prostitution," since she

"writes to a white audience whose chauvinistic tastes she *knows how to satisfy*" (italics mine). As a result, Wright argues that Hurston exploits the political potential of our folklore, turning it into "that phase of Negro life which is 'quaint,' the phase which evokes a piteous smile on the lips of the 'superior' race." See Richard Wright, "Between Laughter and Tears," *New Masses 5* (October 1937): 22–23.

2. Eve Dunbar, *Black Regions of the Imagination: African American Writers between the Nation and the World* (Philadelphia: Temple University Press, 2013), 17.

3. Indeed, James Baldwin makes this connection between Wright's *Uncle Tom's Children* and Harriet Beecher Stowe's *Uncle Tom's Cabin* due to their reliance upon the sentimentality of their "Cause" (i.e., abolitionism), which hides the "secret and violent inhumanity" or "mask of cruelty" at the core of the works. See James Baldwin, "Everybody's Protest Novel," in Baldwin*James Baldwin: Collected Essays*, ed. Toni Morrison (New York: Library of America, 1998), 11–13.

4. Hurston, "Stories of Conflict," *Saturday Review of Literature* 17, no. 2 (1938): 32, italics mine.

5. Hurston, "Stories of Conflict," 32.

6. Hurston, "Stories of Conflict," 32.

7. Hurston, "Stories of Conflict," 32.

8. Wright writes: "Miss Hurston *voluntarily* continues in her novel the tradition which was *forced* upon the Negro in the theatre, that is, the minstrel technique that makes the 'white folks' laugh." See Wright, "Between Laughter and Tears," 13.

9. See Hurston, "What the White Publishers Won't Print," in Hurston, *Zora Neale Hurston*, 951.

10. Hurston, "Art and Such," 908.

11. Hurston, "Stories of Conflict," 33.

12. Hurston, "Art and Such," 908.

13. Hurston, "Court Order Can't Make Races Mix," 956.

14. Hurston, "Court Order Can't Make Races Mix," 956.

15. Hurston, "Art and Such," 907–8.

16. Hurston, "Art and Such," 907–8.

17. Hurston, "Court Order Can't Make Races Mix," 958.

18. Hurston, "Court Order Can't Make Races Mix," 958.

19. Hurston, "Court Order Can't Make Races Mix," 958. While her logic may have been sound, there were benefits to legal desegregation that Hurston did not entertain. For more contemporary discussion of this point, see Kendra Nicole Bryant, "Dear Zora: Letters from the New Literati," in *"The Inside Light": New Critical Essays on Zora Neale Hurston*, ed. Deborah G. Plant (Santa Barbara, CA: Praeger, 2010), 181–96.

20. Hurston to Claude Barnett, February 4? 1943, in Kaplan, *A Life in Letters*, 474.

21. For examples of contemporary work that takes up Zora Neale Hurston's racial politics regarding *Brown vs. Board*, see Moylan, "'A Child Cannot Be Taught by Anyone Who Despises Him'"; and Marcucci, "Zora Neale Hurston and the *Brown* Debate." However, some scholars still hold that Hurston's pro-Southern stance makes her a conservative when it comes to her racial politics.

For instance, Glenda R. Carpio and Werner Sollors attribute Hurston's "conservatism" to her rural roots. And yet, as new evidence has surfaced to the contrary, rather than give up the image of Hurston as a political conservative, they claim that Hurston was simply unable to fit into any political box. See Glenda R. Carpio and Werner Sollors, "The Newly Complicated Zora Neale Hurston," *Chronicle of Higher Education*, January 2, 2011, https://www.chronicle.com/article/The-Newly-Complicated-Zora/125753. As Ernest Julius Mitchell II notes, "over the past decade, Hurston has . . . been assigned a bewildering array of affiliations: a republican, libertarian, radical democrat, reactionary conservative, Black cultural nationalist, anti-authoritarian feminist, and woman-hating protofascist. The woman who once called herself 'Everybody's Zora' has been made all things to all men (often wrongly), and the ongoing controversy has paid little attention to the full corpus of her political writings." See Ernest Julius Mitchell, "Zora's Politics: An Introduction," *Journal of Transnational American Studies* 5, no. 1 (2013), https://escholarship.org/uc/item/38356082#main.

22. Barbara Smith describes this phenomenon in terms of "invisibility." She writes: "This invisibility, which goes beyond anything that either Black men or white women experience and tell about in their writing, is one reason it is so difficult for me to know where to start. It seems overwhelming to break such a massive silence. Even more numbing, however, is the realization that so many of the women who will read this have not yet noticed us missing either from their reading matter, their politics, or their lives." As such, Smith argues that we need to develop both Black feminist criticism and a Black feminist movement, for criticism and politics are linked in this struggle against such "invisibility." See Smith, "Toward a Black Feminist Criticism," 20.

23. See Farrah Jasmine Griffin, "That the Mothers May Soar and the Daughters May Know Their Names: A Retrospective of Black Feminist Literary Criticism," *Signs: Journal of Women in Culture and Society* 32, no. 21 (2007): 486–89.

24. As Barbara Christian writes, "one of the reasons for the surge of Afro-American women's writing during the 1970s and its emphasis on sexism in the Black community is precisely that when the ideologues of the 1960s said *Black*, they meant *Black male*." See Christian, "The Race for Theory," 60. As Mary Helen Washington writes: "What is significant about the all-Black setting is that it enables the novel to escape one of the plagues of Black literature—the handicap of having its most passionate feelings directed at 'The Man.' The Black writer sometimes gets his eyes so fixed on the white world and its ways of acting towards us that his vision becomes constricted. He reflects, if he is not careful, but one aspect of his people's experiences: suffering, humiliation, degradation. And he may fail to show that Black people are more than simply reactors, that, among ourselves, we have laughter, tears, and loving that are far removed from the white horror out there." See Mary Helen Washington, "The Black Woman's Search for Identity," *Black World* 21, no. 10 (1972): 68. Moreover, Griffin notes that "writers and critics as diverse as Morrison, Spillers, and Washington have all noted that, while Black male writers focus their attention on relationships and struggles between Black and white men, Black women most often turn their gaze to the relationships among Black people." See Griffin, "That the Mothers May Soar," 499.

25. Smith, "Sexual Politics," 26.

26. Smith, "Sexual Politics," 26.

27. As Erica Edwards notes, this style of Black male leadership is structured by historical, social, and conceptual violences toward Black women. See Erica Edwards, *Charisma and the Fictions of Black Leadership* (Minneapolis: University of Minnesota Press, 2012), 20–21.

28. Smith, "Sexual Politics," 28.

29. Smith, "Sexual Politics," 28.

30. Plant, *Every Tub Must Sit on Its Own Bottom*, 4.

31. Plant, *Every Tub Must Sit on Its Own Bottom*, 4. Wall also echoes this point. See Cheryl A. Wall, "Zora Neale Hurston: Changing Her Own Words," in *Zora Neale Hurston: Critical Perspectives Past and Present*, ed. Henry Louis Gates Jr. and K. A. Appiah (New York: Amistad, 2000), 96.

32. Plant, *Every Tub Must Sit on Its Own Bottom*, 4.

33. Plant, *Every Tub Must Sit on Its Own Bottom*, 4.

34. Hurston, "Art and Such," 908.

35. Alice Walker notes this in the title of her essay, "On Refusing to be Humbled by Second Place in a Contest You Did Not Design," 1. See also Gay Wilentz, "Defeating the False God: Janie's Self-Determination in *Their Eyes Were Watching God*," in *Faith of a (Woman) Writer*, ed. Alice Kessler-Harris and William McBrien (Westport, CT: Greenwood, 1988), 286–89; and Washington, "Zora Neale Hurston's Work," 68–69.

36. June Jordan writes: "But I would add that the functions of protest and affirmation are not, ultimately, distinct: that, for instance, affirmation of Black values and lifestyle within the American context is, indeed, an act of protest." See Jordan, "Notes toward a Black Balancing of Love and Hatred," 286.

37. See Carla Kaplan, *The Erotics of Talk: Women's Writing and Feminist Paradigms* (New York: Oxford University Press, 1996), 105–13; Edwards, *Charisma*, 76–80, 86–87; and Wall, *On Freedom*, 18–22.

38. For a contemporary discussion of refusal and the politics of recognition, see Hartman, "Intimate History, Radical Narrative."

39. Audra Simpson, "Consent's Revenge," *Cultural Anthropology* 31, no. 3 (2016): 330.

40. It is important to render these terms explicit because, as Kristie Dotson notes, one of the ways that oppression maintains itself is by "process-based invisibilities," i.e., "manufactured forms of invisibility that can be traced by the very processes that affect the disappearances in question." Kristie Dotson, "Radical Black Love: Black Philosophy as Deliberate Acts of Inheritance," *Black Scholar* 43, no. 4 (2013): 39.

41. Hurston, "Negroes without Self-Pity," 933.

42. Toni Morrison, *Beloved* (New York: Vintage International, 2004), 225.

43. Morrison, *Beloved*, 30.

44. Morrison, *Beloved*, 30.

45. Morrison, *Beloved*, 270.

46. As Audra Simpson observes, there often seems to be an "enjoyment" in the performance of refusal on the part of the refuser. See Simpson, *Mohawk Interruptus*, 107.

47. Morrison, *Beloved*, 268. For a discussion of "juba" in *Beloved*, see Teresa N. Washington, "The Sea Never Dies: Yemoja: The Infinitely Flowing Mother

Force of Africana Literature and Cinema," in *Yemoja: Gender, Sexuality, and Creativity in the Latina/o and Afro-Atlantic Diasporas*, ed. Solimar Otero and Toyin Falola (Albany: State University of New York Press, 2013), 218–22.

48. Morrison, *Beloved*, 270.

49. Morrison, *Beloved*, 270.

50. Morrison, *Beloved*, 270.

51. This type of approach is exemplified by Henry Louis Gates Jr. and Jennifer Burton's coverage of the Hurston-Wright debate in their *Call and Response*, an undergraduate textbook for African American studies. The title of the entry—"Do African American artists have an obligation to contribute to a collective political vision—or is the pursuit of an individual vision an equally valid undertaking?"—frames the debate as a matter of political protest versus an emphasis on individuality. For Gates and Burton, the terms of the debate lie in the fundamental tension between the burden of collective politics and the burden of individual achievement. See Henry Louis Gates Jr. and Jennifer Burton, *Call and Response: Key Debates in African American Studies* (New York: W. W. Norton, 2008), 471–72.

52. See also my "Something Akin to Freedom: Black Love, Political Agency, and *Lemonade*," in *The Lemonade Reader: Beyoncé, Black Feminism and Spirituality*, ed. Kinitra Brooks and Kameelah Martin (New York: Routledge, 2019), 21–27.

53. Richard Wright, "Blueprint for Negro Writing," in *Within the Circle: An Anthology of African American Literary Criticism from the Harlem Renaissance to the Present*, ed. Angelyn Mitchell (Durham, NC: Duke University Press, 1994), 100.

54. Wright, "Blueprint for Negro Writing," 100.

55. See Lawrence Levine, *Black Culture and Black Consciousness* (New York: Oxford University Press, 1977), 420.

56. Levine, *Black Culture and Black Consciousness*, 424.

57. See Levine, *Black Culture and Black Consciousness*, 421.

58. Levine, *Black Culture and Black Consciousness*, 421.

59. Levine, *Black Culture and Black Consciousness*, 420.

60. Levine, *Black Culture and Black Consciousness*, 426.

61. James Baldwin, "Alas, Poor Richard," in Baldwin, *James Baldwin: Collected Essays*, 251.

62. Hurston to Alain Locke, July 23, 1943, in Kaplan, *A Life in Letters*, 489.

63. Hurston, "High John de Conquer," 923. During Wright's time, many Black sociologists (such as E. Franklin Frazier) held that African American culture was pathological or damaged due to racism. Wright writes, "[theme] means that Negro writers must have in their consciousness the foreshortened picture of the *whole* culture from which they were torn in Africa, and of the long, complex (and for the most part, unconscious) struggle to regain in some form and under alien conditions a life of *whole* culture again." See Wright, "Blueprint for Negro Writing," 104–5.

64. Hurston, "High John de Conquer," 930.

65. Hurston, "High John de Conquer," 922.

66. Hurston, "High John de Conquer," 922.

67. Hurston, "High John de Conquer," 923.

68. As Plant writes: "Hurston conceived humor and laughter as the wellspring of life and the outward indication of an inner spirituality . . . Hurston considered this wellspring of life a gift from Africa transmitted by High John de Conquer, the 'hopebringer.' This gift High John gave to the enslaved. It allowed them to endure the worst conditions and maintain hope in the face of despair, life in the face of death." See Plant, *Every Tub Must Sit on Its Own Bottom*, 89–90.

69. Hurston, "High John de Conquer," 922.

70. Hurston, "High John de Conquer," 930.

71. Hurston, "High John de Conquer," 924.

72. Toni Morrison and Cecil Brown, "Interview with Toni Morrison," in *Toni Morrison: Conversations*, ed. Carolyn C. Denard (Jackson: University Press of Mississippi, 2008), 109.

73. For example, see Hurston, "The 'Pet Negro' System," 17–18. In this essay, Hurston describes an encounter with Northern white liberals where her refusal prompts them to anger.

74. Walker, "On Refusing to be Humbled by Second Place in a Contest You Did Not Design," 1.

75. For the section heading, see Hurston to Burton Rascoe, September 8, 1944, in Kaplan, *A Life in Letters*, 503.

76. As Susan Meisenhelder notes of Hurston's disappointing encounters with her leftist counterparts: "[Hurston's] lament—'They try to change the whole world, but refuse to let anything change them' (59)—probably speaks to the feeling of more than one woman or person of color coming into many progressive organizations, the feeling of being the object of rather than the creator of theory, the handmaiden of someone else's social analysis rather than the author of one's own." See Meisenhelder, "Gender, Race, & Class in Zora Neale Hurston's Politics."

77. Hurston, *Mules and Men*, 10.

78. As Hurston writes to Alain Locke in a letter: "On the part of northern whites, they have carried over the phraseology of the Abolition struggle. Then, all Negroes were sweet, pure noble people. They knew nothing about them, many of them never having seen a Negro at all. The tales of the Underground Railroad were thrilling and made the white conductors heroes. The doctrine of the 'noble savage' was everywhere. Then came UNCLE TOM'S CABIN and typed the Negro for the North." See Hurston to Alain Locke, July 23, 1943, in Kaplan, *A Life in Letters*, 490.

79. Hurston, "The 'Pet Negro' System," 917–18.

80. "White supremacy" is not the term Hurston uses. However, it is, more or less, the phenomenon to which she is referring by her terms "Jim Crow," "Anglo-Saxon Supremacy," and "(Western) Civilization."

81. Zora Neale Hurston, "My Most Humiliating Jim Crow Experience," in Hurston*Zora Neale Hurston*, 936.

82. Hurston, "My Most Humiliating Jim Crow Experience," 935.

83. See Hurston to Alain Locke, July 23, 1943, 491. Casting racism as a "southern" problem enables northerners to excuse themselves from interrogating their own racist practices. For example, a northern hotel owner can say, upon turning away a Black customer, "it is alright with them, but would upset any Southerners they might service." The imaginary southerner in this example enables the northerner to displace, and thus not claim responsibility for, their racism. Hurston

notes that Blacks as well are tempted to buy into this narrative. Hurston writes, "the Negroes who have gloried in the nort[h] are also caught, so they join in the chorus, 'Them Southerners snuk up here and done it.'"

84. Hurston to Alain Locke, July 23, 1943, 491.

85. Hurston to Alain Locke, July 23, 1943, 491.

86. See Zora Neale Hurston, "Crazy for This Democracy," in Hurston *Zora Neale Hurston*, 947. While some have accused Hurston of being apolitical, in this essay she offers an incisive analysis of the failure of democracy in the United States and abroad due to racism, imperialism, and colonization. She passionately argues for the end of Jim Crow both here and in "colonial Africa, Asia and the Netherlands East Indies."

87. Hurston, "Crazy for This Democracy," 947.

88. Hurston, "Crazy for This Democracy," 947.

89. Hurston, "Crazy for This Democracy," 948.

90. See Hurston, "Crazy for This Democracy," 945–47. Hurston berates the United States for its hypocrisy in participating in World War II for the sake of "democracy," given its own racist conventions at home. Moreover, the United States fights against darker-hued countries that revolt in an attempt to free themselves from Western rule. For more on this topic, see Zora Neale Hurston, "Seeing the World as It Is," in Hurston, *Zora Neale Hurston*, 790–94. This essay was originally part of Hurston's autobiography, *Dust Tracks on a Road*, and was removed due to pressure from her editor.

91. Hurston, "Crazy for This Democracy," 947–48.

92. Hurston, "Crazy for This Democracy," 946.

93. Hurston, "Crazy for This Democracy," 947.

94. Hurston, "Crazy for This Democracy," 948.

95. Hurston, "Crazy for This Democracy," 948.

96. Hurston, "Crazy for This Democracy," 948.

97. Hurston, "Crazy for This Democracy," 948.

98. See Hurston, "Crazy for This Democracy," 948. Hurston writes: "By physical evidence, back seats in trains, backdoors of houses, exclusion from certain places and activities, to promote in the mind of the smallest white child the conviction of First by birth, eternal and irrevocable . . . Talent, capabilities, nothing has anything to do with the case."

99. Hurston, "My Most Humiliating Jim Crow Experience," 936.

100. Hurston, "My Most Humiliating Jim Crow Experience," 936. The pathology Hurston is describing here can be likened to what the social epistemologist José Medina calls "meta-blindness." "Meta-blindness," Medina writes, "can . . . be defined as *the inability to recognize and acknowledge one's limitations and blindspots*." See José Medina, *The Epistemology of Resistance: Gender and Racial Oppression, Epistemic Injustice, and Resistant Imaginations* (New York: Oxford University Press, 2013), 150.

101. See Hurston to Countee Cullen, March 5, 1943, in Kaplan, *A Life in Letters*, 481–82. For more on Hurston's refusal to comply with the mandated liberation strategies of her day, see Carla Kaplan, "The Erotics of Talk: 'That Oldest Human Longing' in *Their Eyes Were Watching God*," in *Zora Neale Hurston's "Their Eyes Were Watching God": A Casebook*, ed. Cheryl A. Wall (New York: Oxford University Press, 2000), 144–45.

102. Hurston, "Crazy for This Democracy," 948.

103. Hurston to Alain Locke, July 23, 1943, 491.

104. Andrew Delbanco, "The Political Incorrectness of Zora Neale Hurston," *Journal of Blacks in Higher Education* 18 (1998): 106.

105. Delbanco, "The Political Incorrectness of Zora Neale Hurston," 106.

106. See Hurston to Claude Barnett, February 4? 1943, in Kaplan, *A Life in Letters*, 474–75.

107. Hurston to Claude Barnett, February 4? 1943, 474.

108. Hurston to Claude Barnett, February 4? 1943, 475.

109. Hurston to Douglass Gilbert, February 4, 1943, in Kaplan, *A Life in Letters*, 475–78.

110. Hurston to Douglass Gilbert, February 4, 1943, 476.

111. Hurston to Douglass Gilbert, February 4, 1943, 477.

112. Hurston to Douglass Gilbert, February 4, 1943, 476. Hurston writes in the letter to Gilbert: "In the matter of segregation, I said that the Negroes had their own theaters and places of amusement, sometimes owned by the Negroes, but often owned by whites and managed by Negroes; that Negroes were happy in their social gatherings and had no more desire to associate with whites than the whites had to associate with them." Hurston also writes in the same letter: "Neither did I say that Negroes are better off in the South than in the North. What I did say was, that there is a large body of Negroes in the South who never get mentioned. They are wealthy, well-educated, and generally doing good for themselves. I said that propagandists always talk about the share-croppers and the like, but never mention these people."

113. Hurston to Douglass Gilbert, February 4, 1943, 477. Hurston also writes: "I told you how I laughed to myself watching northerners, after saying to Negro individuals how distressed they were about the awful conditions down South, trying to keep Negroes from too close a contact with themselves."

114. Hurston to Douglass Gilbert, February 4, 1943, 477.

115. Hurston to Burton Rascoe, September 8, 1944, in Kaplan, *A Life in Letters*, 503.

116. Hurston to Burton Rascoe, September 8, 1944, 503.

117. Hurston to Burton Rascoe, September 8, 1944, 503.

118. Hurston to Burton Rascoe, September 8, 1944, 503.

119. Hurston to Burton Rascoe, September 8, 1944, 503.

120. Hurston to Burton Rascoe, September 8, 1944, 504.

121. Hurston, "How It Feels to Be Colored Me," 829.

Scene 2

1. See Peñate, "Beyoncé's Diaspora Heritage and Ancestry in *Lemonade*," 118; Brooks, "The Lady Sings Her Legacy," 162–63; and Steptoe, "Beyoncé's Western South Serenade," 183–84. See also Simmons, "Landscapes, Memories, and History in Beyoncé's *Lemonade*."

2. We can see examples of this kind of address in abolitionist discourse in slave narratives. See Cruz, *Culture on the Margins*, 111–12.

3. Toni Morrison and Christina Davis, "An Interview with Toni Morrison," in *Conversations with Toni Morrison*, ed. Danille Taylor-Guthrie (Jackson: University Press of Mississippi, 1994), 230.

4. Morrison and Davis, "An Interview with Toni Morrison," 230.

5. For points about the history of racial oppression in *Lemonade*, see Simmons, "Landscapes, Memories, and History in Beyoncé's *Lemonade*"; and Brooks, "The Lady Sings Her Legacy," 162–63.

6. See Simmons, "Landscapes, Memories, and History in Beyoncé's *Lemonade*"; and Beverly, "To Feel like a 'Natural Woman,'" 171, 175–76.

7. See Peñate, "Beyoncé's Diaspora Heritage and Ancestry in *Lemonade*," 118; Beverly, "To Feel like a 'Natural Woman,'" 175; and Steptoe, "Beyoncé's Western South Serenade," 188. See also Highsmith, "Beyoncé Reborn," 137–38; and Gipson, "Interlude E: From Destiny's Child to Coachella," 150.

8. See Peñate, "Beyoncé's Diaspora Heritage and Ancestry in *Lemonade*," 118 19; Highsmith, "Beyoncé Reborn," 137; and Steptoe, "Beyoncé's Western South Serenade," 188.

9. For more on "shouting" and the Sanctified Church, see Hazzard-Donald, *Mojo Workin'*, 96–97, 184–85.

10. As Sharla M. Fett writes, "in African American lore the cosmogram signified power created through connections to one's ancestors. More than a symbol, a cosmogram drawn on the ground or embodied in the form of a forked stick or crossroads drew spiritual power to a particular point on earth. Crossroads and cosmograms traced in the ground marked points of contact between the world of the living and the world of gods and ancestors." See Sharla M. Fett, *Working Cures: Healing, Health, and Power on Southern Slave Plantations* (Chapel Hill: University of North Carolina Press, 2002), 56. For more on the connection between Mardi Gras Indians and hoodoo and Voodoo practices, see Richard Brent Turner, *Jazz Religion, the Second Line, and Black New Orleans: After Hurricane Katrina*, new ed. (Bloomington: Indiana University Press, 2017), 33–34.

Chapter 2

1. Saidiya Hartman makes this point while analyzing the work of abolitionist John Rankin. She notes that "we need to ask why the site of suffering so readily lends itself to inviting identification. Why is pain the conduit of identification?" Rather than illuminate our humanity, Hartman suggests that "if the scene of beating readily lends itself to identification with the enslaved, it does so at the risk of fixing and naturalizing this condition of pained embodiment." See Hartman, *Scenes of Subjection*, 20.

2. Hurston, "Art and Such," 908.

3. As Cheryl A. Wall notes, while Hurston does not explicitly name the men she is criticizing in this passage, "when she refers to the misnaming of the spirituals as 'Sorrow Songs,' she identifies Du Bois as one of her targets." See Wall, *On Freedom*, 108.

4. Hurston, "Art and Such," 908, italics mine.

5. See Wall, *On Freedom*, 18–21, 108–9. See also Kaplan, *A Life in Letters*, 51–52.

6. Zora Neale Hurston, "Spirituals and Neo-Spirituals," in Hurston, *Zora Neale Hurston*, 870.

7. Hurston, "Spirituals and Neo-Spirituals," 870.

8. For more on this position in scholarship, see Wall, *On Freedom*, 113–14. For examples of this type of reading of Hurston's criticism, see Hazel V. Carby, "The Politics of Fiction, Anthropology, and the Folk: Zora Neale Hurston," in

New Essays on "Their Eyes Were Watching God," ed. Michael Awkward (Cambridge: Cambridge University Press, 1991), 75–76; Eric Sundquist, *To Wake the Nations: Race in the Making of American Literature* (Cambridge, MA: Harvard University Press, 1993), 475, 532–33; and Paul Gilroy, *The Black Atlantic: Modernity and Double-Consciousness* (Cambridge, MA: Harvard University Press, 1995), 91–92.

9. See Wall, *On Freedom*, 107–9.

10. Zora Neale Hurston, "The Rise of Begging Joints," in Hurston, *Zora Neale Hurston*, 944.

11. W. E. B. Du Bois, *The Souls of Black Folk*, in *W. E. B. Du Bois: Writings*, ed. Nathan Huggins (New York: Library of America, 1986), 394.

12. Du Bois, *The Souls of Black Folk*, 394.

13. See Sundquist, *To Wake the Nations*, 473–74.

14. Du Bois, *The Souls of Black Folk*, 397–98. As Robert Gooding-Williams argues, Du Bois misrepresents Douglass's politics in order to shore up his *own* advocacy of "assimilation through self-assertion." See Robert Gooding-Williams, *In the Shadow of Du Bois: Afro-Modern Political Thought in America* (Cambridge, MA: Harvard University Press, 2009), 5–7, 165. Notwithstanding Du Bois's misrepresentation of Douglass here, we might consider if there were other ways Du Bois may still be a "spiritual son of the Abolitionists." For instance, Du Bois may still be an intellectual heir of Douglass in how he takes up Douglass's interpretation of the spirituals.

15. Du Bois, *The Souls of Black Folk*, 394.

16. Du Bois, *The Souls of Black Folk*, 398. See also Anderson, *Deep River*, 41–42; and Gooding-Williams, *In the Shadow of Du Bois*, 163.

17. I read "Of the Faith of the Fathers" through "Of the Coming of John," similar to Shamir Zamir and Jonathon S. Kahn. See Shamoon Zamir, *Dark Voices: W. E. B. Du Bois and American Thought, 1888–1903* (Chicago: University of Chicago Press, 1995), 188–89; and Jonathon S. Kahn, *Divine Discontent: The Religious Imagination of W. E. B. Du Bois* (New York: Oxford University Press, 2009), 60–64.

18. Du Bois, *The Souls of Black Folk*, 523.

19. Du Bois, *The Souls of Black Folk*, 522.

20. See Du Bois, *The Souls of Black Folk*, 364–65, for a description of the Veil. See also page 525 for examples of how the Veil occurs in Black John's story. See Howard Winant, *The New Politics of Race: Globalism, Difference, Justice* (Minneapolis: University of Minnesota Press, 2004), 34–38, for a contemporary discussion of race and the Veil.

21. As Farrah Jasmine Griffin notes, Du Bois identifies with the main character of this story; he "sees himself in the young man's strivings"—especially in his experiences of the Veil and Black southern religious practices. See Farah Jasmine Griffin, introduction to W. E. B. Du Bois, *The Souls of Black Folk*, ed. Farah Jasmine Griffin (New York: Barnes and Nobles Classics, 2005), xxiv–xxv. Similarly, Yogita Goyal remarks: "What Du Bois could not resolve as a writer of fiction, he resolves in his own person as the protagonist of the drama of *Souls*." See Goyal, *Romance, Diaspora, and Black Atlantic Literature*, 74–75. See also Anderson, *Deep River*, 39; Gooding-Williams, *In the Shadow of Du Bois*, 115–16; and Sundquist, *To Wake the Nations*, 527–29.

22. Du Bois, *The Souls of Black Folk*, 522.

23. Du Bois, *The Souls of Black Folk*, 523.

24. Du Bois writes of Black John's "happy" nature: "And yet one glance at [John's] face made one forgive him much, that broad, good-natured smile in which lay no bit of art or artifice, but seemed just bubbling good-nature and genuine satisfaction with the world." Du Bois, *Souls of Black Folk*, 522.

25. Du Bois, *The Souls of Black Folk*, 522, italics mine.

26. Du Bois, *The Souls of Black Folk*, 524.

27. Du Bois, *The Souls of Black Folk*, 525.

28. Du Bois, *The Souls of Black Folk*, 525.

29. Du Bois, *The Souls of Black Folk*, 364–67.

30. Du Bois, *The Souls of Black Folk*, 525.

31. Du Bois, *The Souls of Black Folk*, 525.

32. Griffin, introduction to *The Souls of Black Folk*, xxvi.

33. Du Bois, *The Souls of Black Folk*, 534.

34. Du Bois, *The Souls of Black Folk*, 504.

35. Du Bois, *The Souls of Black Folk*, 522.

36. Du Bois, *The Souls of Black Folk*, 528.

37. Du Bois writes: "He had come to save his people, and before he left the depot he had hurt them. He sought to teach them at the church, and had outraged their deepest feelings. He had schooled himself to be respectful to the Judge, and then blundered into his front door. And all the time he had meant right, and yet, and yet, somehow he had found it so hard and strange to fit his old surroundings again, to find his place in the world about him." See Du Bois, *The Souls of Black Folk*, 531.

38. For more discussion of Du Bois's cultural separation from southern Black folk, see Sundquist, *To Wake the Nations*, 527; Anderson, *Deep River*, 36; and Cheryl A. Wall, "Resounding *Souls*: Du Bois and the African American Literary Tradition," *Public Culture* 17, no. 2 (Spring 2005): 219–21.

39. Du Bois notes that many Black southern congregants "firmly believed that without this visible manifestation of the God there could be no true communion with the Invisible." See Du Bois, *The Souls of Black Folk*, 493–95.

40. Du Bois, *The Souls of Black Folk*, 531–33.

41. For more discussion of John Henry and High John de Conquer, see the section titled "Resistance, Refusal, and Root Work" in the previous chapter.

42. Du Bois, *The Souls of Black Folk*, 534.

43. Du Bois, *The Souls of Black Folk*, 535.

44. Du Bois, *The Souls of Black Folk*, 535.

45. Douglass, *Narrative*, 181.

46. Douglass, *Narrative*, 114. See also Hartman, *Scenes of Subjection*, 3–4.

47. McDowell, introduction to *Narrative*, xx. Building upon McDowell's analysis, Angela Davis also surmises that "maimed, flogged, abused Black female bodies are the anchors of [Douglass's] description of slavery." Not only is there a convention to mobilize Black suffering to validate the abolitionist cause, but there is also rhetorical purchase in staging Black *female* bodies as victims of extreme violence. All the same, the cost of this rhetorical maneuver is a lack of representations of Black women's agency in public discourse. See Davis, introduction to *Narrative*, 25–26.

48. As Carby notes, "in this struggle over the control of female sexuality and sexual reproduction, John gains self-respect in his own Black manhood." As a result, this scene illustrates how "the future of Du Bois's imagined Black community is to be determined by the nature of the struggle among men over the bodies of women." See Hazel V. Carby, *Race Men*, W. E. B. Du Bois Lectures (Cambridge, MA: Harvard University Press, 1998), 25. As Susan Gillman and Alys Eve Weinbaum note, even when Du Bois attempts to include Black women in his analyses of oppression, our agency is "summoned, instrumentalized, and ultimately eclipsed by Black 'manhood.' " This is because Du Bois's work is structured by a "politics of juxtaposition," which "positions multiple political issues and related world historical movements for social justice as associate, as necessarily juxtaposed, if not fully interlinked, or self-consciously interwoven." As such, the interconnections of race and gender are often "elided" in Du Bois's treatment of Black women. See Susan Gillman and Alys Eve Weinbaum, "Introduction: W. E. B. Du Bois and the Politics of Juxtaposition," in *Next to the Color Line: Gender, Sexuality, and W. E. B. Du Bois*, ed. Susan Gillman and Alys Eve Weinbaum (Minneapolis: University of Minnesota Press, 2007), 3, 15.

49. For examples, see Zamir, *Dark Voices*, 188; Wall, "Resounding *Souls*," 219–20; and Gillman and Weinbaum, "Introduction," 10.

50. For more on the feminization of the South in other parts of *The Souls of Black Folk*, see Carby, *Race Men*, 38–39. See also James Arthur Manigault-Bryant, "Reimagining the 'Pythian Madness' of *Souls*: W. E. B. Du Bois's Poetics of African American Faith," *Journal of Africana Religions* 1, no. 3 (2013): 336, https://www.jstor.org/stable/10.5325/jafrireli.1.3.0324#metadata_info_tab_contents.

51. Du Bois, *The Souls of Black Folk*, 495.

52. Du Bois, *The Souls of Black Folk*, 505.

53. Although a long and lively debate in scholarship has pitted Du Bois's pragmatism against his Hegelianism, some scholars note that this opposition misses the deep connections between pragmatism and German idealism. Both traditions of philosophical thought would encourage Du Bois to use dialectics in his approach. See Paul Taylor, "What's the Use of Calling Du Bois a Pragmatist?" *Metaphilosophy* 35, no. 1–2 (2004): 99–114. See also Kahn, *Divine Discontent*, 155–56 (esp. footnote 128).

54. Du Bois scholarship usually focuses on the concept of double-consciousness when analyzing the influence of Hegel and German idealism in Du Bois's thought. For examples of this kind of development, see Winant, *The New Politics of Race*, 25–26, 28–29. See also Zamir, *Dark Voices*, 119–32. I shift this focus by reading Du Bois's development of African American religion through Hegel's dialectics as it highlights the role of abolitionism in his analysis of African American religion. For extended discussions of Hegelianism in Du Bois's thought, see Robert Gooding-Williams, "Philosophy of History and Social Critique in *The Souls of Black Folk*," *Information* 26, no. 1 (1987): 99–114; and Stephanie Shaw, *W. E. B. Du Bois and The Souls of Black Folk* (Chapel Hill: University of North Carolina Press, 2013).

55. Du Bois, *The Souls of Black Folk*, 495, italics mine.

56. Eddie Glaude critiques this impulse in Black liberation theology as the "problem of history." See Glaude, *In a Shade of Blue*, 68. Glaude writes: "The

problem, at its root, involves the presumption of a continuous history of African Americans. Much like advocates of the archeological approach to Black identity . . . Black liberation theologians often posit History—in a sense I'll mark with a capital-*H*—as a soulful or spiritual event and as the site for the production of an authentic Black, and in this case Christian, subject."

57. Du Bois, *The Souls of Black Folk*, 497.

58. See Du Bois, *The Souls of Black Folk*, 504–5. Du Bois writes: "Between the two extreme types of ethical attitude which I have thus sought to make clear wavers the mass of millions of Negroes, North and South; and their religious life and activity partake of this social conflict within their ranks . . . But back of this still broods silently the deep religious feeling of the real Negro heart, the stirring, unguided might of powerful human souls who have lost the guiding star of the past and are seeking in the great night a new religious ideal."

59. Du Bois, *The Souls of Black Folk*, 499, italics mine.

60. Du Bois, *The Souls of Black Folk*, 499.

61. See Du Bois, *The Souls of Black Folk*, 498. Du Bois argues that the Voodoo Priest is a prototype of the Black preacher, for "under him the first Afro-American institution, the Negro Church," arose.

62. Du Bois, *The Souls of Black Folk*, 497–98.

63. Du Bois, *The Souls of Black Folk*, 499.

64. Du Bois, *The Souls of Black Folk*, 499.

65. Du Bois, *The Souls of Black Folk*, 500.

66. Du Bois, *The Souls of Black Folk*, 503.

67. Du Bois, *The Souls of Black Folk*, 500.

68. Du Bois, *The Souls of Black Folk*, 503.

69. As Goyal writes, "for Du Bois, the abolitionist impulse provides the spark for a different religious and ethical framework, one in which the fight for freedom itself becomes the deepest expression of spirituality." See Goyal, *Romance, Diaspora, and Black Atlantic*, 79.

70. Du Bois, *The Souls of Black Folk*, 501, italics mine.

71. Du Bois, *The Souls of Black Folk*, 500. Davis also picks up on this theme. She writes: "Christian spirituals created and sung by the masses of slaves were also powerful songs of freedom that demonstrate the extent to which Christianity could be rescued from the ideological context forged by the slaveholders and imbued with a revolutionary content of liberation." Angela Davis, "First Lecture on Liberation," in Douglass, *Narrative*, 63.

72. Du Bois, *The Souls of Black Folk*, 501, italics mine.

73. Du Bois, *The Souls of Black Folk*, 497.

74. Du Bois, *The Souls of Black Folk*, 500.

75. For example, in recounting his famous fight with Mr. Covey (a slave-breaker), Douglass disavows the power of the "root" a fellow slave (Sandy) had given him for protection. See Douglass, *Narrative*, 186–87, 252n53.

76. Du Bois, *The Souls of Black Folk*, 501. In what is essentially a restatement of double-consciousness, Du Bois writes: "From the double life every American Negro must live, as a Negro and as an American . . . from this must arise a painful self-consciousness, an almost morbid sense of personality and moral hesitancy which is fatal to self-confidence . . . this must produce a peculiar wrenching of the soul, a peculiar sense of doubt and bewilderment. Such a double life, with double

thoughts, double duties, and double social classes, must give rise to double words and double ideals, and tempt the mind to pretense or revolt, to hypocrisy or to radicalism." Du Bois, *The Souls of Black Folk*, 501–2.

77. Du Bois, *The Souls of Black Folk*, 502.
78. Du Bois, *The Souls of Black Folk*, 502.
79. Du Bois, *The Souls of Black Folk*, 503.
80. Du Bois, *The Souls of Black Folk*, 503.
81. Du Bois, *The Souls of Black Folk*, 503.
82. Du Bois, *The Souls of Black Folk*, 503.
83. Du Bois, *The Souls of Black Folk*, 503, italics mine.
84. Du Bois, *The Souls of Black Folk*, 503.
85. Du Bois, *The Souls of Black Folk*, 503.
86. Du Bois, *The Souls of Black Folk*, 503.
87. Du Bois, *The Souls of Black Folk*, 504.

88. Indeed, Du Bois's own close association with middle-class aspirations (present in *The Souls of Black Folk*) supports Cornel West's ascription of Du Bois's work to the "exceptionalist" position. See Cornel West, *Prophesy Deliverance! An Afro-Revolutionary Christianity* (Louisville: Westminster John Knox, 2002), 72–76.

89. Du Bois, *The Souls of Black Folk*, 504. I want to be clear, however, that I am not saying something about *all* Black men, since the "spiritual sons of the abolitionists" have a particular intellectual, classed, and regional lineage. Some Black men have found a way to navigate around this pitfall. Namely, they are those who have found the middle path between radical revolt and hypocritical compromise that even Du Bois struggles to find. Consider, for example, James Baldwin's comments on Black life in *The Fire Next Time*. Baldwin writes: "This past, the Negro's past, of rope, fire, torture, castration, infanticide, rape; death and humiliation; fear by day and night, fear as deep as the marrow of the bone; doubt that he was worthy of life, since everyone around him denied it . . . rage, hatred, and murder, hatred for white men so deep it often turned against him and his own, and made all love, all trust, all joy impossible—this past . . . contains, for all its horror, something very beautiful." And this beauty is found in the "great spiritual resilience" needed "not to hate the hater whose foot is on your neck." James Baldwin, "The Fire Next Time," in Baldwin, *James Baldwin: Collected Essays*, ed. Toni Morrison (New York: Library of America, 1998), 343.

90. Hurston, "The 'Pet Negro' System," 921.
91. Du Bois, *The Souls of Black Folk*, 359–60.
92. As Jon Cruz notes, "though the music Douglass introduced was largely alien to white abolitionists, it was understood as harboring an authenticity that was hidden and misunderstood. The songs of sorrow were to be unveiled, and behind that veil was the Black social subject. Shortly after the turn of the century, W. E. B. Du Bois asked the 'gentle readers' of his day—or those among a cultural and literary bourgeoisie who might still possess some of the humanistic pathos now ebbing after the dismantling of slavery, the collapse of Reconstruction, and the rise of social Darwinism—to return to the spirituals of Black Americans." As Cruz notes, slave narratives (such as those by Frederick Douglass) "helped prepare the ground for the sympathetic reception of Black music, beginning with the spirituals." It is fitting, then, that Du Bois also asks the reader to turn to the

spirituals while he subtly invokes tropes of the slave narrative genre. See Cruz, *Culture on the Margins*, 6, 24.

93. As Gooding-Williams notes, the spirituals present a politics that "express . . . a collective, slavery-based racial identity, the essence of which is the unifying, folk-constituting spirit of slave and neo-slave suffering." See Gooding-Williams, *In the Shadow*, 145. Similarly, Gilroy notes, "the Souls is the place where Black music is signaled in its special position of privileged signifier of Black authenticity." See Gilroy, *Black Atlantic*, 91. As such, harnessing the "strange meaning" of Blackness within the "sorrow songs" is what enables Du Bois to say with credibility to his white reader, "I who speak here am bone of the bone and flesh of the flesh of them that live within the Veil." See also Goyal, *Romance, Diaspora, and Black Atlantic*, 67, 75.

94. Cruz, *Culture on the Margins*, 44, 107.

95. "Du Bois appropriated the 'sorrow songs' in *The Souls of Black Folk* as conceptual tools," surmises Anderson, "with which to burrow into the Southern past and the 'soul of the Black slave.'" See Anderson, *Deep River*, 29.

96. See Goyal, *Romance, Diaspora, and Black Atlantic*, 75–76; and Wall, "Resounding *Souls*," 219–23.

97. See Wall, "Resounding *Souls*," 220–23; Zamir, *Dark Voices*, 178–81; Sundquist, *To Wake the Nations*, 465, 527; and Cornel West, "W. E. B. Du Bois: An Interpretation," in *Africana: The Encyclopedia of the African and African American Experience*, ed. Kwame Anthony Appiah and Henry Louis Gates (New York: Basic Books, 1999), 1967–68.

98. See Sundquist, *To Wake the Nations*, 459, 527. See also Goyal, *Romance, Diaspora, and Black Atlantic*, 76–77.

99. Wall, "Resounding *Souls*," 220.

100. See also Sundquist, *To Wake the Nations*, 462.

101. Du Bois, *The Souls of Black Folk*, 536, italics mine. How do these songs belong to Du Bois when he was not born and raised in the South? It is not simply tied to biology, or that he shares the same skin color of Black folk in the South. As Gooding-Williams argues, "racial authenticity" for Du Bois "is not about being faithful and true to a biological racial essence." Rather, "it is a matter of being faithful and true to a racially distinctive identity evident in 'the real Negro heart' and manifest in the sorrow songs." See Gooding-Williams, *In the Shadow*, 151.

102. Du Bois, *The Souls of Black Folk*, 538.

103. See Wall, "Resounding *Souls*," 210, 224–25; and Wall, *On Freedom*, 18. See also Anderson, *Deep River*, 34; Hartman, *Scenes of Subjection*, 48; Zamir, *Dark Voices*, 177; and Sundquist, *To Wake the Nations*, 475–77.

104. Du Bois, *The Souls of Black Folk*, 541.

105. Du Bois, *The Souls of Black Folk*, 544.

106. Du Bois, *The Souls of Black Folk*, 544. This vision's concurrence with the "goals of liberalism" lies in its striking similarity to the norms of justice according to John Rawls's ideal theory of political liberalism. For example, Rawls proposes a thought experiment (the "veil of ignorance") that pushes us to do what Du Bois is suggesting here: to judge society based upon the "soul," not on our "skins" or other social identity markers. For more on this topic, see John Rawls, *Political Liberalism* (New York: Columbia University Press, 2005), 22–29. For an extended discussion of Du Bois and liberalism, see Charles W. Mills, "Toward a

Black Radical Liberalism," in *Black Rights/White Wrongs: The Critique of Racial Liberalism* (New York: Oxford University Press, 2017), 201–16.

107. Sundquist wonders whether Du Bois changed the spelling of a spiritual's title, "My Lord, What a Morning," from "morning" to "mourning" in *The Souls of Black Folk* in order to stress the sorrow of "sorrow songs" even further. See Sundquist, *To Wake the Nations*, 1.

108. Du Bois, *The Souls of Black Folk*, 538.

109. As Goyal notes, in *The Souls of Black Folk*, Du Bois "chooses to represent Africa primarily as a sign of loss—of home, of language, faith, tradition, and heritage. It comes into view fleetingly as a shadow, a barely remembered melody, or a forgotten faith." See Goyal, *Romance, Diaspora, and Black Atlantic*, 78. See also Wall, "Resounding *Souls*," 218, 226.

110. Du Bois, *The Souls of Black Folk*, 541.

111. Du Bois, *The Souls of Black Folk*, 541. As Anderson notes, we can also observe this dismissal of secular music and privileging of the "sorrow songs" in Du Bois's rebuff of contemporary music like jazz. See Anderson, *Deep River*, 35, 48–49.

112. Du Bois, *The Souls of Black Folk*, 538–39. As Cruz notes, even with Douglass's intervention in interpreting Negro spirituals, Black song-making that was not explicitly Christian (such as the ring shout) was still often heard as "noise" by white abolitionists. See Cruz, *Culture on the Margins*, 50, 60, 165.

113. See Sundquist, *To Wake the Nations*, 468, 470, 530–31.

114. See West, "W. E. B. Du Bois: An Interpretation," 1967–68; Anderson, *Deep River*, 20, 49, 53–54; and Kahn, *Divine Discontent*, 56–62.

115. Winters, *Hope Drafted in Black*, 40.

116. See Anderson, *Deep River*, 16, 29–31; Gooding-Williams, *Shadow of Du Bois*, 153–54; and Zamir, *Dark Voices*, 175–77.

117. Winters, *Hope Drafted in Black*, 50.

118. Winters, *Hope Drafted in Black*, 50.

119. Winters, *Hope Drafted in Black*, 54.

120. Winters, *Hope Drafted in Black*, 54.

121. Hurston, "Spirituals and Neo-Spirituals," 869.

122. Hartman, *Scenes of Subjection*, 48.

123. Hurston, "Spirituals and Neo-Spirituals," 870. As Anderson notes, this move allows Hurston to "shift the spirituals' symbolic and emotional valence away from the solemn Du Boisian project of memorializing the inhumanities suffered during slavery." See Anderson, *Deep River*, 199.

124. "Quite apart from the question of authenticity," Wall concurs, "is the reflection on the meaning of the prayer ritual in southern Black churches" in Hurston's "Spirituals and Neo-Spirituals." See Wall, "Zora Neale Hurston's Essays: On Art and Such," *The Scholar and Feminist Online* 3, no. 2 (Winter 2005), http://sfonline.barnard.edu/hurston/wall_01.htm.

125. As Deborah G. Plant writes, by "not being consumed with 'Ole Massa,' Blacks become the center of their own lives." See Plant, *Every Tub Must Sit on Its Own Bottom*, 90. This is a common theme in Hurston scholarship by which to interpret Hurston's politics. See also Jordan, "Notes toward a Black Balancing of Love and Hatred," 287–88; and Washington, "Zora Neale Hurston's Work," 68–69.

126. Hurston, "Art and Such," 910.

127. Hurston, "Characteristics of Negro Expression," 845. Hurston's "Characteristics of Negro Expression" and "Spirituals and Neo-Spirituals" are both part of an excerpt that Hurston prepared for Nancy Cunard's *Negro: An Anthology*.

128. Hurston, "Spirituals and Neo-Spirituals," 870. For an extended discussion of Hurston's "jagged harmonies" and intra-racial dynamics, see Wall, *On Freedom*, 108–17.

129. Hurston, "Characteristics of Negro Expression," 845.

130. Wall, *On Freedom*, 110.

131. Anderson, *Deep River*, 10, 200.

132. Wall, *On Freedom*, 114.

133. Hurston, "Characteristics of Negro Expression," 845.

134. Hurston, "Characteristics of Negro Expression," 845.

135. "Hurston rejected the mainstream New Negro surrogation of the folk spirituals," writes Anderson, "as a harmful appropriation performed for the sake of middle-class uplift and a misguided narrative of cosmopolitan evolution." See Anderson, *Deep River*, 199.

136. Zora Neale Hurston, "The Sanctified Church," in Hurston, *Zora Neale Hurston*, 901–2.

137. Hurston, "The Sanctified Church," 903.

138. Hurston, "The Sanctified Church," 903.

139. Hurston, "The Sanctified Church," 903.

140. "Since music structured his text, Du Bois wished to insert himself into the familiar pattern of African American religion to move his readers to a consciousness of freedom's rhythm," James Arthur Manigault-Bryant writes, "not by shouting, but by creating a myth that invokes it." That is, the cosmology behind the "shouting" of the spirituals (i.e., root work) is supplanted by a myth that Du Bois creates. As "voodooism" is erased in Du Bois's neo-abolitionist interpretation of Black religion, "Africanness" is now reduced to song and rhythm. As such, *music*, not the "voodoism" in Du Bois's account of African American religion, becomes the "harbinger of African spirituality" that "inspired an attitude of judgement against oppressors and vengeful acts against their dominance" See Manigault-Bryant, "Reimagining the 'Pythian Madness' of *Souls*," 335–41.

141. Hurston, "The Sanctified Church," 903.

142. Hurston, "The Sanctified Church," 901.

143. Hurston, "The Sanctified Church," 901.

144. Hurston, "The Sanctified Church," 901–2. For an extended discussion of the use of the drum, dance, and shouting in root work or hoodoo, see Katrina Hazzard-Donald, "Hoodoo Religion and American Dance Traditions: Rethinking the Ring Shout," *Journal of Pan African Studies* 4, no. 6 (September 2011): 194–212, http://www.jpanafrican.org/docs/vol4no6/4.6–11HoodooReligion.pdf.

145. Hurston, "The Sanctified Church," 903.

146. Hurston, "The Sanctified Church," 904.

Scene 3

1. See Emily Epstein Landau, "The Notorious, Mixed-Race New Orleans Madam Who Turned Her Identity into a Brand," Zócalo Public Square, October 1,

2018, https://www.zocalopublicsquare.org/2018/10/01/notorious-mixed-race-new-orleans-madam-turned-identity-brand/ideas/essay/.

2. See Davis, *Blues Legacies and Black Feminism*, 12–15. See also Brooks and Martin, "'I Used to Be Your Sweet Mama,'" 208–12.

3. See Davis, *Blues Legacies and Black Feminism*, 33, 159; and Brooks and Martin, "'I Used to Be Your Sweet Mama,'" 203–6.

4. See Nicholas Jones, "Beyoncé's *Lemonade* Folklore: Feminine Reverberations of *Odú* and Afro-Cuban *Orisha* Iconography," in Brooks and Martin, *The Lemonade Reader*, 95.

5. See LaKisha Simmons, "Pull the Sorrow from between My Legs: *Lemonade* as Rumination on Reproduction and Loss," in Brooks and Martin, *The Lemonade Reader*, 44.

6. See Davis, *Blues Legacies and Black Feminism*, 121. See also Angela Davis, *Women, Race, and Class* (New York: Vintage Books, 1983), 11–12.

7. Deborah G. Plant, afterword to Zora Neale Hurston, *Barracoon: The Story of the Last "Black Cargo,"* ed. Deborah G. Plant (New York: Amistad, 2018), 132.

8. For an example, see Plant, *Every Tub Must Sit on Its Own Bottom*, 3–5.

Chapter 3

1. As the cultural anthropologist Carole McGranahan notes, refusal can take many forms, such as an "ethnographic object, historical possibility, methodological form." McGranahan, "Theorizing Refusal," 321. Indeed, throughout this book, Hurston's refusals take on various forms as well.

2. Cruz, *Culture on the Margins*, 111.

3. Jon Cruz writes: "It gave to white abolitionists a genuinely insightful as well as politically flattering knowledge: cultural interpretation sanctioned by an insider. And with this key, abolitionists could leap to the great presumption that they could apply their ethnosympathy with some shrewd intelligence. Having been given the inside scoop, they could grasp the inner meanings of the slave's song more accurately than could the slaves. The readers' advantage was their position outside the circle; they could be objective . . . Singing slaves had only a limited knowledge of what their practices really meant; they were not able to see and appreciate the very authenticity that characterized their own song making. As chattel, slaves did not have the luxury of repositioning themselves to look in from the outside. Bondage precluded that, and violence held them in check. Presumably, sympathetic outsiders and former slaves were able to make that separation." See Cruz, *Culture on the Margins*, 109–10.

4. With the rise of abolitionism came what Cruz calls "ethnosympathy," or "the new humanitarian pursuit of the inner world of distinctive and collectively classified subjects." This abolitionist development of "ethnosympathy" also encouraged the development of ethnography. Cruz writes: "Emerging from this interest in the discovery of meanings at the cultural margins were modern features of ethnographic interpretation. In the American context, the abolitionist juncture nurtured the orientation toward the study of what we today call 'subcultures.'" Moreover, Cruz notes that the development of the abolitionist interpretation of Negro spirituals (i.e. "sorrow songs") "helped to shape the rise of modern American ethnoscience." See Cruz, *Culture on the Margins*, 3, 12, 20.

5. For instance, Hurston writes in a letter: "It looks as if a Negro shall not be permitted to depart from a standard pattern. As I said, the nation is too sentimental about us to know us. It has a cut and dried formula for us which must not be violated. Either there is no interest in knowing us, or a determination not to destroy the pattern made and provided." See Hurston to Douglas Gilbert, February 4, 1943, in Kaplan, *A Life in Letters*, 477. Hurston also explored this theme in various parts of her work. For instance, see Hurston, "What the White Publishers Won't Print," in Hurston, *Zora Neale Hurston*, 950–56.

6. Simpson, *Mohawk Interruptus*, 105.

7. For examples, see Hurston, "What the White Publishers Won't Print," 951–52; Hurston, *Mules and Men*, 2 3; and Zora Neale Hurston, *Dust Tracks on a Road* (New York: Harper Perennial, 2006), 1–3. The study of her correspondence also demonstrates a sustained interest in the politics and philosophy of Indigenous peoples. For examples, see Hurston's letters in Kaplan, *A Life in Letters*, 97, 121, 326, 334–35, 342, 350, 372, 504, 508, 511, 521, 527, 555–56, 780, and 788–89.

8. Much of the comparative work on Hurston and Indigenous scholarship focuses on Ella Cara Deloria, an Indigenous anthropologist during Hurston's lifetime. In addition to studying under Franz Boas, both anthropologists held an insider-outsider status in their field of research. And both anthropologists often blurred the boundaries of the literary and the scientific as a response, in part, to the racist constraints in the discipline of anthropology. However, it does not appear that Deloria and Hurston ever met, nor is there a trail of correspondence (at least that we know of yet). Moreover, as Maria Eugenia Cotera has criticized, much of the comparative work on these two figures has ignored the specificity of Indigenous contexts. See Maria Eugenia Cotera, *Native Speakers: Ella Deloria, Zora Neale Hurston, Jovita Gonzalez, and the Poetics of Culture* (Austin: University of Texas Press, 2008), 8–10. I maintain that scholarship is right to connect Hurston to Indigenous politics and philosophy. However, I think the connection to Ella Deloria, while interesting, is not the primary connection to be drawn.

9. Hurston to Alain Locke, June 14, 1928, in Kaplan, *A Life in Letters*, 121.

10. Hurston, "How It Feels to Be Colored Me," 827.

11. Ann duCille, "Looking for Zora," *New York Times*, January 5, 2003, https://www.nytimes.com/2003/01/05/books/looking-for-zora.html.

12. Kaplan, *A Life in Letters*, 445.

13. See Mitchell, "Zora's Politics," especially the section "Colonial Violence,"

14. Hurston, "How It Feels to Be Colored Me," 827.

15. For instance, Black feminists such as Alice Walker, June Jordan, Gay Wilentz, and Mary Helen Washington have long noted how Hurston's fierce pride in Black culture is also a refusal of the values of white, mainstream culture. Alice Walker notes this in the title of her essay, "On Refusing to be Humbled by Second Place in a Contest You Did Not Design: A Tradition by Now," 1. See also Jordan, "Notes toward a Black Balancing of Love and Hatred," 286–87; Wilentz, "Defeating the False God," 286–89; and Washington, "Zora Neale Hurston's Work," 68–69.

16. For this section's title, see Hurston to Hamilton Holt, February 11, 1943, in Kaplan, *A Life in Letters*, 478.

17. Simpson, *Mohawk Interruptus*, 177.

18. See Simpson, *Mohawk Interruptus*, 177. Simpson writes: "The story that settler-colonial nation-states tend to tell about themselves is that they are new, they are beneficent; they have successfully 'settled' all issues prior to their beginning."

19. See Kristie Dotson, "On the Way to Decolonization in a Settler Colony: Re-Introducing Black Feminist Identity Politics," *AlterNative: An International Journal of Indigenous Peoples* 14, no. 3 (July 2018): 4–6, https://journals.sagepub .com/doi/abs/10.1177/1177180118783301.

20. See Simpson, *Mohawk Interruptus*, 11–12. See also Audra Simpson, "On Ethnographic Refusal: Indigeneity, 'Voice,' and Colonial Citizenship," *Junctures* 9 (2007): 68–70.

21. Simpson, *Mohawk Interruptus*, 99.

22. Simpson, *Mohawk Interruptus*, 99.

23. Simpson, *Mohawk Interruptus*, 99.

24. Simpson, "On Ethnographic Refusal," 74.

25. Audra Simpson, "Consent's Revenge," *Cultural Anthropology* 31, no. 3 (2016): 328.

26. Simpson, *Mohawk Interruptus*, 177.

27. Simpson, *Mohawk Interruptus*, 7–8.

28. Simpson, *Mohawk Interruptus*, 10.

29. Simpson, *Mohawk Interruptus*, 13–18.

30. Simpson, *Mohawk Interruptus*, 11.

31. Simpson, *Mohawk Interruptus*, 11.

32. Simpson, *Mohawk Interruptus*, 16.

33. Simpson, *Mohawk Interruptus*, 25.

34. See Simpson, *Mohawk Interruptus*, 22. Simpson writes: "Iroquois peoples *remind* nation-states such as the United States (and Canada) that they possess this very history, and within that history and seized space, they possess a *precarious* assumption that their boundaries are permanent, uncontestable, and entrenched. They possess a precarious assumption about their own (just) origins. And by extension, they possess a precarious assumption about themselves."

35. Simpson, *Mohawk Interruptus*, 11.

36. Simpson, *Mohawk Interruptus*, 1.

37. Simpson, *Mohawk Interruptus*, 105.

38. Simpson, *Mohawk Interruptus*, 105.

39. Simpson, "On Ethnographic Refusal," 78.

40. Simpson, "On Ethnographic Refusal," 78.

41. Simpson, *Mohawk Interruptus*, 105.

42. Simpson, *Mohawk Interruptus*, 105.

43. Simpson, *Mohawk Interruptus*, 105.

44. As Kaplan notes, Hurston spent much of her career "more concerned with resisting *pressure* to reveal her inner self, a pressure that came from whites eager to make her into an exotic sensation as well as from Blacks anxious to make her defend her iconoclastic views." See Kaplan, *A Life in Letters*, 430.

45. As Deborah Plant observes, "Hurston's postures of naiveté and ambivalence, her provocative and questionable politics, and her art of dissemblance and silence resulted in a perception of the author as controversial, compromised,

and nonserious." See Plant, *Every Tub Must Sit on Its Own Bottom*, 2. See also Kaplan, *A Life in Letters*, 22–23. Kaplan places Hurston's dissembling in the African American tradition of "double voice and masking, devices central to African American literature since its inception." See also duCille, "Looking for Zora"; and Meisenhelder, *Hitting a Straight Lick*, 2–5, 10–13.

46. For instance, Walker notes that much of Hurston's autobiography, *Dust Tracks on a Road*, "rings false." However, she turns Hurston's dissemblance into a "cautionary tale": "one begins to hear the voice of someone whose life required the assistance of too many transitory 'friends.'" That is, Walker locates one source of Hurston's dissemblance in dependency, "a sign of her powerlessness, her inability to pay back her debts with anything but words." See Walker, "Zora Neale Hurston: A Cautionary Tale and a Partisan View," 91. See also Bordelon, "Zora Neale Hurston: A Biographical Essay," 3.

Other scholars, such as Wall, Kaplan, and Meisenhelder, have also pointed out that when Hurston *did* speak her mind, editors often imposed restrictions that deeply shaped the Hurston we get in print. *Dust Tracks on a Road*, for example, was published without some of the more incisive critiques of racism and imperialism originally included in her chapter "Looking Things Over." See Wall, "Zora Neale Hurston: Changing Her Own Words," 95; Kaplan, *A Life in Letters*, 436–37; Meisenhelder, *Hitting a Straight Lick*, 172–74; and Meisenhelder, "Gender, Race, and Class in Zora Neale Hurston's Politics."

47. As Hurston remarks of her childhood, what she "really loved to hear was the menfolks holding a 'lying' session. That is, straining against each other in telling folk tales." See Hurston, *Dust Tracks on a Road*, 48. Several scholars have thematized how these "lies" become part of Hurston's dissembling strategy. See Cynthia Ward, "Truth, Lies, Mules and Men: Through the 'Spy-Glass of Anthropology' and What Zora Saw There," *Western Journal of Black Studies* 36, no. 4 (2012): 308–11; Keith Walters, "'He Can Read My Writing but He Sho' Can't Read My Mind': Zora Neale Hurston's Revenge in *Mules and Men*," *Journal of American Folklore* (1999): 352; and Meisenhelder, *Hitting a Straight Lick*, 4–5. In addition, some have argued that Hurston's blending of fiction and the "lies" of African American folklore, along with inserting her own self into some of the reports, was a response to problematic "objectivist" mandates of anthropology. See D. A. Boxwell, "'Sis Cat' as Ethnographer: Self-Presentation and Self-Inscription in Zora Neale Hurston's 'Mules and Men,'" *African American Review* 26, no. 4 (1992): 614–15; Walters, "Can't Read My Mind," 348–49; bell hooks, *Yearning: Race, Gender, and Cultural Politics* (Boston: South End, 1999), 137–39; and Cotera, *Native Speakers*, 73–75.

48. See Elaine J. Lawless, "What Zora Knew: A Crossroads, a Bargain with the Devil, and a Late Witness," *Journal of American Folklore* 126, no. 500 (2013): 167; Ward, "Truth, Lies, Mules and Men," 309–11; and Meisenhelder, *Hitting a Straight Lick*, 14–19.

49. Hurston, *Mules and Men*, 2–3.

50. See Kaplan, *A Life in Letters*, 21–22; Plant, *Every Tub Must Sit on Its Own Bottom*, 89–90; and Meisenhelder, *Hitting a Straight Lick*, 5.

51. For examples, see Plant, *Every Tub Must Sit on Its Own Bottom*, 4, 48. See also Lynda Marion Hill, *Social Rituals and the Verbal Art of Zora Neale Hurston* (Washington, DC: Howard University Press, 1996), xvii–xviii, 182–84.

52. Hurston, *Mules and Men*, 3.

53. Hurston, *Mules and Men*, 2.

54. Hurston, *Mules and Men*, 3.

55. Hurston, *Mules and Men*, 3.

56. See Medina, *The Epistemology of Resistance*, 49–51.

57. See Cotera, *Native Speakers*, 81–82, 88. See also hooks, *Yearning*, 137, 140.

58. Hurston, *Dust Tracks on a Road*, 143. Cotera also ponders why Hurston chose to emphasize *this* experience in the research section of her autobiography. It is "extraordinary," Cotera remarks, "that in her autobiography—a text full of demurrals, obfuscations, and outright mistruths regarding her personal history— she chose to *foreground* this parable of ethnographic failure." See Cotera, *Native Speakers*, 82.

59. As Hurston remarks in a letter, "I did not want to write [*Dust Tracks on a Road*] at all, because it is too hard to reveal one's inner self, and still there is no use in writing that kind of book unless you do." See Hurston to Hamilton Holt, February 11, 1943, in Kaplan, *A Life in Letters*, 478. Perhaps this is why, as Maya Angelou notes, "there is, despite its success in certain quarters, a strange distance in the book. Certainly the language is true and the dialogue authentic, but the author stands between the content and the reader. It is difficult, if not impossible, to find and touch the real Zora Neale Hurston." See Maya Angelou, foreword to Zora Neale Hurston, *Dust Tracks on a Road* (New York: Harper Perennial Modern Classics, 1995), xi–xii.

60. See Deborah Jenson, *Beyond the Slave Narrative: Politics, Sex, and Manuscripts of the Haitian Revolution* (Liverpool: Liverpool University Press, 2011), 1–4; and Nicole N. Aljoe, "Introduction: Remapping the Early American Slave Narrative," in *Journeys of the Slave Narrative in the Early Americas*, ed. Nicole N. Aljoe and Ian Finseth (Charlottesville: University of Virginia Press, 2014), 3–7. The genre of slave narratives is more like an umbrella category because several scholars have argued that we need to expand what gets included in this category to include both narratives outside of the United States and other forms of enslaved testimony at that time (such as those included in travelers' notebooks or narratives of spiritual conversion).

61. Plant, afterword to *Barracoon*, 129. See also Hill, *Social Rituals*, 69.

62. See Zora Neale Hurston, *Barracoon: The Story of the Last "Black Cargo,"* ed. Deborah G. Plant (New York: Amistad, 2018), 61. Hurston writes: "But we wait and wait, we heard de guns shootee sometime but nobody don't come to tell us we free. So we think maybe dey fight 'bout something else."

63. Plant, afterword to *Barracoon*, 129.

64. Hurston, *Barracoon*, 61.

65. Plant, afterword to *Barracoon*, 130.

66. See Hurston to Charlotte Osgood Mason, September 25, 1931, in Kaplan, *A Life in Letters*, 228.

67. See Hurston, *Barracoon*, 3. Plant asserts in an interview with Lynn Neary: "We're talking about a language that he had to fashion for himself in order to negotiate this new terrain he found himself in. . . . Embedded in his language is everything of his history. To deny him his language is to deny his history, to deny his experience—which ultimately is to deny him, period. To deny what happened to him." See Lynn Neary, "In Zora Neale Hurston's 'Barracoon,' Language Is the

Key to Understanding," last modified May 8, 2018, *NPR*, https://www.npr.org /2018/05/08/609126378/in-zora-neale-hurstons-barracoon-language-is-the-key -to-understanding.

68. In addition, Hill and Plant suggest that Hurston's plagiarism concerning this text may have also been a form of refusal. See Plant, afterword to *Barracoon*, 123–24; and Hill, *Social Rituals*, 64.

69. Hurston, *Barracoon*, 3.

70. Hurston, *Barracoon*, 3.

71. Morrison, "The Site of Memory," 237–38. Morrison draws this metaphor from a quote in Hurston's *Dust Tracks on a Road*: "Like the dead-seeming, cold rocks, I have memories within that came out of the material that went to make me." See Hurston, *Dust Tracks on a Road*, 1. Morrison writes: "These 'memories within' are the subsoil of my work."

72. Morrison, "The Site of Memory," 39.

73. Morrison, "The Site of Memory," 236.

74. Morrison, "The Site of Memory," 238.

75. Robinson, *This Ain't Chicago*, 21, 32–33.

76. Hurston, *Barracoon*, 25, 37, 51, 83, 93. Hurston writes: "I had spent two months with Kossula, who is called Cudjo, trying to find the answers to my questions. Some days we ate great quantities of clingstone peaches and talked. Sometimes we ate watermelon and talked. Once it was a huge mess of steamed crabs. Sometimes we just ate. Sometimes we just talked."

77. Hurston, *Barracoon*, 40–41.

78. Alice Walker, foreword to *Barracoon*, xii.

79. See Cotera, *Native Speakers*, 95. Manufacturing a shared identity with her respondents was also part of Hurston's research method. Cotera analyzes this as a response to her "outsider" status as an ethnographer, and she calls this response "ethnographic research as aesthetic exchange."

80. Walker, foreword to *Barracoon*, x–xi.

81. See Hurston, *Barracoon*, 37, 40–41.

82. Hurston, *Barracoon*, 16.

83. Hurston, *Barracoon*, 94.

84. Hurston, "The Sanctified Church," 901.

85. See Hurston, *Dust Tracks on a Road*, 254–56. See also Meisenhelder, *Hitting a Straight Lick*, 169–70; and Mitchell, "Zora's Politics" (especially the section "Political Theology").

86. Walker, foreword to *Barracoon*, x.

87. Hurston, *Dust Tracks on a Road*, 165.

88. Hurston, *Barracoon*, 18–19.

89. Hurston, *Barracoon*, 41. Hurston draws a connection between "juju" in West Africa and spirit work practices in the United States. She writes: "Veaudeau is the European term for African magic practices and beliefs, but it is unknown to the American Negro. His own name for his practices is hoodoo, both terms being related to the West African term *juju*." See Hurston, "Hoodoo in America," 317.

90. Hurston, *Barracoon*, 62–63.

91. Hurston, *Barracoon*, 20.

92. Hurston, *Barracoon*, 20–21.

93. Hurston, *Barracoon*, 51, 57.

94. Hurston, *Barracoon*, 18–19.

95. Plant, afterword to *Barracoon*, 132–33. For examples, see Hurston, *Barracoon*, 18–19, 49, 87.

96. See Hurston, *Barracoon*, 24, 26, 69.

97. Hurston, *Barracoon*, 57.

98. Hurston, *Barracoon*, 57.

99. Hurston, *Barracoon*, 35, 45.

100. Hurston, *Barracoon*, 73–74.

101. Hurston, *Barracoon*, 62.

102. Hurston, *Barracoon*, 69. For more examples, see Hurston, *Barracoon*, 73–74.

103. Hurston, *Barracoon*, 69.

104. Toni Morrison, *A Mercy* (New York: First Vintage International, 2009), 194.

105. Simpson, *Mohawk Interruptus*, 19.

106. Simpson, *Mohawk Interruptus*, 66.

107. Plant, afterword to *Barracoon*, 135.

108. Hurston, *Barracoon*, 6.

109. Hurston, *Barracoon*, 68. See also Sylvanie A. Diouf's discussion of the establishment of Africatown in *Dreams of Africa in Alabama: The Slave Ship "Clotilda" and the Story of the Last Africans Brought to America* (New York: Oxford University Press, 2007), 72–90.

110. Hurston, *Barracoon*, 72.

111. Hurston, *Barracoon*, 74.

112. Hurston, *Barracoon*, 74.

113. Hurston, *Barracoon*, 74.

114. Simpson, *Mohawk Interruptus*, 109.

115. Simpson, "On Ethnographic Refusal," 78.

116. Simpson, "On Ethnographic Refusal," 78.

117. Hurston, *Barracoon*, 73.

118. Hurston, *Barracoon*, 16.

119. Hurston, *Barracoon*, 94.

120. Hurston, *Barracoon*, 98, italics mine.

121. Hurston, *Barracoon*, 57.

122. See Plant, afterword to *Barracoon*, 133. Plant discusses this struggle in terms of the enslaved "grappling for a sense of sovereignty over their own bodies ever since slavery was institutionalized."

123. Hurston, *Dust Tracks on a Road*, 254.

124. Hurston, *Dust Tracks on a Road*, 254. See also Mitchell, "Zora's Politics" (esp. the section titled "Colonial Violence").

125. Hurston, *Dust Tracks on a Road*, 254. Additionally, Hurston writes: "While I have a handkerchief over my eyes crying over the landing of the first slaves in 1619, I might miss something swell that is going on in 1942. Furthermore, if somebody were to consider my grandmother's ungranted wishes, and give *me* what *she* wanted, I would be too put out for words." See Hurston, *Dust Tracks on a Road*, 230.

126. Hurston, *Dust Tracks on a Road*, 254.

127. Hurston, *Dust Tracks on a Road*, 254.

128. See Kaplan, *A Life in Letters*, 436–37. As Kaplan notes, *Dust Tracks on a Road* was written for a primarily white audience and was wildly successful as such.

129. Hurston, *Dust Tracks on a Road*, 254.

130. Hurston, *Dust Tracks on a Road*, 254. Similarly, in "My People! My People!" Hurston also makes a disavowal of slavery in the context of rape. She writes: "I neither claim Jefferson as my grandpa nor exclaim 'Just look how that white man took advantage of my grandma!' It does not matter in the first place, and then in the next place, I do not know how it came about. Since nobody ever told me, I give my ancestress the benefit of the doubt. She probably ran away from him just as fast as she could. But if that white man could run faster than my grandma, that was no fault of hers. Anyway, you must remember, he didn't have a thing to do but keep on running forward. She, being pursued, had to look back over her shoulder every now and then to see how she was doing. And you know your ownself, how looking backwards slows people up." See Hurston, *Dust Tracks on a Road*, 191.

131. Hurston, *Dust Tracks on a Road*, 263. See also Plant, *Every Tub Must Sit on Its Own Bottom*, 47. As Plant notes, "the card game is a recurring leitmotif in Hurston's work, particularly as it symbolizes unfair play in American sociopolitical life."

132. Hurston, *Dust Tracks on a Road*, 262. As Meisenhelder notes, by introducing this "broadened definition" of slavery, "what appears to be vindication of [the slaver's grandson's] personal guilt" earlier in the chapter "is, in fact, a much broader political indictment of his world." Moreover, "without Hurston's broadened definition of slavery [criticism of how America has moved the slave quarters farther away from the house], her remaining depiction of American slavery as a finished chapter looks naïve and even reactionary." See Meisenhelder, *Hitting a Straight Lick*, 172–74.

133. Hurston admits this in a letter to Hamilton Holt. See Hurston to Hamilton Holt, February 11, 1943, in Kaplan, *A Life in Letters*, 478. As Lawless surmises, even the title of Hurston's book may suggest that she was trying to "hoodoo" (by a dust tracks hoodoo ritual) her audience away while giving them very little. Lawless writes: "Her autobiography might well be her way of saying 'I'll give you a little but not a lot.'" See Lawless, "What Zora Knew," 166–67.

134. See Angelou, foreword to *Dust Tracks on a Road*, xii; Bordelon, "Zora Neale Hurston: A Biographical Essay," 3–9; Kaplan, *A Life in Letters*, 36–37, 436–37; and Meisenhelder, *Hitting a Straight Lick*, 144.

135. Plant, afterword to *Barracoon*, 124.

136. See Hurston, *Dust Tracks on a Road*, 192, 237.

137. For examples, see Hurston, *Dust Tracks on a Road*, 177–81, 184–85, 235–40.

138. Hurston, *Dust Tracks on a Road*, 179.

139. See Hurston, *Dust Tracks on a Road*, 184–85.

140. Hurston, *Dust Tracks on a Road*, 188.

141. Hurston, *Dust Tracks on a Road*, 190.

142. Hurston, *Dust Tracks on a Road*, 190.

143. Hurston, *Dust Tracks on a Road*, 192. Hurston often drummed up intraracial conflicts as a way to dispel the notions of racial essentialism. For these

reasons, Wall challenges the reading that Hurston's views on race were essential-ist. Referring to Hurston's 1934 essay "Characteristics of Negro Expression," Wall writes that even when, "like her peers, Hurston refers to *the* Negro, which encourages readings of her work as essentialist," in the essay itself "intraracial differences are foregrounded in terms of class and gender. Geography is always a factor in Hurston's analysis as well; some of her observations are clearly specific to rural Black southerners." See Wall, *On Freedom*, 110.

144. As Plant writes, Hurston's ventures to "collect, preserve, and celebrate" Black cultural traditions were also a "refutat[ion]" of "the tenets of biological determinism that were at the heart of the Great Race theory." See Plant, after-word to *Barracoon*, 137.

145. See Simpson, *Mohawk Interruptus*, 19.

146. Hurston, *Dust Tracks on a Road*, 1. Hurston was also studying the folk-lore of the Seminoles in Florida while revising *Dust Tracks on a Road*. See also Meisenhelder, *Hitting a Straight Lick*, 146–47.

147. Hurston, *Dust Tracks on a Road*, 2.

148. Hurston, *Dust Tracks on a Road*, 237.

149. Simpson, *Mohawk Interruptus*, 78.

150. "When God was assigning skin color to all the different peoples of the earth, everyone crowded around the throne. With all the commotion, God said "Get back! Get back." But Blacks misheard Him, thinking he said 'Git Black!' " Hurston writes, "so they got Black and just kept the thing agoing." See Hurston, *Dust Tracks on a Road*, 244–45.

151. Hurston, *Dust Tracks on a Road*, 244.

152. See Walters, "Can't Read My Mind," 360–63. As Walters notes, Hurston could camouflage criticism of her white readers through folktales that they would find inoffensive.

153. Du Bois, *The Souls of Black Folk*, 363.

154. Wall, *On Freedom*, 19.

155. For an extended recent discussion of this, see Wall, *On Freedom*, 16–20.

156. Du Bois, *The Souls of Black Folk*, 364.

157. Du Bois, *The Souls of Black Folk*, 364.

158. Du Bois, *The Souls of Black Folk*, 364.

159. For a discussion of this experience, see, for example, James Baldwin, "The American Dream and the American Negro," in Baldwin, *James Baldwin: Col-lected Essays*, 714–15.

160. Du Bois, *The Souls of Black Folk*, 364.

161. Du Bois, *The Souls of Black Folk*, 364.

162. Du Bois, *The Souls of Black Folk*, 364.

163. While Du Bois certainly recognizes that there are positive affects in Afri-can American life, he emphasizes sorrow via his privileging of "sorrow songs" as the exemplar of African American expression.

164. See Simpson, *Mohawk Interruptus*, 106.

165. As Joseph R. Winters writes: "The basic survival of communities and selves relies on the protection of their rights and freedoms, the ability to partici-pate in society's central institutions and practices, and the extension of respect and affirmation—especially to groups that have been systematically injured and disrespected—from other members of the broader community. At the same time,

there is an underside to this desire for recognition. Recognition comes with a price. In order to be recognized and affirmed by those in power, one has to accept and consent to the terms and conditions of power (even as those terms and conditions might change and shift)." See Winters, *Hope Drafted in Black*, 38–39.

166. Simpson, "On Ethnographic Refusal," 74.

167. Simpson, "On Ethnographic Refusal," 74.

168. Simpson, *Mohawk Interruptus*, 107.

169. As Walker notes, Hurston "came to 'delight' in the chaos she sometimes left behind." See Walker, "On Refusing to Be Humbled," in Walker, *I Love Myself*, 1. And, as Kaplan observes, "[Hurston] might gain recognition only to turn around and attack its very grounds. Or she'd work her way into a group, only to blast it as pretentious." See Kaplan, *A Life in Letters*, 24.

170. Hurston, *Mules and Men*, 3.

171. As Kaplan notes, a similar dynamic occurs in Hurston's *Their Eyes Were Watching God*. Janie's "song" exists "independent of either the misrecognitions or recognitions of its possible listeners." See Kaplan, *The Erotics of Talk*, 105–22.

172. Kaplan, *A Life in Letters*, 14, 51.

173. Du Bois, *The Souls of Black Folk*, 501–2; Hurston, "How It Feels to Be Colored Me," 829.

174. Hurston, "How It Feels to Be Colored Me," 829.

175. Hurston, "Art and Such," 908.

176. Hurston, "How It Feels to Be Colored Me," 826. As Wall notes, Hurston begins the essay with a joke to "deflat[e] the artifice that then attended most discourse on race . . . The joke is aimed both at those whites who would assume that Blackness is a problem requiring a solution, or at least an explanation, and at those Blacks, almost certainly including race-conscious New Negroes, who want it understood that they are *not merely* Black." See Wall, "Zora Neale Hurston's Essays."

177. Hurston, "How It Feels to Be Colored Me," 827.

178. Hurston, "How It Feels to Be Colored Me," 829.

179. See Hurston, *Dust Tracks on a Road*, 190–91. Hurston writes in "My People, My People" in *Dust Tracks on a Road*: "I learned that skins were no measure of what was inside people." This is because Hurston "sensed early, that the Negro race was not one band of heavenly love. There was stress and strain inside as well as out. Being Black was not enough. It took more than a community of skin color to make your love come down on you."

180. Hurston, "How It Feels to Be Colored Me," 827.

181. Hurston, "How It Feels to Be Colored Me," 826.

182. Hurston, "How It Feels to Be Colored Me," 827.

183. Du Bois, *The Souls of Black Folk*, 538.

184. As Wall notes, "liberal-leaning white Americans" were a major part of the readership of *The World Tomorrow*, where the essay was published. See Wall, "Zora Neale Hurston's Essays."

185. Hurston, "How It Feels to Be Colored Me," 826.

186. Hurston, *Dust Tracks on a Road*, 34.

187. Hurston, *Dust Tracks on a Road*, 34.

188. Hurston, *Dust Tracks on a Road*, 54.

189. Hurston, *Dust Tracks on a Road*, 54.

190. Hurston, "How It Feels to Be Colored Me," 827.
191. Hurston, "How It Feels to Be Colored Me," 827.
192. Hurston, "How It Feels to Be Colored Me," 827.
193. Walker, foreword to *Barracoon*, x.
194. Walker, foreword to *Barracoon*, xii.
195. Hurston, "How It Feels to Be Colored Me," 827.
196. Hurston, "How It Feels to Be Colored Me," 828.
197. Hurston, "How It Feels to Be Colored Me," 828.
198. Hurston, "How It Feels to Be Colored Me," 828.
199. For examples, see Hurston, *Barracoon*, 54–56, 67, and 73–74.
200. Hurston, "How It Feels to Be Colored Me," 828.
201. Hurston, "How It Feels to Be Colored Me," 828–29.
202. Hurston, "How It Feels to Be Colored Me," 829.
203. Hurston, "How It Feels to Be Colored Me," 829.
204. Kaplan, *A Life in Letters*, 445.
205. Kaplan, *A Life in Letters*, 445.
206. McGranahan, "Theorizing Refusal," 321.

Scene 4

1. See Peñate, "Beyoncé's Diaspora Heritage and Ancestry in *Lemonade*," 120–21; Highsmith, "Beyoncé Reborn," 139–40; L. Michael Gipson, "Interlude E: From Destiny's Child to Coachella," 152; and Brooks, "The Lady Sings Her Legacy," 162–63. See also Kevin Allred, "Back by Popular Demand: Beyoncé Harnesses the Power of Conjuring in 'Formation,'" bitchmedia, June 11, 2019, https://www.bitchmedia.org/article/bcyonce-conjuring-ghosts-formation-excerpt.
2. See Davis, *Blues Legacies and Black Feminism*, 101, 113.
3. Melanie Jones defines "slay" as "an outer display of sartorial grace and an inner courage for Black women who leverage their power (i.e., resources, talents, gifts, wealth, etc.) to command the moment." See Melanie Jones, "The *Slay* Factor: Beyoncé Unleashing the Black Feminine Divine in a Blaze of Glory," in Brooks and Martin, *The Lemonade Reader*, 99.
4. As Jones observes, "slay is a way of being in the world that encourages Black women to command the moment and claim their power by self-possession." See Jones, "The *Slay* Factor," 106.
5. Lorde, "Uses of the Erotic," 54.
6. Lorde, "Uses of the Erotic," 58.
7. Lorde, "Uses of the Erotic," 57.
8. See Brooks and Martin, "'I Used to Be Your Sweet Mama,'" 209–10; and Tanisha Ford, "Beysthetics: 'Formation' and the Politics of Style," in Brooks and Martin, *The Lemonade Reader*, 198.
9. Part of the Black southern aesthetic that Beyoncé is developing involves the blending of different spiritual traditions across the African diaspora. See Highsmith, "Beyoncé Reborn," 133, 139–40. For more on the Maman Brigette connection, see Janelle Hobson, "Getting to the Roots of 'Becky with the Good Hair' in Beyoncé's *Lemonade*," in Brooks and Martin, *The Lemonade Reader*, 38.
10. Highsmith, "Beyoncé Reborn," 142.
11. Hurston, "High John de Conquer," 924.
12. Hurston, "High John de Conquer," 924.

Chapter 4

1. Du Bois, *The Souls of Black Folk*, 494. I focus on the "frenzy" or ring shout here, but for more on the preacher and the spirituals in Hurston's essay, see Hurston, "The Sanctified Church," 901–2.

2. In his discussion of his experience of a southern religious revival, Du Bois notes that he witnessed what appeared to be "a pythian madness, a demoniac possession that lent terrible reality to song and word." This "possession" was accompanied by the "shouting" of a "gaunt-cheeked brown woman" who "suddenly leaped straight into the air and shrieked like a lost soul, while round about came wail and groan and outcry, and a scene of human passion such as I had never conceived before." See Du Bois, *The Souls of Black Folk*, 494.

3. Du Bois, *The Souls of Black Folk*, 493; and Hurston, "The Sanctified Church," 902.

4. Du Bois, *The Souls of Black Folk*, 498; and Hurston, "The Sanctified Church," 901.

5. Du Bois, *The Souls of Black Folk*, 499.

6. Hurston, "The Sanctified Church," 901.

7. Du Bois, *The Souls of Black Folk*, 495.

8. Hurston, "The Sanctified Church," 901.

9. Hurston, "The Sanctified Church," 903–4.

10. Hurston, "The Sanctified Church," 904. See also Du Bois, *The Souls of Black Folk*, 493–95. As Paul Allen Anderson notes, Du Bois had "little sympathy" for the Sanctified Church. See Anderson, *Deep River*, 49, 53. This is because, as Cornel West observes, "Du Bois, owing to his Puritan New England origins and Enlightenment values, found it difficult to not view common Black folk as some degraded 'other' or 'alien' no matter how hard he resisted." See West, "W. E. B. Du Bois: An Interpretation," 1968.

11. For an extended example and development of this point, see Edwards, *Charisma and the Fictions of Black Leadership*, 6–12.

12. Hurston, "The Sanctified Church," 901.

13. Hurston, "The Sanctified Church," 902. Regarding the "actual rendition in the congregations who make the [spirituals]," Hurston writes: "So the congregation is restored to its primitive altars under the new name of Christ. Then there is the expression known as 'shouting' which is nothing more than a continuation of the African 'Possession' by the gods . . . This is still prevalent in most Negro protestant churches and is universal in the Sanctified churches." See Hurston, "The Sanctified Church," 902.

14. Hurston, "The Sanctified Church," 903.

15. See the section titled "The Development of Neo-Abolitionism."

16. As Eddie Glaude writes: "Perhaps the problem, at least for those of us who write about African Americans, rests with a view that, whatever the particular situation, always presents agency as politically liberatory. That is to say, we invoke the trope of agency, as Walter Johnson has so brilliantly argued, as a way of defending the humanity of a subject people—as a way of holding off the claim that they were mere pawns in the action of men." See Glaude, *In a Shade of Blue*, 97. Glaude especially notes this dynamic in scholarly discussions of Black Christianity, such as Ira Berlin's *Generations of Captivity: A History of African-American Slaves*. See Glaude, *In a Shade of Blue*, 90–92, 99–105. For more

contemporary examples of this trend in scholarship, see Jason Young, *Rituals of Resistance: African Atlantic Religion in Kongo and the Lowcountry South in the Era of Slavery* (Baton Rouge: Louisiana State University Press, 2007), 1–24; and Jasmine Syedullah, "Beyond the Battlefields of Institutions: Everyday Abolitionism from the Antebellum South," in *Let Spirit Speak! Cultural Journeys through the African Diaspora*, ed. Vanessa Valdés (Albany: State University of New York Press, 2012), 119–25.

17. One notable example of this kind of argument is found in Albert Raboteau's famous *Slave Religion: The "Invisible Institution" in the Antebellum South* (New York: Oxford University Press, 2004). Several scholars have also tried to show that even the acceptance of Christianity by the enslaved could be used to criticize their slave masters. See Angela Davis, "Lectures on Liberation," in *Narrative of the Life of Frederick Douglass, An American Slave*, ed. Angela Davis (San Francisco: Open Media Series, 2010), 67–73. See also Cruz, *Culture on the Margins*, 73, 90–92.

18. For example, see Young, *Rituals of Resistance*, 12. Against the specter of pro-slavery arguments, Young "argue[s] further that slave cultural resistance was not only defensive in nature, as it helped slaves shield themselves from some of the horrid conditions of enslavement, but also offensive, enabling them to attack directly the ideological underpinnings of slavery. That is, slave cultural practice may be read as something of a political tract denouncing the varied justifications that members of the master class expounded in support of slave labor."

19. Though this concern about the limitations of resistance has reached across disciplines, I take up this concern within strains of cultural anthropology and pragmatist philosophy. Indeed, these disciplines' shared orientation toward lived experience makes them especially apt to launch this kind of concern. See also Denise James, "The Burden of Integration," *Symposium on Gender, Race, and Philosophy* 9, no. 2 (Fall 2013): 1–2, http://web.mit.edu/sgrp/2013/no2/James0913.pdf; and Patricia Hill Collins, "Social Inequality, Power, and Politics: Intersectionality and American Pragmatism in Dialogue," *Journal of Speculative Philosophy* 26, no. 2 (2012): 443–49, http://eds.a.ebscohost.com.ezproxy.memphis.edu/eds/pdfviewer/pdfviewer?vid=3&sid=a31c1bd1-28e4-4f64-90fc-3bd693568d49%40sdc-v-sessmgr01.

20. Sherry B. Ortner, "Resistance and the Problem of Ethnographic Refusal," *Comparative Studies in Society and History* 37, no. 1 (1995), 190.

21. Ortner, "Resistance and the Problem of Ethnographic Refusal," 190.

22. Ortner, "Resistance and the Problem of Ethnographic Refusal," 175.

23. Ortner, "Resistance and the Problem of Ethnographic Refusal," 175.

24. Ortner, "Resistance and the Problem of Ethnographic Refusal," 175. For a similar analysis in the context of African American life and politics, see Eddie Glaude, *Exodus! Religion, Race, and Nation in Early Nineteenth-Century Black America* (Chicago: University of Chicago Press, 2000), 30–34.

25. Ortner, "Resistance and the Problem of Ethnographic Refusal," 178, 190.

26. As Ortner writes: "There seems a virtual taboo on putting these pieces together, as if to give a full account of the Mayan political order, good and bad, would be to give some observers the ammunition for saying that the Maya deserved what they got from the Spanish. But this concern is ungrounded. Nothing about Mayan politics, however bloody and exploitative, would condone the

looting, killing, and cultural destruction wrought by the Spanish." See Ortner, "Resistance and the Problem of Ethnographic Refusal," 178.

27. Ortner, "Resistance and the Problem of Ethnographic Refusal," 182.

28. Ortner, "Resistance and the Problem of Ethnographic Refusal," 177.

29. Ortner, "Resistance and the Problem of Ethnographic Refusal," 180.

30. Ortner, "Resistance and the Problem of Ethnographic Refusal," 180.

31. Saba Mahmood, another cultural anthropologist, also criticizes this trend in resistance studies. Through an analysis of the women's mosque movement (within the larger Islamic Revival in Egypt), Mahmood argues that there are modes of agency that get erased when we read all actions through the lens of resistance. For Mahmood, the pressure to reduce the agency of the oppressed to resistance arises from a narrative of "progressive politics" in liberal feminist discourse. Within this liberal framework, our autonomy is indicated by our ability to form our own desires, choices, projects and interests free from the coercion of others, associations, traditions, and so on. When this framework is applied to the lives of the oppressed, resistance gets privileged as a mode of agency. Because liberation is equated with what the oppressed *do* have under their power, resistance becomes the clearest expression of our will (or the subjects' "true" interests). See Mahmood, *The Politics of Piety*, 5–17.

32. Glaude, *In a Shade of Blue*, 90.

33. Glaude, *In a Shade of Blue*, 92.

34. Glaude, *In a Shade of Blue*, 78.

35. Glaude, *In a Shade of Blue*, 91.

36. Glaude, *In a Shade of Blue*, 99.

37. Glaude, *In a Shade of Blue*, 92. Glaude turns to John Dewey for an account of agency that is rooted in the experiences of the actors themselves. The meaning of actions, under this account, cannot be properly understood without taking account of the transactions made between the demands of the environment upon actors and the desires of such actors formed *within* that environment. Therefore, "to attribute agency a specified form and content prior to the actual experiences," writes Glaude, "is to abjure the active work individuals do in intelligently transforming situations." See Glaude, *In a Shade of Blue*, 99.

38. Glaude, *In a Shade of Blue*, 109.

39. Glaude, *In a Shade of Blue*, 104.

40. Glaude, *In a Shade of Blue*, 109.

41. Glaude, *In a Shade of Blue*, 109.

42. Glaude, *In a Shade of Blue*, 108.

43. Ortner, "Resistance and the Problem of Ethnographic Refusal," 179.

44. Hurston to Fannie Hurst, December 1933, in Kaplan, *A Life in Letters*, 286.

45. Hurston to Fannie Hurst, December 1933, 286.

46. Some notable examples include Mark P. Leone and Gladys-Marie Fry, "Conjuring in the Big House Kitchen: An Interpretation of African American Belief Systems Based on the Uses of Archaeology and Folklore Sources," *Journal of American Folklore* 112, no. 445 (Summer 1999): 381, https://www.jstor.org /stable/541368; Young, *Rituals of Resistance*, 1–24; Rucker, "Conjure, Magic, and Power"; and Walter Rucker, *The River Flows On: Black Resistance, Culture, and Identity Formation in Early America* (Baton Rouge: Louisiana State University Press, 2006), 1–14. Moreover, the introduction of the concept of "indirect

resistance" by James Scott has deeply encouraged this automatic attribution of resistance to the actions of the oppressed; namely, Scott's *Weapons of the Weak: Everyday Forms of Peasant Rebellion* and *Domination and the Arts of Resistance: Hidden Transcripts.* For examples of how scholars take up these works in discussions of Black spirituality to expand the category of "everyday resistance," see Syedullah, "Beyond the Battlefields of Institutions," 120–21; Young, *Rituals of Resistance*, 12–13; and Fett, *Working Cures*, 12.

47. For examples, see Plant, *Every Tub Must Sit on Its Own Bottom*, 45–46; Bordelon, "Zora Neale Hurston: A Biographical Essay," 27; Meisenhelder, *Hitting a Straight Lick*, 4, 18–23; and Hazzard-Donald, *Mojo Workin'*, 68–73.

48. For examples, see Rucker, "Conjure, Magic, and Power"; Rucker, *The River Flows On*; Gwendolyn Midlo Hall, *Africans in Colonial Louisiana: The Development of Afro-Creole Culture in the Eighteenth Century* (Baton Rouge: Louisiana State University Press, 1992), 162; Raboteau, *Slave Religion*, 26; Katrina Hazzard-Gordon, *Jookin': The Rise of Social Dance Formations in African American Culture* (Philadelphia: Temple University Press, 1990), 37–38; and Freddi Williams Evans, *Congo Square: African Roots in New Orleans* (Lafayette: University of Louisiana at Lafayette Press, 2011), 32–33.

49. See Wendy Dutton, "The Problem of Invisibility: Voodoo and Zora Neale Hurston," *Frontiers: A Journal of Women Studies* 13, no. 2 (1993): 131–33, https://www.jstor.org/stable/3346733. Perhaps Hurston only "scratch[ed] on the surface" in the essay because she was also participating in the "silence of the initiated" that hoodoo practitioners observe. See Hurston, *Mules and Men*, 185. This silence was partly due to the social stigma and illegal status of hoodoo. "Hoodooism is in disrepute," Hurston writes, "and certain of its practices are forbidden by law." See Hurston, "Hoodoo in America," 319.

50. Hurston confides to Alain Locke: "Besides, the editor had to have it sugared up to flatter the war effort. That certainly was not my idea, but sometimes you have to give something to get something. So I wrote in an opening paragraph and closing paragraph as requested. You will see what I mean when you read it." Hurston to Alain Locke, July 23, 1943, in Kaplan, *A Life in Letters*, 490.

51. Hurston to Alain Locke, July 23, 1943, 489.

52. Hurston to Alain Locke, July 23, 1943, 489–90.

53. Hazzard-Donald develops eight components of the "African Religion Complex" that "link the New World to the Old" in hoodoo religious practices. These are as follows: counterclockwise sacred circle dancing (which developed into the ring shout in the New World), spirit possession, the principle of sacrifice, ritual water immersion, divination, ancestor reverence, belief in spiritual cause of malady, and herbal and naturopathic medicine. See Hazzard-Donald, *Mojo Workin'*, 40. As Hazzard-Donald also observes, several of these elements and influences, such as water immersion, have similar emphases and overlaps within Christianity. See Hazzard-Donald, *Mojo Workin'*, 35–36, 43. For more on the overlap between Christianity and conjure, see Martin, *Conjuring Moments in African American Literature*, 90–91; Young, *Rituals of Resistance*, 115–17; and Tracey E. Hucks, "'Burning with a Flame in America': African American Women in African-Derived Traditions," *Journal of Feminist Studies* 17, no. 2 (2001): 97.

54. Hurston, "High John de Conquer," 931.

55. As Jeffrey E. Anderson observes, "other common forms of *minkisi* were roots . . . According to Kongo belief, the first *nkisi* was the spirit Funza, who dwelt in twisted roots. John the Conquer root, reputably one of the most powerful of all charms and found throughout the nineteenth-century South, was the American derivation of the African Funza." See Anderson, *Conjure in African American Society*, 39. See also Fett, *Working Cures*, 102–3; and Timothy Ruppel, Jessica Neuwirth, Mark P. Leone, and Gladys-Marie Fry, "Hidden in View: African Spiritual Spaces in North American Landscapes," *Antiquity* 77, no. 296 (2003): 328.

56. Hazzard-Donald writes: "Whether the charm is constructed from leather, from a tiny gourd encased in raffia, from animal skin, or from a piece of cloth, the similarities of bags, from the African American mojo to the Kongo *nkisi*, are undeniable." See Hazzard-Donald, *Mojo Workin'*, 67. See also Young, *Rituals of Resistance*, 105–45.

57. As Hazzard-Donald observes, "water immersion in the form of either baptism or ritual bath for medicinal or initiatory purposes, the practices of guarding discarded hair and fingernail clippings as well as other personal effects, the 'feeding' of spirits, pouring libations, as well as belief in spiritual causation for malady were part of traditional West African religious practice." See Hazzard-Donald, *Mojo Workin'*, 30.

58. Hurston, "High John de Conquer," 930. As John S. Mbiti notes, in many African religions, "the land provides [the descendants] with the roots of existence, as well as binding them metaphysically to their departed." See John S. Mbiti, *African Religions and Philosophy* (Portsmouth, NH: Heinemann, 1990), 26.

59. Leone and Fry note that mojo bags contained a number of different items. For instance, there was graveyard dust, riverbed clay, or funeral paraphernalia that acted "metonymically" to "provide direct access to the spirit." Their closeness to death makes objects in the this category "alive with a spirit," and as such, allow us to touch the dead. See Leone and Fry, "Conjuring in the Big House Kitchen," 380. As Hazzard-Donald writes, "the practice of honoring one's ancestors, seizing the power of the departed, is universal in West and Central West Africa and would carry over into the Americas in a variety of forms, including grave site decoration and the magical use of internment soil, known in Hoodoo as graveyard dirt." See Hazzard-Donald, *Mojo Workin'*, 26. See also Young, *Rituals of Resistance*, 124; and Fett, *Working Cures*, 102–3, for an extended discussion of the items used in the construction of *minkisi*.

60. I particularly like Hazzard-Donald's definition of luck: "a general spiritual condition believed to influence overall aspects of an individual's existence." See Hazzard-Donald, *Mojo Workin'*, 4. As Anderson notes, *minkisi* were the "benevolent side of Kongo magic." See Anderson, *Conjure in African American Society*, 39.

61. Hurston, "High John de Conquer," 923.

62. Hazzard-Donald, *Mojo Workin'*, 44. Additionally, in BaKongo cultural traditions, when these spaces were interior, such as rooms in a house, the magical objects were sometimes hidden. In this scenario, the rooms themselves became "separate dwellings, with few furnishings other than the charm or nkisi (medicine of the gods) carefully placed in vessels, on the earth, and closed." See Ruppel et al., "Hidden in View," 328. See also Young, *Rituals of Resistance*, 115.

63. For an extended discussion of the cosmogram, see Fett, *Working Cures*, 56.

64. Ruppell et al., "Hidden in View," 329.

65. See Hazzard-Donald, *Mojo Workin'*, 35, 45–48; and K. Zauditu-Selassie, *African Spiritual Traditions in the Novels of Toni Morrison* (Gainesville: University Press of Florida, 2009), x–xi.

66. Ruppel et al., "Hidden in View," 329. This also known as the *kalunga* line. See Zauditu-Selassie, *African Spiritual Traditions*, x.

67. Ruppel et al., "Hidden in View," 329.

68. Morrison also dramatizes this blending of religious meanings of the symbol of the cross in her novel *Paradise*. See Toni Morrison, *Paradise* (New York: Vintage Books, 2014), 145–46.

69. See also Mark Leone, Gladys-Marie Fry, and Timothy Ruppel, "Spirit Management among Americans of African Descent," in *Race and the Archeology of Identity*, ed. Charles Orser (Salt Lake City: University of Utah Press, 2001), 151.

70. Ruppel et al., "Hidden in View," 328.

71. Ruppel et al., "Hidden in View," 328

72. Ruppel et al., "Hidden in View," 329.

73. Ruppel et al., "Hidden in View," 329.

74. See also Fett, *Working Cures*, 52–56. Fett writes: "In African American folklore the cosmogram signified power created through connections to one's ancestors. More than a symbol, a cosmogram drawn on the ground or embodied in the form of a forked stick or crossroads drew spiritual power to a particular point on earth. Crossroads and cosmograms traced in the ground marked points of contact between the world of the living and the world of gods and ancestors."

75. Ruppel et al., "Hidden in View," 329.

76. Ruppel et al., "Hidden in View," 329.

77. Hurston, "High John de Conquer," 923, 925.

78. As Hurston writes, "wherever West African beliefs have survived in the New World, this place of the dead has been maintained." See Hurston, "Hoodoo in America," 319.

79. Namely, James Scott's *Domination and the Arts of Resistance: Hidden Transcripts*. See Young, *Rituals of Resistance*, 12–14.

80. Young, *Rituals of Resistance*, 12.

81. Young, *Rituals of Resistance*, 13.

82. Young writes: "In this way, every act of conjure from one slave against another represented a critical form of resistance, and the depletion of the plantation workforce due to conjure amounted to a blow against the system." See Young, *Rituals of Resistance*, 130.

83. Young writes: "Unlike Scott, who argues that the 'infrapolitics of the powerless' very rarely reaches the eyes and ears of the dominant class, I argue that slaveholders not only acknowledged but also responded to the political implications of slave cultural practices. The cultural resistance of slaves exhibited in the realm of material culture, folklore, and religion directly affected the larger political discourse in the country in general and, in particular, the ways in which the powerful justified their control over the mechanisms of oppression and violence. This is certainly evident throughout this book as members of the master class responded to the prevalence of ritual medicines and poisons or to the slaves' particular interpretation of Christianity." See Young, *Rituals of Resistance*, 12.

84. For more on the reactions of slave owners to Black conjure, see Yvonne P. Chireau, *Black Magic: Religion and the African American Conjuring Tradition* (Berkeley: University of California Press, 2003), 18–20; and Hazzard-Donald, *Mojo Workin'*, 136–40.

85. Young, *Rituals of Resistance*, 114.

86. Young, *Rituals of Resistance*, 114.

87. Young, *Rituals of Resistance*, 114.

88. See also Majorie Pryse's discussion of this phenomenon with regard to early Black women preachers/speakers: Marjorie Pryse, "Zora Neale Hurston, Alice Walker, and the 'Ancient Power' of Black Women," in Pryse and Spillers, *Conjuring*, 8–13.

89. Ortner, "Resistance and the Problem of Ethnographic Refusal," 186.

90. Davis, *Blues Legacies and Black Feminism*, 113.

91. Davis, "Lectures on Liberation," 56.

92. Davis, "Lectures on Liberation," 52.

93. As Leone, Fry, and Ruppel note, "hoodoo served as a survival tool, one that offered hope for an alternative to a regime of oppression and implied that these conditions were finite and ultimately surmountable." See Leone, Fry, and Ruppel, "Spirit Management," 153. Similarly, Chireau observes that "black Americans utilized conjuring traditions not only because they saw them as a valuable resource for resistance," but because the spirit-world "offered alternative possibilities for empowerment." See Chireau, *Black Magic*, 18. In addition, Fett notes that "herein lay the political importance of African American doctoring [i.e., conjure], for its active practice on southern plantations was a constant reminder that slaveholder power was only partial." See Fett, *Working Cures*, 107–8.

94. Davis writes: "Because the slaveocracy had sought to extinguish the collective cultural memory of Black people in order to confine them to an inferior social space, music, folktales, and hoodoo practices were always important ways Black people could maintain connections—conscious or not—with the traditions of their ancestors." See Davis, *Blues Legacies and Black Feminism*, 155.

95. For most of the novel, Sethe is chased by memories she desperately tries to forget. For examples, see Toni Morrison, *Beloved* (New York: Vintage International, 2004), 6–7, 82–83.

96. Morrison, *Beloved*, 111–12.

97. Morrison, *Beloved*, italics mine, 111–12.

98. This insight is similar to Michel Foucault's insistence on the distinction between liberation and "practices of freedom." See Michel Foucault, "The Ethics of Concern for Self as a Practice of Freedom," in *Ethics: Subjectivity and Truth*, ed. Paul Rabinow (London: Penguin, 1997). In this interview, Foucault raises the point that liberation (such as in a traditional colonial context) is a necessary but insufficient act for full emancipation. That is, oppression works at all levels, from orchestrating institutional practices to inculcating collective habits, to keep the oppressed in a state of oppression. Ladelle McWhorter extends this discussion of practices of freedom within a feminist context. For McWhorter, practices of freedom are on a different register of engagement than systems of oppression, since practices of freedom "help protect their practitioners from the damaging effects of oppressive forces" and are "transformative and creative" without the specific target of resistance. McWhorter turns to "practices of freedom" over resistance,

in part, because overturning the system of oppression does not guarantee that the "liberated" will be free from the pernicious effects of the oppression they have *already* undergone. See Ladelle McWhorter, "Post-Liberation Feminism and Practices of Freedom," *Foucault Studies* 16 (September 2013): 54–73, https://rauli.cbs.dk/index.php/foucault-studies/article/view/4117/4534.

99. Morrison, *Beloved*, 111.

100. See Evans, *Congo Square*, 20–24.

101. Morrison, *Beloved*, 102. See Zauditu-Selassie, *African Spiritual Traditions*, 158–59. For more on the importance of the woods for hoodoo practices, see Hazzard-Donald, *Mojo Workin'*, 44.

102. Morrison, *Beloved*, 103.

103. Morrison, *Beloved*, 111.

104. See Hazzard-Donald, "Hoodoo Religion," 199–201; and Hazzard-Donald, *Mojo Workin'*, 40, 47–48.

105. Further, many of the songs, instruments, foods, and even dress-wear of the gatherers at these secret meetings had their origins in spirit work practices. See Evans, *Congo Square*, 47–76. See also Eileen Southern, *The Music of Black Americans: A History* (New York: W. W. Norton, 1997), 139–40; and Hazzard-Donald, "Hoodoo Religion," 204–5.

106. Morrison, *Beloved*, 116.

107. See Zauditu-Selassie, *African Spiritual Traditions*, 158; Martin, *Conjuring Moments*, 95; and Washington, "'The Sea Never Dies,'" 221.

108. Morrison, *Beloved*, 108.

109. For more on how African American women blend Christianity and conjure together in their religious practices, see Huck, "Burning with a Flame in America," 90, 97; Chireau, *Black Magic*, 25–26; Martin, *Conjuring Moments*, 89–92; and Hazzard-Donald, *Mojo Workin'*, 43–44.

110. Morrison, *Beloved*, 102–3.

111. Hazzard-Donald, "Hoodoo Religion," 205.

112. As Morrison writes, ancestors are to be distinguished from parents, because they are "a timeless people whose relationships" to us are "benevolent, instructive, and protective, and they provide a certain kind of wisdom." See Toni Morrison, "Rootedness, the Ancestor as Foundation," in *What Moves at the Margin: Selected Nonfiction*, ed. Carolyn C. Denard (Jackson: University Press of Mississippi, 2008), 62. While elders are living and ancestors are among the dead, there is a conceptual relationship between the two. Hazzard-Donald also notes that "ancestral spiritual power is consulted and invoked as it was when the elders were in their earthly existence." See Hazzard-Donald, *Mojo Workin'*, 25. And as Mbiti notes, elders of the community are reverenced, in part, *because* of their closeness to death. This closeness to death, in turn, puts them closer to the living-dead or ancestors. See Mbiti, *African Religions and Philosophy*, 80–81.

113. Morrison, "Rootedness: The Ancestor as Foundation," in Morrison, *What Moves at the Margins*, 61.

114. In fact, the very rock upon which Baby Suggs prayed and preached is considered sacred by others. For instance, Sethe returns to Baby Suggs's "preaching rock" for help and guidance after Baby Suggs has died, marking the rock as a sacred object. The rock becomes an altar, a physical location transformed through ritual into a meeting place between the living and the dead. For when

Sethe physically touches the rock, she feels the ghost of Baby Suggs massage her neck. See Morrison, *Beloved*, 112.

115. Morrison, *Beloved*, 112, italics mine.

116. The relationship between imagination and capacities to resist has been of long-standing interest to those who theorize on liberation praxis. For recent work, see Medina, *The Epistemology of Resistance*; and Vivian M. May, *Pursuing Intersectionality, Unsettling Dominant Imaginaries* (New York: Routledge, 2015).

117. Morrison, *Beloved*, 83.

118. Morrison writes: "the butter-smeared face of a man God made none sweeter than demanded more: an arch build or a robe sewn. Some fixing ceremony. Sethe decided to go to the Clearing, back where Baby Suggs had danced in sunlight." See Morrison, *Beloved*, 101.

119. Genevieve Fabre is also working with a notion of Black dance that is infused with West and Central African spirituality here. See Genevieve Fabre, "The Slave Ship Dance," in *Black Imagination and the Middle Passage*, ed. Maria Diedrich, Henry Louis Gates Jr., and Carl Pedersen (New York: Oxford University Press, 1999), 33–34, 38, 44.

120. Morrison, *Beloved*, 103.

121. Morrison, *Beloved*, 103.

122. Morrison, *Beloved*, 103–4.

123. At these dances, folklorist Robert Tallant notes that a "Voodoo priestess" would stand in the center of the group and call out different dances for the group to perform. An observant informs Tallant, "[the Priestess] would call the numbers—you know what I mean? She would tell the dancers what to do and holler all kinds of funny things." See Robert Tallant, *Voodoo in New Orleans* (New York: Collier Books, 1967), 72. Hazzard-Donald also comments on this dance tradition of "calling the numbers." See Hazzard-Donald, "Hoodoo Religion," 205–7. While Baby Suggs is not literally standing in the center of the group during this passage, she is *figuratively* centered, since all look to and await her bodily instructions.

124. Morrison, *Beloved*, 103–4.

125. Glaude, *In a Shade of Blue*, 42.

126. Hurston, "High John de Conquer," 931.

127. Morrison, *Beloved*, 103.

128. Ortner, "Resistance and the Problem of Ethnographic Refusal," 180. See also note 94 in this chapter.

129. Hazzard-Donald writes: "The seeds of all future Black dance movement, as well as those fundamental postures and gestures which were both rhythmically ordered and held in esteem, in African American culture, would be contained in the 'shout ceremony.' There, they could be preserved until their rebirth in a variety of modified forms. The shout ritual was the arena in which the motor muscle memory of African movement could be learned, sustained, relexified, and reborn eventually as secular dance forms. These forms would go on to become the famous African American dances that have circulated around the world; dances like the 'Twist,' the 'Black Bottom,' the 'Pony,' and, of course, the touch response partnering dance known as the 'Lindy Hop' and all its various forms." See Hazzard-Donald, "Hoodoo Religion," 200. See also Hazzard-Donald, *Mojo Workin'*, 46–48.

130. Hazzard-Donald, "Hoodoo Religion," 203. For instance, Raboteau remarks on the various borrowing and blending of disparate religious traditions that mark cultures formed by the African diaspora. The "similar patterns of response—rhythmic clapping, ring-dancing, styles of singing, all of which result in or from the state-of-possession trance," Raboteau writes, "reveals the slaves' African religious background." For Raboteau, these physical gestures are codes by which even people across different religious traditions in the African diaspora can "recognize immediately" what is happening. See Raboteau, *Slave Religion*, 36–37, 72.

131. It is interesting that Morrison also draws upon the grammar of dance when defining Black joy elsewhere. She writes: "Finally, in this long trek through three hundred years of Black life, there was joy, which is what I mostly remember. That part of our lives that was spent neither on our knees nor hanging from trees. The idleness of the day broken by Black boys doing the hambone. Our bodies in motion at public dances that pulled Black people from as far as a hundred miles away. A glorious freedom of movement in which rites of puberty were acted out on a dance floor to the sound of brass, strings and ivory. For dancing was relief and communication, control of the body and its letting go. We danced in public and alone, on the porches and in the yards. Wherever the sound found us. And, of course, there was the music. Not only the 'race records' and the live bands but the shout songs and the remnants of slave jubilees." In this quote, Morrison links generations of dance-talk, from the ring shout of the enslaved to the "race records" of the blues and jazz. See Toni Morrison, "Rediscovering Black History," in Morrison, *What Moves at the Margin*, 54. As Zauditu-Selassie notes, the dance-talk continues on, as elements of the ring shout dance remain in communal dances such as the "bus stop" or the "electric slide" performed at weddings of cousins and family reunions. See Zauditu-Selassie, *African Spiritual Traditions*, xi.

132. As Davis writes, "the articulation of a specifically Black aesthetic—the announced aim of the Harlem Renaissance—cannot locate itself in the living tradition of African-American culture without taking seriously the practices variously called conjure, voodoo, or hoodoo." See Davis, *Blues Legacies and Black Feminism*, 159. See also Sterling Stuckey, *Slave Culture: Nationalist Theory, and the Foundations of Black America* (New York: Oxford University Press, 2013), 12–16; Rucker, *The River Flows On*, 7, 198–99; Hazzard-Donald, "Hoodoo Religion," 197; and Hazzard-Donald, *Mojo Workin'*, 8, 46.

133. It cannot be overstated that the relationship African Americans have held toward conjure is rife with contradictions and tensions. There were those who held the position that conjure held the race back, those who saw it as antithetical to Christianity (and therefore evil), and those who blended both conjure and Christianity into their own unique religious practices. See Hazzard-Donald, "Hoodoo Religion," 202; and Hazzard-Donald, *Mojo Workin'*, 64. See also Chireau, *Black Magic*, 3, 12; Davis, *Blues Legacies and Black Feminism*, 154–60; and Anderson, *Conjure in African American Society*, 1–24.

134. See Martin, *Conjuring Moments*, 91; and Hazzard-Donald, *Mojo Workin'*, 19–33.

135. As Davis writes of Hurston's study of spirit work practices, "the folk tales or 'lies' Hurston wrote down and the spiritual power of hoodoo that she directly experienced as well as analyzed, together with the blues, holds the key to

an understanding of the foundations of African-American popular culture." See Davis, *Blues Legacies and Black Feminism*, 155.

136. Morrison, *Beloved*, 234.

137. Morrison, *Beloved*, 234.

138. As Saidiyah Hartman observes, "acts of resistance exist within the context of relations of domination and are not external to them," which is why "they acquire their character from these relations, and vice versa." See Hartman, *Scenes of Subjection*, 8.

139. See Hurston, "High John de Conquer," 927. See also Hurston to Alain Locke, July 23, 1943, 489; and Plant, *Every Tub Must Sit on Its Own Bottom*, 45.

140. For example, see Hazzard-Donald, *Mojo Workin'*, 75–83. In the chapter titled "The Search for High John the Conquer," Hazzard-Donald searches for the origins of this figure. She speculates that the figure was originally a slave rebellion leader. See also Meisenhelder, *Hitting a Straight Lick*, 4–5, 18–23.

141. Instead, Plant writes, "in Hurston's version of the tale . . . High John is amicable and even moves 'Ole Massa' to laughter." See Plant, *Every Tub Must Sit on Its Own Bottom*, 90.

142. I take it that Plant means that there don't seem to be any "hard feelings" in the trickery and ruses of High John de Conquer in Hurston's essay. Plant writes: "There are several ways to read Hurston's conciliatory tone. Perhaps Hurston suggests that a little humor could work wonders on the human soul—no matter whose it is. Perhaps the laughter coming from someone as indurate as a slaveholder creates a dramatic irony that releases tension. Perhaps, also, Hurston suggests that revenge isn't necessary, as is the case of Lester's version, and that whites, symbolized by 'Ole Massa,' really aren't the threat they are believed to be; that time might be better spent building one's own barn than burning down another's; and that by not being consumed with 'Ole Massa,' Blacks become the center of their own lives." See Plant, *Every Tub Must Sit on Its Own Bottom*, 90.

143. Hurston, "High John de Conquer," 927.

144. Hurston, "High John de Conquer," 927.

145. Hurston, "High John de Conquer," 927.

146. Hurston, "High John de Conquer," 923.

147. Wall, *On Freedom*, 20. See also Plant, *Every Tub Must Sit on Its Own Bottom*, 47, for a discussion of Hurston's use of "games" as a metaphor for racial politics. The stance toward politics that Wall describes is precisely what earned Hurston criticism. As Henry Louis Gates Jr. writes: "It seems that Hurston draws on [High John de Conquer] as a basis for a certain philosophy of life. An anti-materialist and carefree attitude, she suggests, offers political and economic power. This view, implying that Blacks had not succumbed to a culture of poverty, is at the core of accusations against Hurston that she was not politically correct." See Henry Louis Gates, "Introduction: Zora Neale Hurston: Establishing the Canon," in Zora Neale Hurston, *The Complete Stories* (New York: HarperCollins, 1995), xx.

148. Toni Morrison, "A Knowing So Deep," in Morrison, *What Moves at the Margin*, 32. This is also how "hope for the hopeless," as Davis writes, has been "magically conjured up by the various trickster figures in Black folklore" such as John de Conquer. See Davis, *Blues Legacies and Black Feminism*, 157.

149. Hurston, "High John de Conquer," 927.

150. Hurston, "High John de Conquer," 929.
151. Hurston, "High John de Conquer," 930.
152. Hurston, "High John de Conquer," 924.
153. Hurston, "High John de Conquer," 924.
154. Hurston, "High John de Conquer," 922.
155. Lorde, "Uses of the Erotic," 54.
156. Lorde, "Uses of the Erotic," 56.
157. Lorde, "Uses of the Erotic," 56.
158. Lorde, "Uses of the Erotic," 57.
159. Lorde, "Uses of the Erotic," 54.
160. Lorde writes: "When we live outside ourselves, and by that I mean on external directives only rather than from our internal knowledge and needs, when we live away from those erotic guides from within ourselves, then our lives are limited by external and alien forms, and we conform to the needs of a structure that is not based on human need, let alone an individual's. But when we begin to live from within outward, in touch with the power of the erotic within ourselves, and allowing that power to inform and illuminate our actions upon the world around us, then we begin to be responsible to ourselves in the deepest sense." See Lorde, "Uses of the Erotic," 58.
161. Hurston, "High John de Conquer," 930–31.
162. There is a long tradition in Black feminist scholarship that discusses Hurston's use of folklore as a means of cultural self-definition. For examples, see Walker, "On Refusing to Be Humbled by Second Place in a Contest You Did Not Design," 1–6; Wilentz, "Defeating the False God," 285–91; and Wall, "Zora Neale Hurston: Changing Her Own Words," 78–97.
163. Hurston, "High John de Conquer," 924.
164. Hurston, "High John de Conquer," 924.
165. Hurston, "High John de Conquer," 924. As Plant observes, laughter is "an independent force whose contagious presence acts as a curative and a restorative. Hurston considered humor and laughter the wellspring of life and the outward indication of an inner spirituality." See Plant, *Every Tub Must Sit on Its Own Bottom*, 89.
166. Hurston, "High John de Conquer," 924.
167. Fett argues that hoodoo folktales form a special subgenre of African American folktales. Many of them shared a specific form and perform certain functions within African American communities. Fett notes four "stages" in hoodoo tales that focus on healing. First, the identification of a conflict between the "afflicted" (or sick) and some member of the community. Second, the description of the ailment by "mapping out the bodily effects of the hoodoo 'dose.'" If the client was truly "hoodooed," then the diagnosis of the "real" source of the ailment would disavow Western medicine and science. That is, if the ailment was considered "not natural," the conjurer would warn their client that medical doctors "won't do you no good" or might actually make it worse. In these cases, the diagnosis is an acknowledgment of different *sources* of power at work, and, as such, different sets of practices that are required to attend to the problem. Third, the search for the "conjurer." And in this interaction with the conjurer, we can begin to see their role of leadership within the community. For instance, conjurers bear the authority to call their clients into question. In hoodoo tales, conjurers

often accuse their clients of lying, having problematic motives, or being foolish for lack of knowledge. Moreover, they may warn the client of future danger if their instructions are not followed. Alleviation of the ailment which prompted the consultation depended on the client's obedience to the conjurer's instruction, as noted by Fett in her fourth stage, the removal of the sickness by following the instructions of the conjurer. See Fett, *Working Cures*, 86.

168. As bell hooks notes, Hurston's return to the South for fieldwork was a "gesture of self-recovery" from the alienating Northern landscapes of her education. hooks writes: "[Hurston's] return 'home' to do field work was on one level a gesture of self-recovery; Hurston was returning to that self she had been forced to leave behind in order to survive the public world of a huge Northern city." This return had an important impact on Hurston's research as well. hooks writes: "The return home had such an impact on Hurston's psyche that she could not simply transcribe the material uncovered there as though it were only scientific data. It was vividly connected in her mind to habits of being and a way of life." See hooks, *Yearning*, 141.

169. Many have demonstrated the medical industry's (and certain areas of science's) role in the construction and perpetuation of racism. For example, see Cornel West's *Prophesy Deliverance!* 47. West argues that "the very structure of modern discourse *at its inception* produced forms of rationality, scientificity, objectivity as well as aesthetic and cultural ideals which require the constitution of the idea of white supremacy." In their disavowal of the power of certain medical practices to truly heal their clients, conjurers were able to redirect their patients to a different set of practices. Further, I would argue that this redirection, *in effect*, enabled the production of very different subjects than those subjected to the gaze of "science" through "proper" medical treatment.

170. Hurston, "High John de Conquer," 925.

171. Hurston, "High John de Conquer," 925.

172. As Martin writes, "[a] string of bad luck, a decrease in health, harm done to loved ones, and a myriad of other disharmonies of life can occur when one refuses to believe [the conjurer]." See Martin, *Conjuring Moments*, 7.

173. Hurston, "High John de Conquer," 928.

174. Hurston, "High John de Conquer," 929.

175. Hurston, "High John de Conquer," 923.

176. Hurston, "High John de Conquer," 931.

177. See Hurston, "High John de Conquer," 922–23. Hurston writes: "It was sure to be heard when and where the work was the hardest, and the lot most cruel." And so, "maybe [High John de Conquer] was in Texas when the lash fell on a slave," Hurston continues, "but before the blood was dry on the back he was there." Indeed, High John de Conquer was even a witness and symbol of our memory of the Middle Passage: "The sea captains knew that they brought slaves in their ships. They knew about those Black bodies huddled down there in the middle passage, being hauled across the waters to helplessness. John de Conquer was walking the very winds that filled the sails of the ships. He followed over them like the albatross."

178. Hurston, "High John de Conquer," 923, 927.

179. Hurston to Alain Locke, July 23, 143, 489.

180. Hurston, "High John de Conquer," 923.

181. Hurston, "High John de Conquer," 930. For an extended discussion of this phenomenon, see Chireau, *Black Magic*, 122–23, 127–29; and Anderson, *Conjure in African American Society*, 1–24.

182. Hurston, "High John de Conquer," 930.

Conclusion

1. Simpson, "On Ethnographic Refusal," 73.

2. This section's title is a poignant remark that my mother, Alisia Stewart-Coleman, made while we were discussing the coronavirus during our weekly Sunday phone chats.

3. David Benoit, "Coronavirus Devastates Black New Orleans: 'This Is Bigger Than Hurricane Katrina,'" *Wall Street Journal*, May 23, 2020, https://www.wsj .com/articles/coronavirus-is-a-medical-and-financial-disaster-for-Blacks-in-new -orleans-11590226200.

4. For an example of this type of coverage, see James Glanz et al., "Where America Didn't Stay Home Even as the Virus Spread," *New York Times*, April 2, 2020, https://www.nytimes.com/interactive/2020/04/02/us/coronavirus-social -distancing.html. Bob Bryan criticizes the map used in this report for its regional bias. See Bob Bryan, "Stop Shaming the South over the Coronavirus," Business Insider, April 2, 2020, https://www.businessinsider.com/stop-shaming-the-south -over-coronavirus-pandemic-social-distancing-2020-4.

5. For an example of this type of analysis, see Edna Bonhomme, "Racism: The Most Dangerous 'Pre-Existing Condition,'" *Al Jazeera*, April 16, 2020, https:// www.aljazeera.com/indepth/opinion/racism-dangerous-pre-existing-condition -200414154246943.html.

6. Hurston, "Art and Such," 908.

7. Richard Fausset, Katy Reckdahl, and Campbell Robertson, "New Orleans Faces a Virus Nightmare, and Mardi Gras May Be Why," *New York Times*, April 13, 2020, https://www.nytimes.com/2020/03/26/us/coronavirus-louisiana-new -orleans.html.

8. Hurston, "Negroes without Self-Pity," 933.

9. Zeeshan Aleem, "The Problem with the Surgeon General's Controver-sial Coronavirus Advice to Americans of Color," Vox, April 11, 2020, https:// www.vox.com/2020/4/11/21217428/surgeon-general-jerome-adams-big-mama -coronavirus.

10. Aleem, "The Problem with the Surgeon General's Controversial Corona-virus Advice."

11. For an example of such criticisms, see Curtis Brown, "Black Health Experts Say Surgeon General's Comments Reflect Lack of Awareness of Black Commu-nity," *NBC News*, April 15, 2020, https://www.nbcnews.com/news/nbcblk/Black -health-experts-say-surgeon-general-s-comments-reflect-lack-n1183711.

12. Aleem, "The Problem with the Surgeon General's Controversial Corona-virus Advice."

13. We can see this, for example, in the essay on women-whipping indexed to Harriet Tubman and Sarah Bradford's *Scenes in the Life of Harriet Tubman*. In this essay, S. M. Hopkins notes that "it is very pleasant to lay upon Nature or Providence what belongs only to will or institutions. A man indulges in violent passions with little restraint or remorse, so long as he can persuade himself he is

merely what certain positive natural laws made him. What an opiate for a conscience defiled with lust and blood, to think that [slavery] is only natural to the
'sunny South.'" See S. M. Hopkins, "Essay on Woman-Whipping, Ethically and
Esthetically Considered," in Sarah Bradford and Harriet Tubman, *Scenes in the
Life of Harriet Tubman* (London: Forgotten Books, 2012), 126.

14. Hopkins writes: "There is every reason to hope, therefore, that the Southern character, both male and female, will become gradually ameliorated by the
changed condition [i.e., abolition of slavery] under which it will hereafter be
formed. It is a common error, one in which Southern people themselves share,
that there is something in their climate [i.e., something natural] to nurse and justify" the institution of slavery. See Hopkins, "Essay on Woman-Whipping," 126.

15. After Hopkins makes the argument that it is institutions rather than
nature that forms our social and moral characters, he pivots to what he hopes
the abolition of slavery will do for white southerners. "It may require several
generations;" Hopkins writes, "but *institutions* ceasing to corrupt them, the loss
of wealth, the necessity of work and a new Gospel of peace, better than their
old slaveholding Christianity, will gradually educate [white southerners] into a
law-abiding, orderly, and virtuous people." Moreover, the path of white southern reform is modeled after their northern white counterparts: "In short, there
neither is nor ever was any reason, slavery excepted, why the Southern whites
should not possess a character for industry, peacefulness, and religion, equal to
that of the rural districts of New York and New England." See Hopkins, "Essay
on Woman-Whipping," 128–29.

16. Fausset, Reckdahl, and Robertson, "New Orleans Faces a Virus Nightmare."

17. See also Richard Fausset and Derek Kravitz, "Why New Orleans Pushed
Ahead with Mardi Gras, Even as It Planned for Coronavirus," April 15, 2020,
https://www.nytimes.com/2020/04/13/us/coronavirus-new-orleans-mardi-gras
.html.

18. See Ramon Antonio Vargas, "CDC: Mardi Gras Quickened Spread of
Coronavirus in Louisiana; Canceling Was Never Recommended," Nola, April
11, 2020, https://www.nola.com/news/coronavirus/article_dedfb5e4–7c2a-11ea
-901f-6720fa25be5a.html.

19. See Benedict Carey and James Glanz, "Travel from New York City Seeded
Wave of U.S. Outbreaks," *New York Times*, May 7, 2020, https://www.nytimes
.com/2020/05/07/us/new-york-city-coronavirus-outbreak.html.

20. As Lynell Thomas observes, "for many whites, this idea of New Orleans
provides a safe, sanctioned space to indulge in Black culture and unite with Black
bodies, if only vicariously." Moreover, "in the context of New Orleans tourism,
racialized consumption is afforded without censure and with the added benefit of
absolving whites of guilt and culpability for a racist past and present." This consumption of Black New Orleans culture is also motivated by a sense of regional
escapism. Thomas writes: "Strikingly, the image of New Orleans in the twenty-
first century differed very little from the mythologized South that had attracted
northern tourists in the decades following the Civil War. Pre-Katrina white tourists, like their postbellum predecessors, sought in New Orleans an escape from
class uncertainties and racial problems and the promise of established tradition,
romantic history, and social stability seemingly lacking from their own lives." See
Thomas, *Desire and Disaster in New Orleans*, 14, 33.

21. See Fausset, Reckdahl, and Robertson, "New Orleans Faces a Virus Nightmare."

22. Turner, *Jazz Religion*, 3.

23. See Turner, *Jazz Religion*, 115–17.

24. See Turner, *Jazz Religion*, xxi, 69.

25. Hurston, "High John de Conquer," 922.

BIBLIOGRAPHY

Aleem, Zeeshan. "The Problem with the Surgeon General's Controversial Coronavirus Advice to Americans of Color." Vox, April 11, 2020. https://www.vox.com/2020/4/11/21217428/surgeon-general-jerome-adams-big-mama-coronavirus.

Alexander, Michelle. *The New Jim Crow: Incarceration in the Age of Color Blindness*. New York: New Press, 2012.

Aljoe, Nicole N. "Introduction: Remapping the Early American Slave Narrative." In *Journeys of the Slave Narrative in the Early Americas*, edited by Nicole N. Aljoe and Ian Finseth, 1–15. Charlottesville: University of Virginia Press, 2014.

Allen, Reniqua. "Racism Is Everywhere, So Why Not Move South?" *New York Times*, July 8, 2017. https://www.nytimes.com/2017/07/08/opinion/sunday/racism-is-everywhere-so-why-not-move-south.html.

Allred, Kevin. "Back by Popular Demand: Beyoncé Harnesses the Power of Conjuring in 'Formation.'" bitchmedia, June 11, 2019. https://www.bitchmedia.org/article/beyonce-conjuring-ghosts-formation-excerpt.

Anderson, Jeffrey E. *Conjure in African American Society*. Baton Rouge: Louisiana State University Press, 2008.

Anderson, Paul Allen. *Deep River: Music and Memory in Harlem Renaissance Thought*. Durham, NC: Duke University Press, 2001.

Andrews, William L. Introduction to *Slave Narratives after Slavery*, edited by William L. Andrews, vii–xxiii. New York: Oxford University Press, 2011.

Angelou, Maya. Foreword to *Dust Tracks on a Road*, by Zora Neale Hurston, vii–xii. New York: Harper Perennial Modern Classics, 1995.

Baldwin, James. "Alas, Poor Richard." In *James Baldwin: Collected Essays*, edited by Toni Morrison, 247–68. New York: Library of America, 1998.

———. "The American Dream and the American Negro." In Baldwin, *James Baldwin: Collected Essays*, 714–20.

———. "Everybody's Protest Novel." In Baldwin, *James Baldwin: Collected Essays*, 11–18.

———. "The Fire Next Time." In Baldwin, *James Baldwin: Collected Essays*, 291–348.

Baraka, Amiri. *Blues People: Negro Music in White America*. New York: William Morrow, 1999.

Benoit, David. "Coronavirus Devastates Black New Orleans: 'This Is Bigger Than Katrina.'" *Wall Street Journal*, May 23, 2020. https://www.msn.com/en-us/news/us/coronavirus-devastates-Black-new-orleans-this-is-bigger-than-katriina/ar-BB14uu5r?ocid=sf2.

Berlin, Ira. *Generations of Captivity: A History of African-American Slaves*. Cambridge, MA: Harvard University Press, 2003.

Beverly, Michele Prettyman. "To Feel like a 'Natural Woman': Aretha Franklin, Beyoncé and the Ecological Spirituality of *Lemonade*." In Brooks and Martin, *The Lemonade Reader*, 166–82.

Bonhomme, Edna. "Racism: The Most Dangerous 'Pre-Existing Condition.'" *Aljazeera*, April 16, 2020. https://www.aljazeera.com/indepth/opinion/racism -dangerous-pre-existing-condition-200414154246943.html.

Bordelon, Pamela. *Go Gator and Muddy the Water: Writings by Zora Neale Hurston from the Federal Writers' Project*, edited by Pamela Bordelon. New York: W. W. Norton, 1999.

———. "Zora Neale Hurston: A Biographical Essay." In Bordelon, *Go Gator and Muddy the Water*, 1–60.

Boxwell, D. A. "'Sis Cat' as Ethnographer: Self-Presentation and Self-Inscription in Zora Neale Hurston's 'Mules and Men.'" *African American Review* 26, no. 4 (1992): 605–17.

Brooks, Daphne A. "The Lady Sings Her Legacy: Introduction." In Brooks and Martin, *The Lemonade Reader*, 161–65.

Brooks, Kinitra D., and Kameelah L. Martin. "'I Used to Be Your Sweet Mama': Beyoncé at the Crossroads of Blues and Conjure in *Lemonade*." In Brooks and Martin, *The Lemonade Reader*, 202–214.

———. "Introduction: Beyoncé's *Lemonade* Lexicon." In Brooks and Martin, *The Lemonade Reader*, 1–5.

———, eds. *The Lemonade Reader*. New York: Routledge, 2019.

Bryan, Bob. "Stop Shaming the South over the Coronavirus." Business Insider, April 2, 2020. https://www.businessinsider.com/stop-shaming-the-south-over -coronavirus-pandemic-social-distancing-2020-4.

Bryant, Kendra Nicole. "Dear Zora: Letters from the New Literati." In *"The Inside Light": New Critical Essays on Zora Neale Hurston*, edited by Deborah G. Plant, 181–96. Santa Barbara, CA: Praeger, 2010.

Bunn, Curtis. "Black Health Experts Say Surgeon General's Comments Reflect Lack of Awareness of Black Community." *NBC News*, April 15, 2020. https:// www.nbcnews.com/news/nbcblk/Black-health-experts-say-surgeon-general -s-comments-reflect-lack-n1183711.

Campt, Tina. "Black Visuality and the Practice of Refusal." Women and Performance, February 25, 2019. https://www.womenandperformance.org /ampersand/29–1/campt.

Carby, Hazel V. "The Politics of Fiction, Anthropology, and the Folk: Zora Neale Hurston." In *New Essays on "Their Eyes Were Watching God,"* edited by Michael Awkward, 71–74. New York: Cambridge University Press, 1991.

———. *Race Men*. W. E. B. Du Bois Lectures. Cambridge, MA: Harvard University Press, 1998.

Carpio, Glenda R., and Werner Sollors. "The Newly Complicated Zora Neale Hurston." *Chronicle of Higher Education*, January 2, 2011. https://www .chronicle.com/article/The-Newly-Complicated-Zora/125753.

Cary, Benedict, and James Glanz. "Travel from New York City Seeded Wave of U.S. Outbreaks. *New York Times*, May 7, 2020. https://www.nytimes.com /2020/05/07/us/new-york-city-coronavirus-outbreak.html.

Cary, Benedict, James Glanz, Josh Holder, Derek Watkins, Jennifer Valentino-DeVries, Rick Rojas, and Lauren Leatherby. "Where America Didn't Stay

Home Even as the Virus Spread." *New York Times*, April 2, 2020. https://www
.nytimes.com/interactive/2020/04/02/us/coronavirus-social-distancing.html.

Chireau, Yvonne P. *Black Magic: Religion and the African American Conjuring Tradition*. Berkeley: University of California Press, 2003.

Christian, Barbara. "The Race for Theory." *Cultural Critique* 6 (1987): 51–63. https://www.jstor.orga/stable/1354255.

Collins, Patricia Hill. *Black Feminist Thought*. New York: Routledge Classics, 2009.

———. "Social Inequality, Power, and Politics: Intersectionality and American Pragmatism in Dialogue." *Journal of Speculative Philosophy* 26, no. 2 (2012): 442–57.

Cotera, Maria Eugenia. *Native Speakers: Ella Deloria, Zora Neale Hurston, Jovita Gonzalez, and the Poetics of Culture*. Austin: University of Texas Press, 2008.

Crawley, Ashton T. *Black Pentecostal Breath: The Aesthetics of Possibility*. New York: Fordham University Press, 2017.

Cruz, Jon. *Culture on the Margins: The Black Spiritual and the Rise of American Cultural Interpretation*. Princeton, NJ: Princeton University Press, 1999.

Davis, Angela Y. *Blues Legacies and Black Feminism*. New York: Vintage Books, 1999.

———. Introduction to Frederick Douglass, *Narrative of the Life of Frederick Douglass, an American Slave, Written by Himself*, edited by Angela Y. Davis, 21–40. San Francisco: Open Media Series, 2010.

———. "Second Lecture on Liberation." In Douglass, *Narrative of the Life of Frederick Douglass*, 65–86.

———. *Women, Race, and Class*. New York: Vintage Books, 1983.

Delbanco, Andrew. "The Political Incorrectness of Zora Neale Hurston." *Journal of Blacks in Higher Education* 18 (1998): 103–8.

Denard, Carolyn C., ed. *Toni Morrison: Conversations*. Jackson: University Press of Mississippi, 2008.

Diouf, Sylviane A. *Dreams of Africa in Alabama: The Slave Ship "Clotilda" and the Story of the Last Africans Brought to America*. New York: Oxford University Press, 2007.

Dorrien, Gary. *The New Abolition: W. E. B. Du Bois and the Black Social Gospel*. New Haven, CT: Yale University Press, 2015.

Dotson, Kristie. "On the Way to Decolonization in a Settler Colony: Re-Introducing Black Feminist Identity Politics." *AlterNative: An International Journal of Indigenous Peoples* 14, no. 3 (2018): 1–10.

———. "Querying Leonard Harris' Insurrectionist Standards." *Transactions of the Charles S. Pierce Society: A Quarterly Journal in American Philosophy* 49, no. 1 (2013): 74–92.

———. "Radical Love: Black Philosophy as Deliberate Acts of Inheritance." *Black Scholar* 43, no. 4 (2013): 38–45.

———. "Tracking Epistemic Violence, Tracking Practices of Silencing." *Hypatia* 26, no. 2 (2011): 236–57.

Douglass, Frederick. *My Bondage and My Freedom*. 1885. New York: Modern Library, 2003.

———. *Narrative of the Life of Frederick Douglass, an American Slave, Written by Himself*. Edited by Angela Y. Davis. San Francisco: Open Media Series, 2010.

Du Bois, W. E. B. *Du Bois on Religion*. Edited by Phil Zuckerman. Walnut Creek, CA: Altamira, 2000.

———. *The Souls of Black Folk*. In *W. E. B. Du Bois: Writings*, edited by Nathan Huggins, 357–548. New York: Library of America, 1986.

DuCille, Ann. "Looking for Zora." *New York Times*, January 5, 2003.

———. "The Mark of Zora: Reading between the Lines of Legend and Legacy." *The Scholar and Feminist Online* 3, no. 2 (2005). http://sfonline.barnard.edu/hurston/ducille_02.htm.

Dunbar, Eve. *Black Regions of the Imagination: African American Writers between the Nation and the World*. Philadelphia: Temple University Press, 2013.

Dutton, Wendy. "The Problem of Invisibility: Voodoo and Zora Neale Hurston." *Frontiers: A Journal of Women Studies* 13, no. 2 (1993): 131–52.

Edwards, Erica. *Charisma and the Fictions of Black Leadership*. Minneapolis: University of Minnesota Press, 2012.

Evans, Curtis. "W. E. B. Du Bois: Interpreting Religion and the Problem of the Negro Church." *Journal of the American Academy of Religion* 75, no. 2 (2007): 268–97.

Evans, Freddi Williams. *Congo Square: African Roots in New Orleans*. Lafayette: University of Louisiana at Lafayette Press, 2011.

Fabre, Genevieve. "The Slave Ship Dance." In *Black Imagination and the Middle Passage*, edited by Maria Diedrich, Henry Louis Gates, and Carl Pedersen, 33–46. New York: Oxford University Press, 1999.

Fausset, Richard, and Derek Kravitz. "Why New Orleans Pushed Ahead with Mardi Gras, Even as It Planned for Coronavirus." *New York Times*, April 13, 2020. https://www.nytimes.com/2020/04/13/us/coronavirus-new-orleans-mardi-gras.html.

Fausset, Richard, Katy Reckdahl, and Campbell Robertson. "New Orleans Faces a Virus Nightmare, and Mardi Gras May Be Why." *New York Times*, April 13, 2020. https://www.nytimes.com/2020/03/26/us/coronavirus-louisiana-new-orleans.html.

Fett, Sharla M. *Working Cures: Healing, Health, and Power on Southern Slave Plantations*. Chapel Hill: University of North Carolina Press, 2002.

Ford, Tanisha C. "Beysthetics: 'Formation' and the Politics of Style." In Brooks and Martin, *The Lemonade Reader*, 192–201.

Foucault, Michel. "The Ethics of the Concern for Self as a Practice of Freedom." In *Ethics: Subjectivity and Truth, Essential Works of Foucault, 1954–1984, Vol. 1*, edited by Paul Rabinow, translated by Robert Hurly and others. New York: New Press, 1994.

Gambrell, Alice. *Women Intellectuals, Modernism, and Difference: Transatlantic Culture, 1919–1945*. Cambridge: Cambridge University Press, 1997.

Gates, Henry Louis. Afterword to Zora Neale Hurston, *Dust Tracks on a Road*, 287–99. New York: First Harper Perennial Modern Classics, 2006.

———. Introduction to Zora Neale Hurston, *The Complete Stories*, ix–xxiii. New York: HarperCollins, 1995.

Gates, Henry Louis, Jr., and Jennifer Burton. *Call and Response: Key Debates in African American Culture*. New York: W. W. Norton, 2008.

Gilroy, Paul. *The Black Atlantic: Modernity and Double-Consciousness*. Cambridge, MA: Harvard University Press.

Gillman, Susan, and Alys Weinbaum, eds. "Introduction: W. E. B. Du Bois and the Politics of Juxtaposition." In Gilman and Weinbaum, *Next to the Color Line*, 1–34.

———. *Next to the Color Line: Gender, Sexuality, and W. E. B. Du Bois.* Minneapolis: University of Minnesota Press, 2007.

Gipson, L. Michael. "Interlude E: From Destiny's Child to Coachella: On Embracing Then Resisting Others' Respectability Politics." In Brooks and Martin, *The Lemonade Reader*, 144–54.

Glaude, Eddie. *Exodus! Religion, Race, and Nation in Early Nineteenth-Century Black America.* Chicago: University of Chicago Press, 2000.

———. *In a Shade of Blue: Pragmatism and the Politics of Black America.* Chicago: University of Chicago Press, 2007.

Gooding-Williams, Robert. *In the Shadow of Du Bois: Afro-Modern Political Thought in America.* Cambridge, MA: Harvard University Press, 2009.

———. "Philosophy of History and Social Critique in *The Souls of Black Folk.*" *Information (International Social Science Council)* 26, no. 1 (1987): 99–114.

Goyal, Yogita. *Romance, Diaspora, and Black Atlantic Literature.* Cambridge: Cambridge University Press, 2010.

———. *Runaway Genres: The Global Afterlives of Slavery.* New York: New York University Press, 2019.

Greenlee, Cynthia. "Just Say No Thanks to #ThanksAlabama and 'Magical Negro' Narratives." Rewire.News, December 14, 2017. https://rewire.news /article/2017/12/14/just-say-no-thanks-alabama-magical-negro/.

Griffin, Farah Jasmine. Introduction to W. E. B. Du Bois, *The Souls of Black Folk*, edited by Farah Jasmine Griffin, xv–xxviii. New York: Barnes and Noble Classics, 2005.

———. "That the Mothers May Soar and the Daughters May Know Their Names: A Retrospective of Black Feminist Literary Criticism." *Signs: Journal of Women and Culture* 32, no. 21 (2007): 483–504.

Gumbs, Alexis Pauline. *Spill: Scenes of Black Feminist Fugitivity.* Durham, NC: Duke University Press, 2016.

Hall, Gwendolyn Midlo. *Africans in Colonial Louisiana: The Development of Afro-Creole Culture in the Eighteenth Century.* Baton Rouge: Louisiana State University Press, 1992.

Hart, William D. "Three Rival Narratives of Black Religion." In *A Companion to African-American Studies*, edited by Lewis R. Gordon and Jane Anna Gordon, 476–93. Malden, MA: Blackwell, 2006.

Hartman, Saidiya V. "Intimate History, Radical Narratives." Black Perspectives, May 22, 2020. https://www.aaihs.org/intimate-history-radical-narrative/.

———. *Scenes of Subjection: Terror, Slavery, and Self-Making in Nineteenth-Century America.* New York: Oxford University Press, 1997.

Hartman, Saidiya V., and Fred Moten. "To Refuse That Which Has Been Refused to You." Chimurenga Chronic, October 19, 2018. https://chimurengachronic .co.za/to-refuse-that-which-has-been-refused-to-you-2/.

Hazzard-Donald, Katrina. "Hoodoo Religion and American Dance Traditions: Rethinking the Ring Shout." *Journal of Pan African Studies* 4, no. 6 (2011): 194–212.

———. *Jookin': The Rise of Social Dance Formations in African American Culture.* Philadelphia: Temple University Press, 1990.

———. *Mojo Workin': The Old African American Hoodoo System*. Urbana: University of Illinois Press, 2013.

Higginbotham, Evelyn Brooks. *Righteous Discontent: The Women's Movement in the Black Baptist Church, 1880–1920*. Cambridge, MA: Harvard University Press, 1993.

Highsmith, L. V. "Beyoncé Reborn: *Lemonade* as Spiritual Enlightenment." In Brooks and Martin, *The Lemonade Reader*, 133–43.

Hill, Lynda Marion. *Social Rituals and the Verbal Art of Zora Neale Hurston*. Washington, DC: Howard University Press, 1996.

Hobson, Janell. "Getting to the Roots of 'Becky with the Good Hair' in Beyoncé's *Lemonade*." In Brooks and Martin, *The Lemonade Reader*, 31–41.

Hoefel, Roseanne. "'Different by Degree': Ella Cara Deloria, Zora Neale Hurston, and Franz Boas Contend with Race and Ethnicity." *American Indian Quarterly* 25, no. 2 (2001): 181–204.

hooks, bell. "Moving beyond Pain." bell hooks Institute, May 9, 2016. http://www.bellhooksinstitute.com/blog/2016/5/9/moving-beyond-pain.

———. *Yearning: Race, Gender, and Cultural Politics*. Boston: South End, 1990.

Hopkins, S. M. "Woman-Whipping, Ethically and Esthetically Considered." In Sarah H. Bradford and Harriet Tubman, *Scenes in the Life of Harriet Tubman*. London: Forgotten Books, 2012.

Hucks, Tracey E. "'Burning with a Flame in America': African American Women in African-Derived Traditions." *Journal of Feminist Studies in Religion* 17, no. 2 (2001): 89–106.

Hull, Akasha Gloria. *Soul Talk: The New African Spirituality of African American Women*. Rochester, NY: Inner Traditions International, 2001.

Hurston, Zora Neale. "Art and Such." 1938. In *Zora Neale Hurston: Folklore, Memoirs, and Other Writings*. Edited by Cheryl A. Wall, 905–11. New York: Library of America, 1995.

———. *Barracoon: The Story of the Last "Black Cargo."* Edited by Deborah G. Plant. New York: Amistad, 2018.

———. "Characteristics of Negro Expression." 1934. In Hurston, *Zora Neale Hurston*, 830–46.

———. "Court Order Can't Make Races Mix." 1955. In Hurston, *Zora Neale Hurston*, 956–58.

———. "Crazy for This Democracy." 1945. In Hurston, *Zora Neale Hurston*, 945–49.

———. *Dust Tracks on a Road*. 1942. New York: Harper Perennial, 2006.

———. "High John de Conquer." 1943. In Hurston, *Zora Neale Hurston*, 922–31.

———. "Hoodoo in America." *Journal of American Folklore* 44, no. 174 (October–December 1931): 317–417. https://www.jstor.org/stable/535394.

———. "How It Feels to Be Colored Me." 1928. In Hurston, *Zora Neale Hurston*, 826–29.

———. *Mules and Men*. 1938. New York: Harper Perennial Modern Classics, 2008.

———. "My Most Humiliating Jim Crow Experience." 1944. In Hurston, *Zora Neale Hurston*, 935–36.

———. "Negroes without Self-Pity." 1943. In Hurston, *Zora Neale Hurston*, 932–34.

————. "The 'Pet Negro' System." 1943. In Hurston, *Zora Neale Hurston*, 914–21.

————. "The Rise of Begging Joints." 1945. In Hurston, *Zora Neale Hurston*, 937–44.

————. "The Sanctified Church." 1938. In Hurston, *Zora Neale Hurston*, 901–4.

————. "Shouting." 1934. In Hurston, *Zora Neale Hurston*, 851–54.

————. "Spirituals and Neo-Spirituals." 1934. In Hurston, *Zora Neale Hurston*, 869–74.

————. "Stories of Conflict." *Saturday Review of Literature* 17, no. 2 (1938): 32–33.

————. "What the White Publishers Won't Print." 1950. In Hurston, *Zora Neale Hurston*, 950–55.

————. *Zora Neale Hurston: Folklore, Memoirs, and Other Writings*, edited by Cheryl A. Wall. New York: Library of America, 1995.

Hutchinson, George. *Harlem Renaissance in Black and White*. Cambridge, MA: Harvard University Press, 1995.

James, Denise. "The Burdens of Integration." *Symposium on Gender, Race, and Philosophy* 9 (2013): 1–5.

James, Joy. *Transcending the Talented Tenth: Black Leaders and American Intellectuals*. New York: Routledge, 1997.

Jenson, Deborah. *Beyond the Slave Narrative: Politics, Sex, and Manuscripts in the Haitian Revolution*. Liverpool: Liverpool University Press, 2011.

Jones, Maris. "Dear Beyoncé, Katrina Is Not Your Story." *Black Girl Dangerous*, February 10, 2016. https://www.bgdblog.org/2016/02/dear-beyonce-katrina-is-not-your-story/.

Jones, Melanie C. "The *Slay* Factor: Beyoncé Unleashing the Black Feminine Divine in a Blaze of Glory." In Brooks and Martin, *The Lemonade Reader*, 98–110.

Jones, Nicholas R. "Beyoncé's *Lemonade* Folklore: Feminine Reverberations of *Odù* and Afro-Cuban *Orisha* Iconography." In Brooks and Martin, *The Lemonade Reader*, 88–87.

Jordan, June. "Notes toward a Black Balancing of Love and Hatred." In *Some of Us Did NOT Die: New and Selected Essays of June Jordan*, 284–89. New York: Basic Civitas Books, 2003.

————. "On Richard Wright and Zora Neale Hurston: Notes toward a Balancing of Love and Hatred." *Black World* 23, no. 10 (1974): 4–8.

Kahn, Jonathon S. *Divine Discontent: The Religious Imagination of W. E. B. Du Bois*. New York: Oxford University Press, 2009.

Kaplan, Carla. "The Erotics of Talk: 'That Oldest Human Longing' in *Their Eyes Were Watching God*." In *Zora Neale Hurston's "Their Eyes Were Watching God": A Casebook*, edited by Cheryl A. Wall, 137–63. New York: Oxford University Press, 2000.

————. *The Erotics of Talk: Women's Writing and Feminist Paradigms*. New York: Oxford University Press, 1996.

————, ed. *Zora Neale Hurston: A Life in Letters*. New York: Anchor, 2003.

Kirkland, Paul E. "Sorrow Songs and Self-Knowledge: The Politics of Recognition and Tragedy in Du Bois's 'Souls of Black Folk.'" *American Political Thought* 4, no. 3 (2015): 412–37.

Landau, Emily Epstein. "The Notorious, Mixed-Race New Orleans Madam Who Turned Her Identity into a Brand." Zócalo, October 1, 2018. https://www.zocalopublicsquare.org/2018/10/01/notorious-mixed-race-new-orleans -madam-turned-identity-brand/ideas/essay/.

Lawless, Elaine J. "What Zora Knew: A Crossroads, a Bargain with the Devil, and a Late Witness." *Journal of American Folklore* 126, no. 500 (2013): 152–73.

Lee, Valerie. *Black Midwives and Black Women Writers: Double-Dutched Readings*. New York: Routledge, 1996.

Leone, Mark P., and Gladys-Marie Fry. "Conjuring in the Big House Kitchen." *Journal of American Folklore* 112, no. 445 (1999): 372–403.

———. "Spirit Management among Americans of African Descent." In *Race and the Archeology of Identity*, edited by Charles E. Orser. Salt Lake City: University of Utah Press, 2001.

Levine, Lawrence W. *Black Culture and Black Consciousness*. New York: Oxford University Press, 2007.

Lewis, David Levering. *When Harlem Was in Vogue*. New York: Penguin, 1997.

Locke, Alain. "Book Reviews." *Opportunity: A Journal of Negro Life* (1938): 26–27.

Lorde, Audre. "Use of the Erotic: The Erotic as Power." In *Sister Outsider: Essays and Speeches*. Berkeley: Crossing, 2007.

Luke, Jenny M. *Delivered by Midwives: African American Midwifery in the Twentieth-Century South*. Jackson: University Press of Mississippi, 2018.

Mahmood, Saba. *Politics of Piety: The Islamic Revival and the Feminist Subject*. Princeton, NJ: Princeton University Press, 2005.

Manigault-Bryant, James Arthur. "Reimagining the 'Pythian Madness' of *Souls*: W. E. B. Du Bois's Poetics of African American Faith." *Journal of Africana Religions* 1, no. 3 (2013): 324–47.

Marcucci, Olivia. "Zora Neale Hurston and the *Brown* Debate: Race, Class, and the Progressive Empire. *Journal of Negro Education* 86, no. 1 (2017): 13–24.

Marshall, J. B. T. *The Story of the Jubilee Singers*. Boston: Houghton, Mifflin, 1881.

Martin, Kameelah. *Conjuring Moments in African American Literature: Women, Spirit Work, and Other Such Hoodoo*. New York: Palgrave Macmillan, 2013.

———. *Envisioning Black Feminist Voodoo Aesthetics: African Spirituality in American Cinema*. Lanham, MD: Lexington Books, 2016.

May, Vivian M. "Writing the Self into Being: Anna Julia Cooper's Textual Politics." *African American Review* 43, no. 1 (2009): 17–34.

Mbiti, John S. *African Religions and Philosophy*. Portsmouth, NH: Heinemann Educational Books, 1990.

McBride, Dwight A. *Impossible Witness: Truth, Abolitionism, and Slave Testimony*. New York: New York University Press, 2001.

McDowell, Deborah. Introduction to Frederick Douglass, *Narrative of the Life of Frederick Douglass, an American Slave*, edited by Deborah McDowell, vii–xxvii. New York: Oxford University Press, 1999.

McGee, Alexis. "The Language of *Lemonade*: The Sociolinguistic and Rhetorical Strategies of Beyoncé's *Lemonade*." In Brooks and Martin, *The Lemonade Reader*, 55–68.

McGranahan, Carole. "Theorizing Refusal: An Introduction." *Cultural Anthropology* 31, no. 3 (2016): 319–25. https://journal.culanth.org/index.php/ca /article/view/ca31.3.01.

McWhorter, John H. "Thus Spake Zora: Zora Neale Hurston's Writing Challenged Black People as well as White." *City Journal*, Summer 2009.

———. "Why Zora Neale Hurston Was a Conservative." The Root, January 5, 2011. https://www.theroot.com/why-zora-neale-hurston-was-a-conservative-1790862242.

McWhorter, Ladelle. "Post-Liberation Feminism and Practices of Freedom." *Foucault Studies* 16 (2013): 54–73.

Medina, José. "Color-Blindness, Meta-Ignorance, and the Racial Imagination." *Critical Philosophy of Race* 1, no. 1 (2013): 38–67.

———. *The Epistemology of Resistance: Gender and Racial Oppression, Epistemic Injustice, and Resistant Imaginaries.* New York: Oxford University Press, 2013.

Meisenhelder, Susan E. "Gender, Race, and Class in Zora Neale Hurston's Politics." *Solidarity: A Socialist, Feminist, Anti-Racist Organization* 55 (1995). https://www.solidarity-us.org/node/2838.

———. *Hitting a Straight Lick with a Crooked Stick: Race and Gender in the Work of Zora Neale Hurston.* Tuscaloosa: University of Alabama Press, 2001.

Mills, Charles W. *Black Rights/White Wrongs: The Critique of Racial Liberalism.* New York: Oxford University Press, 2017.

Mitchell, Ernest Julius, II. "Zora's Politics: A Brief Introduction." *Journal of Transnational American Studies* 5, no. 1 (2013). https://escholarship.org/uc/item/38356082#main.

Moody-Turner, Shirley. *Black Folklore and the Politics of Racial Representation.* Jackson: University Press of Mississippi, 2013.

Morrison, Toni. *Beloved.* New York: Vintage International, 2004.

———. "A Knowing So Deep." In Morrison, *What Moves at the Margin*, 31–33.

———. *A Mercy.* New York: First Vintage International, 2009.

———. *The Origin of Others.* Cambridge, MA: Harvard University Press, 2017.

———. *Paradise.* New York: Vintage Books, 2014.

———. "Rediscovering Black History." In Morrison, *What Moves at the Margin*, 39–55.

———. "Rootedness: The Ancestor as Foundation." In Morrison, *What Moves at the Margin*, 56–64.

———. "The Site of Memory." In *The Source of Self-Regard*, 233–45. New York: Alfred A Knopf, 2019.

———. "A Slow Walk of Trees (as Grandmother Would Say); Hopeless (as Grandfather Would Say)." In Morrison, *What Moves at the Margin*, 3–14.

———. *What Moves at the Margin: Selected Nonfiction*, edited by Carolyn C. Denard. Jackson: University Press of Mississippi, 2008.

Moylan, Lynn. "'A Child Cannot Be Taught by Anyone Who Despises Him': Hurston versus Court-Ordered School Integration." In *"The Inside Light": New Critical Essays on Zora Neale Hurston*, edited by Deborah G. Plant, 215–24. Santa Barbara, CA: Praeger, 2010.

Neary, Lynn. "In Zora Neale Hurston's 'Barracoon,' Language Is the Key to Understanding." Last modified May 8, 2018. *NPR.* https://www.npr.org/2018/05/08/609126378/in-zora-neale-hurstons-barracoon-language-is-the-key-to-understanding.

O'Brien, John, and Alice Walker. "Alice Walker: An Interview." In *Alice Walker: Critical Perspectives, Past and Present,* edited by Henry Louis Gates Jr. and K. A. Appiah, 326–47. New York: Amistad, 1993.

Ortner, Sherry B. "Resistance and the Problem of Ethnographic Refusal." *Comparative Studies in Society and History* 37, no. 1 (1995): 173–93.

Patterson, Orlando. *Slavery and Social Death: A Comparative Study.* Cambridge, MA: Harvard University Press, 1982.

Patterson, Tiffany Ruby. *Zora Neale Hurston and a History of Southern Life.* Philadelphia: Temple University Press, 2005.

Peñate, Patricia Coloma. "Beyoncé's Diaspora Heritage and Ancestry in *Lemonade.*" In Brooks and Martin, *The Lemonade Reader,* 111–22.

Perry, Imani. "As the South Goes, So Goes the Nation." *Harper's Magazine,* July 2018. https://harpers.org/archive/2018/07/as-goes-the-south-so-goes-the-nation/.

———. *Vexy Thing: On Gender and Liberation.* Durham, NC: Duke University Press, 2018.

Pinn, Anthony B. "Du Bois' Souls: Thoughts on 'Veiled' Bodies and the Study of Black Religion." *The North Star: A Journal of African American Religious History* 6, no. 2 (2003): 1–5.

Plant, Deborah G. Afterword to Zora Neale Hurston, *Barracoon: The Story of the Last "Black Cargo,"* edited by Deborah G. Plant, 117–38. New York: Amistad, 2018.

———. *Every Tub Must Sit on Its Own Bottom: The Philosophy and Politics of Zora Neale Hurston.* Urbana: University of Illinois Press, 1995.

———. *Zora Neale Hurston: A Biography of the Spirit.* Westport, CT: Praeger, 2007.

Pryse, Marjorie, and Hortense J. Spillers. *Conjuring: Black Women, Fiction, and Literary Tradition.* Bloomington: Indiana University Press, 1985.

Raboteau, Albert J. *Slave Religion: The "Invisible Institution" in the Antebellum South.* New York: Oxford University Press, 2004.

Rawls, John. *Political Liberalism.* New York: Columbia University Press, 2005.

Robinson, Zandria. "Beyoncé's Black Southern 'Formation.'" *Rolling Stone,* February 8, 2016, https://www.rollingstone.com/music/music-news/beyonces-Black-southern-formation-235827/.

———. *This Ain't Chicago: Race, Class, and Regional Identity in the Post-Soul South.* Chapel Hill: University of North Carolina Press, 2014.

———. "We Slay, Part 1." New South Negress, February 7, 2016. https://newsouthnegress.com/southernslayings/.

Rucker, Walter. "Conjure, Magic, and Power: The Influence of Afro-Atlantic Religious Practices on Slave Resistance and Rebellion." *Journal of Black Studies* 32, no. 1 (2001): 84–103. https://www-jstor.org/stable/2668016.

———. *The River Flows On: Black Resistance, Culture, and Identity Formation in Early America.* Baton Rouge: Louisiana State University Press, 2006.

Ruppell, Timothy, Jessica Neuwirth, Mark P. Leone, and Gladys-Marie Fry. "Hidden in View: African Spiritual Spaces in North American Landscapes." *Antiquity* 77, no. 296 (2003): 321–35.

Salamone, Frank A. "His Eyes Were Watching Her: Papa Franz Boas, Zora Neale Hurston, and Anthropology." *Anthropos* 109, no. 1 (2014): 217–24.

Samuel, Sigal. "The Witches of Baltimore: Young Black Women Are Leaving Christianity and Embracing African Witchcraft in Digital Covens." *The Atlantic*, November 5, 2018. https://www.theatlantic.com/international/archive /2018/11/Black-millennials-african-witchcraft-christianity/574393/.

Sexton, Jared. *Black Masculinity and the Cinema of Policing*. New York: Palgrave Macmillan, 2017.

———. "The Social Life of Social Death: On Afro-Pessimism and Black Optimism." *Tensions* 5 (2011): 1–47.

Sharpe, Christina. *In the Wake: On Blackness and Being*. Durham, NC: Duke University Press, 2016.

Shaw, Stephanie J. *W. E. B. Du Bois and "The Souls of Black Folk."* Chapel Hill: University of North Carolina Press, 2013.

Simmons, LaKisha M. "Landscapes, Memories, and History in Beyoncé's *Lemonade*." *UNC Press Blog*, April 28, 2016. https://uncpressblog.com/2016/04/28 /lakisha-simmmons-beyonces-lemonade/.

———. "Pull the Sorrow from between My Legs: *Lemonade* as Rumination on Reproduction and Loss." In Brooks and Martin, *The Lemonade Reader*, 42–54.

Simpson, Audra. "Consent's Revenge." *Cultural Anthropology* 31, no. 3 (2016): 326–33.

———. *Mohawk Interruptus: Political Life across the Borders of Settler States*. Durham, NC: Duke University Press, 2014.

———. "On Ethnographic Refusal: Indigeneity, 'Voice,' and Colonial Citizenship." *Junctures* 9 (2007): 67–80.

———. "The Ruse of Consent and the Anatomy of 'Refusal': Cases from Indigenous North America and Australia." *Postcolonial Studies* 20, no. 1 (2017): 18–33.

Smith, Barbara. "Sexual Politics and the Fiction of Zora Neale Hurston." *Radical Teacher* 8 (1978): 26–30.

———. "Toward a Black Feminist Criticism." *Radical Teacher* 7 (1978): 20–27.

Southern, Eileen. *The Music of Black Americans: A History*. New York: W. W. Norton, 1997.

Stepto, Robert B., Michael S. Harper, and Ralph Ellison. "Study and Experience: An Interview with Ralph Ellison." In *Conversations with Ralph Ellison*, edited by Maryemma Graham and Amritjit Singh, 319–41. Jackson: University Press of Mississippi, 1995.

Steptoe, Tyina. "Beyoncé's Western South Serenade." In Brooks and Martin, *The Lemonade Reader*, 183–91.

Stewart, Lindsey. "Something Akin to Freedom: Black Love, Political Agency, and *Lemonade*." In Brooks and Martin, *The Lemonade Reader*, 19–30.

Story, Ralph D. "Gender and Ambition: Zora Neale Hurston in the Harlem Renaissance." *Black Scholar* 20, no. 3–4 (1989): 25–31.

Stuckey, Sterling. *Slave Culture: Nationalist Theory and the Foundations of Black America*. New York: Oxford University Press, 2013.

Sundquist, Eric J. *To Wake the Nations: Race in the Making of American Literature*. Cambridge, MA: Harvard University Press, 1993.

Syedullah, Jasmine. "Beyond the Battlefield of Institutions: Everyday Abolitionism from the Antebellum South." In *Let Spirit Speak! Cultural Journeys through the African Diaspora*, edited by Vanessa Kimberly Valdés, 119–25. Albany: State University of New York Press, 2012.

Tallant, Robert. *Voodoo in New Orleans*. New York: Macmillan, 1967.

Taylor, Paul. "What's the Use of Calling Du Bois a Pragmatist?" *Metaphilosophy* 35, no. 1–2 (2004): 99–114.

Taylor-Guthrie, Danille, ed. *Conversations with Toni Morrison*. Jackson: University Press of Mississippi, 1994.

Thomas, Lynnell L. *Desire and Disaster in New Orleans: Tourism, Race, and Historical Memory*. Durham, NC: Duke University Press, 2014.

Turner, Richard Brent. *Jazz Religion, the Second Line, and Black New Orleans after Hurricane Katrina*. Bloomington: Indiana University Press, 2017.

Valdés, Vanessa K. *Oshun's Daughters: The Search for Womanhood in the Americas*. Albany: State University of New York Press, 2014.

Vargas, Ramon Antonio. "CDC: Mardi Gras Quickened Spread of Coronavirus in Lousiana; Canceling Was Never Recommended." Nola.com, April 11, 2020. https://www.nola.com/news/coronavirus/article_dedfb535–7c2a-11ea-901f -6720fa25be5a.html.

Walker, Alice. Foreword to Zora Neale Hurston, *Barracoon: The Story of the Last "Black Cargo,"* edited by Deborah G. Plant, ix–xii. New York: Amistad, 2018.

———. "Looking for Zora." In *In Search of Our Mothers' Gardens*. San Diego, CA: Harcourt Brace, 1983.

———. "On Refusing to be Humbled by Second Place in a Contest You Did Not Design: A Tradition by Now." In *I Love Myself When I Am Laughing and Then Again When I'm Looking Mean and Impressive*, edited by Alice Walker, 1–6. New York: Feminist, 1979.

———. "Zora Neale Hurston: A Cautionary Tale and a Partisan View." In Walker, *In Search of Our Mothers' Gardens*, 83–92.

Wall, Cheryl A. Introduction to *Zora Neale Hurston's "Their Eyes Were Watching God": A Casebook*, edited by Cheryl A. Wall, 3–18. New York: Oxford University Press, 2000.

———. *On Freedom and the Will to Adorn: The Art of the African American Essay*. Chapel Hill: University of North Carolina Press, 2018.

———. "Resounding *Souls*: Du Bois and the African American Literary Tradition." *Public Culture* 17, no. 2 (2005): 217–34.

———. "Zora Neale Hurston: Changing Her Own Words." In *Zora Neale Hurston: Critical Perspectives Past and Present*, edited by Henry Louis Gates Jr. and K. A. Appiah, 78–97. New York: Amistad, 2000.

———. "Zora Neale Hurston's Essays: On Art and Such." *The Scholar and Feminist Online* 3, no. 2 (2005). https://sfonline.barnard.edu/hurston/printcwa.htm.

Wallace, Michele. *In Invisibility Blues: From Pop to Theory*. New York: Verso, 1990.

Walters, Keith. "'He Can Read My Writing but He Sho' Can't Read My Mind': Zora Neale Hurston's Revenge in Mules and Men." *Journal of American Folklore* 112, no. 445 (1999): 343–71.

Ward, Cynthia. "Truth, Lies, Mules and Men: Through the 'Spy-Glass of Anthropology' and What Zora Saw There." *Western Journal of Black Studies* 36, no. 4 (2012): 301–13.

Ward, Jesmyn. "My True South: Why I Decided to Return Home." *Time*, July 26, 2018. https://time.com/5349517/jesmyn-ward-my-true-south/.

Washington, Mary Helen. "The Black Woman's Search for Identity: Zora Neale Hurston's Work." *Black World* 21, no. 10 (1972): 68–75.

Washington, Teresa N. "The Sea Never Dies: Yemoja: The Infinitely Flowing Mother Force of Africana Literature and Cinema." In *Yemoja: Gender, Sexuality, and Creativity in the Latina/o and Afro-Atlantic Diasporas*, edited by Solimar Otero and Toyin Falola, 215–66. Albany: State University of New York Press, 2013.

Weigel, Moira. "The Iconic Images behind Beyoncé's 'Formation' Video." *The New Republic*, February 12, 2016. https://newrepublic.com/article/129814 /iconic-images-behind-beyonces-formation-video.

Weinbaum, Alys. "Interracial Romance and Black Internationalism." In Gillman and Weinbaum, *Next to the Color Line*, 96–123.

West, Cornel. *Prophesy Deliverance! An Afro-American Revolutionary Christianity*. Louisville: Westminster John Knox, 2002.

———. "W. E. B. Du Bois: An Interpretation." In *Africana: The Encyclopedia of the African and African American Experience*, edited by Kwame Anthony Appiah and Henry Louis Gates Jr., 1967–82. New York: Basic Books, 1999.

Wilderson, Frank B., III. "Afro-Pessimism and the End of Redemption." Humanities Futures, March 30, 2016. https://humanitiesfutures.org/papers/afro -pessimism-end-redemption/.

———. *Incognegro: A Memoir of Exile and Apartheid*. Durham, NC: Duke University Press, 2015.

Wilentz, Gay. "Defeating the False God: Janie's Self-Determination in Zora Neale Hurston's *Their Eyes Were Watching God*." In *Faith of a (Woman) Writer*, edited by Alice Kesser-Harris and William McBrien, 285–91. Westport, CT: Greenwood, 1988.

Winant, Howard. *The New Politics of Race: Globalism, Difference, Justice*. Minneapolis: University of Minnesota Press, 2004.

Winters, Joseph R. *Hope Drafted in Black: Race, Melancholy, and the Agony of Progress*. Durham, NC: Duke University Press, 2016.

Wright, Richard. "Between Laughter and Tears." *New Masses* 25 (1937): 22–25.

———. "Blueprint for Negro Writing." In *Within the Circle: An Anthology of African American Literary Criticism from the Harlem Renaissance to the Present*, edited by Angelyn Mitchell, 97–106. Durham, NC: Duke University Press, 1994.

Young, Jason R. *Rituals of Resistance: African Atlantic Religion in Kongo and the Lowcountry South in the Era of Slavery*. Baton Rouge: Louisiana State University Press, 2007.

Zamir, Shamoon. *Dark Voices: W. E. B. Du Bois and American Thought, 1888– 1903*. Chicago: University of Chicago Press, 1995.

———. "'The Sorrow Songs'/'Songs of Myself': Du Bois, the Crisis of Leadership, and Prophetic Imagination." In *The Souls of Black Folk: W. E. B. Du Bois*, edited by Henry Louis Gates and Terri Hume Oliver, 346–64. New York: W. W. Norton, 1999.

Zauditu-Selassie, K. *African Spiritual Traditions in the Novels of Toni Morrison*. Gainesville: University Press of Florida, 2009.

INDEX

abolitionism, 6–8, 56–57, 151n112; Black male, 135n139; Christianity and, 61, 65; discourse of, 15–24, 28–30, 38, 42–49, 53, 61, 69–71, 78–79, 86, 91, 98–99, 116–20, 132n86, 133n103; propaganda of, 31; radical white, 17; resurgence of the norms of, 47; romanticism in the service of, 20; tragedy of Black life in, 91. *See also* neo-abolitionism; slavery

Adams, Surgeon General Jerome, 120

African American literature, 8, 156n45

African American philosophy, 24, 48

African Americans: Americanization of, 89; and anthropologists, 75; folk ethos of, 32; folktales of, 175n167; lore of, 144n10; northern, 50; persecution of African Americans by, 79, 81

African American studies, 140n51

agency: account of, 166n37; analyses of, 25, 79; and autonomy, 16; Black, 25, 123, 125n2; conjuring, 103–7; of the enslaved, 53; expressions of, 99–100; freedom and, 101; modes of, 9, 24–25, 35, 99, 102–3, 106–7, 111–13, 166n31; narratives of, 125n2; resistance and, 35, 106–7, 117; submission to divine, 102, 106

Alabama, 4

Aleem, Zeeshan, 120

Allen, Shamarr: "Quarantine and Chill" (YouTube video), 122–23

American Mercury, 103

Angelou, Maya, 157n59

anthropology: African Americans and, 75; Hurston's work in, 10, 13, 102, 130n50; Indigenous, 154n8; "objectivist" mandates of, 156n47. *See also* ethnography

Baldwin, James, 35, 137n3, 149n89

Barnett, Claude, 31, 43

Benoit, David, 118

Black art, 24; norms of, 44

Black Arts Movement, 32

Black emancipatory politics, 4, 6, 21. *See also* progressive politics

Black feminism, 4–5, 24–25, 53, 131n82, 138n22, 154n15; interventions of, 30–33; literature of, 45; recovery of Hurston by, 31–32; root work in, 21, 25; scholarship of, 175n162. *See also* Black women; feminism

Black folklore: emancipatory potential of, 34

Black liberation, 5–6, 24, 99; ethnographic accounts of, 111; goals of, 123; neo-abolitionist narratives of, 94; and northern liberal intervention, 52; strategies for, 41–42, 49, 54; vision of, 41, 98. *See also* freedom

Black Lives Matter, 4, 27

Black nationalism, 5, 32

Black northern life, 58

Black Panther Party, 4

Black southern aesthetic: 11, 14, 45, 117, 127n17, 163n9; and John de Conquer, 23. *See also* Black southern life; southern Black culture

Black southern life: analyses of, 10, 21; celebration of, 3–4, 6; complex story about, 43; food-ways of, 78, 92, 158n76; histories of, 2; narrative of, 46; nostalgia and, 2–4; pity and, 1, 15, 19; representations of, 7–8, 13–18, 25, 28–30, 42–48, 84, 98, 117–18; as a site of joy, 24, 27–28, 116, 123; sorrow and tragedy of, 30, 61–62, 91. *See also* Black southern aesthetic; joy; Negro spirituals; South; southern Black culture

Indigenous peoples, 15, 70–73, 85–86,
155n34; and anthropologists, 75,
161n146; politics and philosophy of,
154n7

Jim Crow, 6, 31, 41, 43, 49, 119,
142n86; defiance of, 53; era of, 91;
intellectual, 43; as a national and
global system of oppression, 40–
42. *See also* lynching; racism; white
supremacy
John de Conquer, 10, 22–23, 36–37,
97, 103–5, 112–16, 123, 134n127,
176n177. *See also* hoodoo; root work
Jones, Senator Doug, 4
Jordan, June: "Notes toward a Black
Balancing of Love and Hatred," 33,
139n36
joy: Black, 1–11, 18, 32–33, 37–39,
43–46, 52, 90–92, 101, 117, 121–22,
173n131; disavowal of Black, 61; the
erotic and, 113; of Mardi Gras, 121;
resistance and, 14, 21–22; spaces of,
46. *See also* Black southern life
juju. *See* hoodoo

Kaepernick, Colin, 73
Kaplan, Carla, 71; Works: *The Erotics
of Talk*, 33, 162n171; *Zora Neale
Hurston: A Life in Letters* of, 11,
155n44
Knowles, Beyoncé: *Lemonade* (visual
album), 4, 6, 24, 27–28, 45–46, 67–68,
95–96, 117, 127n17, 135n1, 136n3

language: African, 110–11; and history,
157n67; oral, 110; religious, 12; of
resistance, 75–76; of witchcraft, 21
Levine, Lawrence: *Black Culture and
Black Consciousness*, 35
Locke, Alain, 8, 40–42, 70, 103
Lorde, Audre, 9, 95, 113–14, 128n28,
175n160
Louisiana, 1–2, 118
lynching, 19, 29, 50, 53–54. *See also* Jim
Crow

Malcolm X, 4
McBride, Dwight: *Impossible Witness*,
15–16

McDowell, Deborah, 53, 131n82
McGranahan, Carole, 9, 153n1
Meisenhelder, Susan: *Hitting a Straight
Lick with a Crooked Stick*, 10,
141n76, 160n132
Middle Passage, 36, 115, 176n177. *See
also* slavery
minkisi, 104–7, 168n55, 168n59. *See
also* root work
minstrel tradition, 30, 43, 61, 90–91,
136n1, 137n8
Morrison, Toni, 25, 37, 45, 113,
171n112, 173n131; Works: *Beloved*,
34, 107–12, 139n47; *A Mercy*, 81;
Paradise, 169n68; "Rediscovering
Black History," 1–2; "Rootedness: The
Ancestor as Foundation," 109; "The
Site of Memory," 77, 131n78, 132n84

Negro spirituals, 17–19, 21, 56–57,
149n92; abolitionist interpretation
of, 60–62, 65, 153n4; debate between
Hurston and Du Bois over, 24, 48,
62–65, 98–99; as joyous religious
expression, 115; politics of the, 24,
150n93; as songs of freedom, 148n71;
as "sorrow songs," 46, 48, 59–62,
98–99, 115, 150n93, 151n107,
151n111, 161n163; in southern Black
communities, 63–64. *See also* Black
southern life
neo-abolitionism, 8, 10, 15–21, 28–29,
45, 115; Black sorrow and, 45, 48,
62, 64, 86–90, 115; criticisms of, 15,
21, 48; dangers of, 25; development
of, 62; ethnographic refusals of the
norms of, 77–78, 84–90, 93; images
of abjection that arise from, 33; rise
of, 47–65; southern Black tragedy as
the mandate of, 23, 75, 90, 93, 97,
116–19. *See also* abolitionism
New Orleans, 3–4, 67, 118–22, 178n20;
Black population in, 125n5
New York City, 40, 118, 121
North: Black masculinity in the, 58–59;
notion of racial justice in the, 130n64;
racism in the, 40, 43
northern white liberals, 4, 13, 16–
17, 33, 37–43, 71, 87, 162n184;
conscience of, 40, 42; empathy of, 84;